SAMS Teach Yourself Today

e-Politics

e-Politics

Using the Internet to participate in politics and interact with your government

Allison Hayward

201 West 103rd Street, Indianapolis, Indiana 46290

Sams Teach Yourself e-Politics Today

International Standard Book Number: 0-672-31981-0

Library of Congress Catalog Card Number: 00-105549

Printed in the United States of America

First Printing: August 2000

03 02 01 00 4 3 2 1

Trademarks

All terms mentioned in this book that are known to be trademarks or service marks have been appropriately capitalized. Sams Publishing cannot attest to the accuracy of this information. Use of a term in this book should not be regarded as affecting the validity of any trademark or service mark.

Warning and Disclaimer

Every effort has been made to make this book as complete and as accurate as possible, but no warranty or fitness is implied. The information provided is on an "as is" basis. The author and the publisher shall have neither liability nor responsibility to any person or entity with respect to any loss or damages arising from the use of programs accompanying it, or from the information contained in this book or from the use of programs accompanying it.

Acquisitions Editor
Jeff Schultz

Development Editor
Laura N. Williams

Managing Editor
Charlotte Clapp

Project Editor
Elizabeth Finney

Copy Editor
Michael Henry

Indexer
Eric Schroeder

Proofreader
Maryann Steinhart
Daniel Ponder

Team Coordinator
Amy Patton

Interior Designer
Gary Adair

Cover Designer
Aren Howell

Production
Steve Geiselman

Table of Contents

Introduction 1

Part I Exploring Inside the Beltway: The Federal Government Online

1 Where It All Started: The Declaration of Independence and the Constitution 7

2 Going Online with the U.S. Senate and the House of Representatives 15

3 The Wired White House and Bitmap Bureaucracy 27

4 A Web Court Appearance 43

Part II Beyond Washington: State, Local, and International Governments Online

5 State Sites on the Web 59

6 All Politics Is Local—And Online 69

7 The Web IS Worldwide: International Political Research on the WWW 79

Part III Sites with Attitude

8 Left-Brain Activity: Progressives and Liberals on the Web 95

9 Place Your Right Hand over Your Keyboard: Conservative Web Sites 107

10 Is There a Ministry of Silly Walks? Iconoclastic, Humorous, and Hard-To-Describe Political Sites 117

11 Surfing for the Cause: Interest Groups on the World Wide Web 127

12 The Cyber-Swiss Army Knife: Sites That Put It All Together 143

Part IV Come to the Party Online

13 Democrats Online 157

14 Republicans Online 171

15 Other Parties Online 185

16 The Money Game Online 195

Part V The Future

17 The Future of the Internet in Politics 213

18 Campaigns in the Future: Campaign Finance Reform 221

Appendices

A Web Site Directory 233

B Glossary of e-Politics Terms 261

Index 271

Acknowledgments

In this day and age, especially with a book that depends so heavily on online resources, it is important to acknowledge the people whose opinions steered the project. Particularly, as in this case, where they might be unaware of their participation.

Accordingly, I should thank my many friends who endeavored to give me good Web leads and otherwise helped—directly or indirectly—in the writing of this manual. An incomplete list includes Mark Acton, Jack Ayer, Alex Azar, Jan Baran, Ginger Bruner, Trevor Potter, and Alex Vogel. A special acknowledgement must be made to my colleagues at Bell, McAndrews, Hiltachk & Davidian, especially Chuck Bell, for patience with me during deadline time.

My editors at Macmillan were a terrific help in the completion of this book. Special thanks to Jeff Schultz for his advice on the scope of the book, and Laura Williams for her edits and comments.

I would also like to acknowledge the support and advice from my good friend and loving husband Steve Hayward, and the critique from my mother, Natalie Rittenhouse. I finally should thank dear Winston, without whose naps this book could not have been written.

INTRODUCTION

Government, Politics, and Information

For a new visitor to the Web world, the choices seem daunting. First, there are the many different ways of getting and using Web information. What browser? What service provider? What search engine? What start page? And what does that error message mean? The simple fact is that you can fiddle with your browser, switch your providers, and redo your start page as often as you want. And, frankly, no one knows what the error messages mean.

This book won't make these preliminary decisions any easier for you. What it will do is help you figure out where to go on the Web, by showing you what you'll find out there.

It's What You Know

A threadbare quote oft repeated in politics is, "It's not what you know, it's who you know." I'd like to suggest that in this age, the quote is exactly backwards. For most people, information is essential in dealing with government, and for succeeding in politics.

Campaigns have always been about the collection and distribution of information. In early American campaigns, partisan newspapers and pamphlets traded barbs on behalf of candidates and parties. The candidates themselves began spreading the word through devices such as whistle-stop campaigning via train. Many political commentators point to the 1960 Nixon-Kennedy presidential debate as a watershed event in the impact of television on politics.

Influencing officials after they are in office is a big part of politics, and information can make or break your policy arguments. Sure, just knowing a lot won't make you the Big Daddy of your state, but for most of us, government and politics is all about knowing what is going on, who is doing it, forming an opinion about it, and deciding what to do about it.

The Internet, and particularly the Web, has made answering these questions easier than ever before. As with television, the Internet gives you information in the comfort of your own homes. But—better than television—you have complete control over what information you get from the Internet and when you get it. In the old days, you called your congressperson or state legislature to get a copy of legislation. Now you can pull it up at home whenever you want. Did the rain ruin your newspaper? Before, you had to call the distributor for a new one. Now, you can in all likelihood pull up your paper on the Web and read it there. Then, you can take a peek at what other papers are saying, as well as news wires, columnists, and on and on.

Need the text of a law? Before, you hoofed over to a law library. Now, you can choose from among several sites for federal statutes, state statutes, and regulations. Then, you can pull the court decisions interpreting the laws. Want the latest information on your favorite candidate's activities or schedule? Before, you called campaign HQ and hoped that the person on the other end of the phone knew the information you needed. Now, you can check the Web page or subscribe to campaign updates via email, and the chances are good that the person authoring the update has accurate information. Want to contribute to an organization or candidate you believe in? Don't wait for the solicitation in the mail—find the appropriate site and make your contribution online.

In the next few years, you might even have the opportunity to vote online. Democrats in Arizona voted online in their 2000 primary, and voter turnout increased beyond what anyone expected.

People Still Matter...a Lot

Does the growth of the e-politics universe mean the end of person-to-person activism? I seriously doubt it. Involvement in government and politics, as any activist can testify, is a splendid way to meet people with common interests, build loyalties, hone opinions, and develop political sophistication. I have a hard time envisioning the "people" part of politics disappearing. In my experience, email is a quirky and unsatisfying substitute for meeting someone in person.

Nevertheless, governmental and political research is more convenient than ever before. So, people should take advantage of this convenience to get educated, get informed, and then get out of the house and participate.

Moreover, some of us will never take a shine to doing things online. Either because of budget, temperament, or physical impairments, computers won't be a universal tool. The "digital divide" will shrink, but it won't disappear. Even in the cyber-future, your government will keep offices open for delivering services, your legislator will appear at community events to meet people, and volunteers will walk door-to-door with campaign literature and voter registration materials.

The Ever-Changing World in Which We Live

This book should help you along the way, by giving you a good overview of the Web resources available on government and politics. Please remember that this is a rapidly changing area. Don't despair if you meticulously follow the book, and find that a site I've described can't be retrieved. Try the name of the site or group in a Web browser—it could be that the site has moved. Perhaps the site is now defunct. Or the host server for the site might be too busy to handle your request, in which case, you should try again later.

You could also find a site you love, on a topic I discussed, but that site is not mentioned in the book. It might be that the site is new. It might be that the site wasn't retrievable during the composition of this book, or when I found the site, it looked inactive. I couldn't mention every site on every topic, and it might be that it was omitted for space reasons. Or, I simply might not have found it. But you did, and you can use the site for your activities. That's what matters.

Additionally, you might pull up a site and the content has changed for the worse. I can promise that every effort was made to include sites containing useful, accurate, up-to-date information, but these qualities can change over time. My advice, if you find a site is unhelpful, annoying, or offensive, is to move on. Sites justify their existence by attracting visitors. So, don't go there.

I trust that this book will help you find what you need and to do what you want in government and politics. Take some time with a chapter that discusses an area of interest to you, and have some fun. Public and private organizations have put time and resources into making all this material available, but it doesn't do anyone any good unless you take your mouse in your hand and jump in.

PART I

Exploring Inside the Beltway: The Federal Government Online

CHAPTER 1

Where It All Started: The Declaration of Independence and the Constitution

Any review of American government and politics should start with its founding documents: the Declaration of Independence and the Constitution. Both documents have greatly influenced how our government has developed. There are many places you can go to learn about the Declaration and the Constitution—certainly more than can be covered in a single chapter. This chapter not only shows you some of the places where you can learn about these important documents, but also gives you a sense of the different ways the same information might be presented.

What You'll Learn in This Chapter:

- Where to find the Declaration and the U.S. Constitution on the Web
- How to use links to move from document to document
- How URLs, bookmarking, and search pages can make your research faster and easier
- The variety of different places you can look for information about the Declaration and the Constitution

Visit the Real McCoy at the National Archives

The actual Declaration of Independence and Constitution are both housed at the National Archives in Washington, D.C. It's not surprising, then, that the National Archives and Records Administration (NARA) Web site also features these documents.

At *www.nara.gov*, you'll find a link to The Online Exhibit Hall, where you can see scanned images of the Declaration and the Constitution.

The Declaration

The Declaration is at *www.nara.gov/exhall/charters/declaration/decmain.html*.

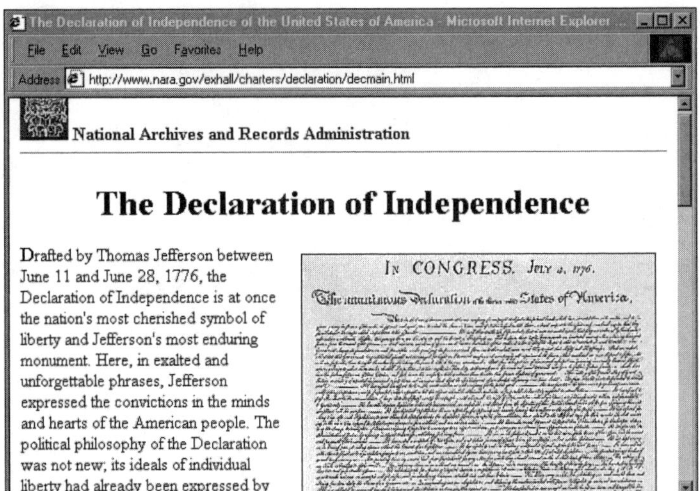

This National Archives page shows you the image of the actual Declaration of Independence. Of course, reading it in this form is extremely difficult. A full transcription of the Declaration is at the URL www.nara.gov/exhall/charters/declaration/declaration.html.

Here at the transcribed Declaration, you can find the words that moved our nation to independence, and the words many of us still have memorized from high school government class: "We hold these truths to be self-evident, that all men are created equal, that they are endowed by their Creator with certain unalienable Rights, that among these are Life, Liberty and the Pursuit of Happiness." You will also find here the names of the 56 signatories to the Declaration, and notations indicating the position of each signature.

The Declaration was drafted by Thomas Jefferson in June of 1776, with the assistance of Benjamin Franklin and John Adams. The Second Continental Congress adopted the Declaration on July 4, 1776; hence, our celebration of Independence Day on the Fourth of July. The engrossed version was signed by 56 delegates to the Congress, starting with John Hancock. Hancock's signature is the bold one easily visible below the text of the Declaration.

What's a URL?

URL stands for *Uniform Resource Locator*, which is a standardized address for Web pages, files, newsgroups, and email users. Here the URLs you'll reference all lead you to specific Web pages. Ahandy reference for other e-related definitions and explanations is *www.whatis.com*.

The Constitution

The National Archives also provides the image of the Constitution, at *www.nara.gov/exhall/charters/constitution/conmain.html*.

Additionally, from this page you can follow links to pages with high-resolution images of each of the four pages of the actual Constitution, and the Letter of Transmittal. This page also links you to The Founding Fathers, a page containing the biographies of the 55 delegates to the Constitutional Convention, an article titled "A More Perfect Union" containing an account of the Constitutional Convention and the subsequent ratification process, and a page titled Questions and Answers Pertaining to the Constitution. You can identify these links on the National Archives page because they are printed in blue and underlined. On most pages the links to other pages will look like this—but don't be surprised if, from time to time, you see a different color.

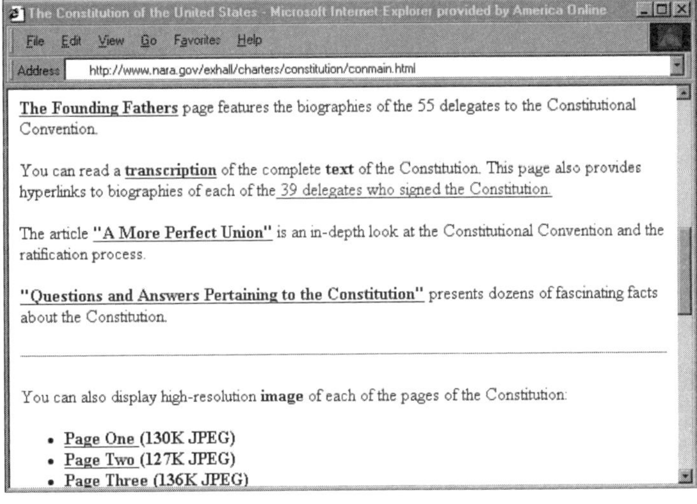

The Constitution on the NARA site.

Notice the links provided on this page, which enable you to find additional information about the Constitution. If you'd rather find these items directly, their URLs (addresses on the Web) are

The Founding Fathers: *www.nara.gov/exhall/charters/constitution/confath.html*

"A More Perfect Union": *www.nara.gov/exhall/charters/constitution/conhist.html*

Jumping from Document to Document

You can access a different page on the Web by clicking on the link indicated in the Web page. Links are usually set off by being underlined and in a contrasting color. Each page has a unique URL—typing that address into your browser and pressing the Enter key will also get you to your destination.

Questions and Answers Pertaining to the Constitution: *www.nara.gov/exhall/charters/constitution/conqa.html*

The Constitutional Convention met in Philadelphia in the summer of 1787. It began as an effort to revise the Articles of Confederation, which contained inadequate provisions to fund the national government or to allow the national regulation of commerce. James Madison is considered the father of the Constitution because of his considerable influence and participation in the formation of the text, but the Constitution has no single author. To create an acceptable Constitution, a number of compromises were required; among the compromises was the treatment of small states in the national legislature. This issue was satisfied by providing each state with two senators—regardless of the state's population. After the Convention adopted the Constitution, it was sent to the states for ratification by state convention. Ratification was especially heated in Massachusetts, New York, and Virginia.

Just as with the Declaration of Independence, the Constitution's transcription is also posted, at *www.nara.gov/exhall/charters/constitution/constitution.html*. This transcription provides the text of the Preamble and the articles of the Constitution. When most people refer to the "Constitution," they also mean the amendments—the first ten of which are the Bill of Rights.

Use Bookmarking to Save Research Time

Bookmark sites that you want to visit again. You don't need to remember a title or URL, and you don't need to resort to a search engine to get where you want to go. Name your bookmark yourself—the default names are often obscure codes or are not too meaningful. Later, organize your bookmarks into folders by project to save time sifting through the list you've accumulated.

The image of the Bill of Rights can be found at *www.nara.gov/exhall/charters/billrights/billmain.html*. A transcription of the Preamble to the Bill of Rights is at *www.nara.gov/exhall/charters/billrights/preamble.html*. The Bill of Rights transcription is at *www.nara.gov/exhall/charters/billrights/billrights.html*, and amendments 11–27 are at *www.nara.gov/exhall/charters/constitution/amendments.html*.

You will notice that many of the documents we've found are also referenced in other pages, and links are provided to take you directly to them. You should practice accessing a document first by entering the URL in your Web browser, and second by clicking on a link in another document. Either way should work; although clicking a link involves less typing, it isn't always obvious from a link's name what you will see when you reach the other document. When you type an address to a Web page in your browser, you can be sure you will be sent where you want to go.

After you find the page you want, try bookmarking it (called "Add to Favorites" in Internet Explorer). You can give it a name (or accept the default name) and add it to your list of links. Later, just select the item from your Bookmark pull-down menu and you can go directly to that page.

Other Sites with the Constitution and the Declaration of Independence

One of the helpful—or exasperating—aspects of Web-based research is the fact that the same document can be found in several places. This is helpful when you need to find something quickly and don't have a URL. If you put the name of the document in a commercial search engine, your chances are good that at least one of the pages with that document will be listed at the top of your results. But this can be exasperating if you are looking for a particular version. For instance, imagine that you wanted the Constitution as delivered by the National Archives Web site because you remember liking the Archives' commentary. Unless you can remember that it was the Archives page on which the version was featured, you might be surfing around a number of different Constitutions before you find the one you want. Nevertheless, here are other sites at which you can find the Constitution, Declaration, and other useful information from our nation's founding.

USConstitution.net

USConstitution.net provides the text of the Constitution at *www.usconstitution.net/const.html*. This version contains links in the text of the Constitution that lead you to a constitutional glossary. It also indicates where the text of the original Constitution has been superceded by amendments. The Web site also has the text of the Declaration at *www.usconstitution.net/declar.html*. The home page also has links to the Articles of Confederation (at *www.usconstitution.net/articles.html*) and other historical documents. Among other documents you might want to look up is the Emancipation Proclamation, *www.usconstitution.net/eman.html*.

Consider the Source

As more and more research and governmental organizations invest serious time and talent on Web pages, the World Wide Web is becoming a powerful historical research tool. As you wander the Web, here's a word of caution. Not every group purporting to feature the Constitution—or other early American legal or historical documents—has good intentions. Some are fringe groups that seek to add legitimacy to their cause by including these documents along with their own literature. Others use these documents to attract "hits" from researchers, and then bombard them with explicit or offensive advertising. (No doubt at a tidy profit!) My advice is to consider the source when doing your research. Government sites, libraries, and other large, well-known institutions are reliable places to obtain basic historical documents and commentary.

Avalon Project at Yale Law School

This site contains a large number of historic legal documents. From the home page at *elsinore.cis.yale.edu/lawweb/avalon/avalon.htm*, select the heading for 18th Century Documents. This link takes you to not only the Constitution and Declaration, but also to many other documents and search pages that will lead you to still more material.

Take a minute to read the text of the Massachusetts Ratification of the Constitution, and remember that after the Constitutional Convention, a heated campaign was waged to secure the ratification of the Constitution.

If you want to review the *Federalist Papers*, which were written to advocate the Constitution's ratification, the search page is at *elsinore.cis.yale.edu/lawweb/avalon/federal/fed.htm*. Here you can run a keyword search through the *Federalist Papers* or select a specific paper by its number.

The Avalon Project provides a search page that enables you to search the Federalist Papers by keyword or by number.

Many law school libraries have excellent resource pages. Check out, for instance, the *Federalist Papers* as presented by the Emory School of Law, at *www.law.emory.edu/FEDERAL/federalist*, which lists the papers, summarizes each, and features a search function at the bottom of the page. The links provided by the University of Oklahoma Law Center, at *www.law.ou.edu/hist/*, are also worth a look.

Library of Congress Web Site

The Library of Congress offers copies of the Constitution and Declaration, and additional documents you might want to review. You will find a number of interesting links at *memory.loc.gov/ammem/amhome.html*. Click the Collection Finder link to see the collection of the Library of Congress organized by topic. You might want to try a few collections just to get a sense of the large amount of material presented here.

Some specific documents of interest at the Library of Congress site are the *Journals of the Continental Congress*, at *memory.loc.gov/ammem/amlaw/lwjc.html*, and Farrand's *Records of the Federal Convention of 1787*, at *memory.loc.gov/ammem/amlaw/lwfr.html*.

You can browse through these documents, but if you are interested in researching a specific topic, browsing can prove time-consuming and laborious.

Instead, the Library of Congress has a page that enables you to search any one of or all its collections of legal history, including the Continental Congress, the Constitutional Convention, and the First through Twenty-fourth Congresses (to 1837). This page is at *memory.loc.gov/ammem/hlawquery.html*.

Keyword Searches

If you are researching lengthy online documents, you might want to use a search page, if one is offered, to execute a keyword search using specific terms that reflect your interest. If the Web site doesn't have a search function of its own, you can use the Find function in your own Web browser. It can execute a crude keyword search of the page you have active on your computer. Your browser will take you to each occurrence of the word you've entered (just like the Find function on your word processor).

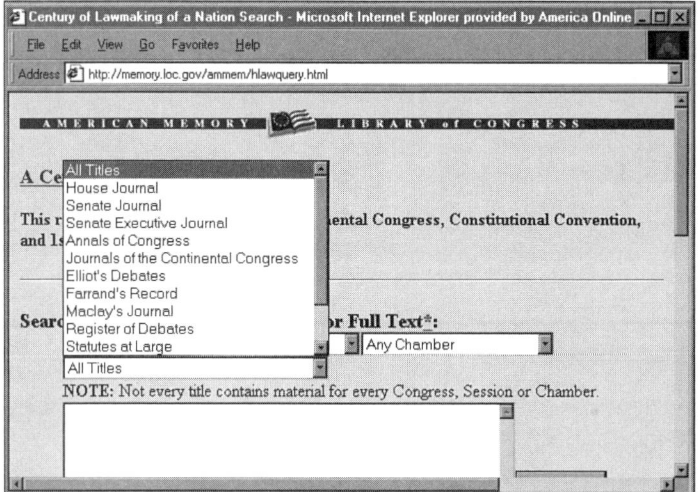

This is the search page for the Library of Congress's collection of important documents from the nation's founding.

At this search page, you can search the *Journals of the Continental Congress*, Farrand's *Records*, the House and Senate journals from the period, Elliot's debates, and numerous other documents by keyword.

Wrapping It Up

- The Constitution and the Declaration of Independence are available in many places on the Web.
- These same sites can lead you to a wealth of additional information about these documents.
- Sites such as those provided by the National Archives and the Library of Congress can also lead you to information about American history, law, and the founding.
- You can move from site to site and document to document by surfing links found in these documents, by entering a specific URL into your browser, and by bookmarking sites for easy reference.

CHAPTER 2

Going Online with the U.S. Senate and the House of Representatives

In the last chapter, we discussed how to find the foundational documents of our government—the Declaration of Independence and the Constitution. We also covered some general search techniques, and saw the variety of places in which you can locate information about these documents. In the next three chapters, we will look at the three coequal branches established in the Constitution: the legislative, executive, and judicial branches of the federal government. In this chapter, we look at the legislative branch, made up of the U.S. Senate and the House of Representatives.

What You'll Learn in This Chapter:

- How to identify your senators and representative in Congress
- How to write your member of Congress, and why
- How to find out what your member of Congress has been doing in Washington by researching bills on the Internet
- What other congressional offices have useful information on the activities of the federal government

The Senate

The U.S. Senate is comprised of 100 members, two from each state. Each member serves for a six-year term. These terms are staggered, so only one-third of the Senate is up for election in any even-numbered election year.

The Senate's Home Page

The Senate's Web page is at *www.senate.gov*. This page features a number of useful links.

First, look at the button at the top called Senators. This button takes you to an alphabetical list of the senators, with links to each senator's own Web page. These pages vary in quality—some contain useful information about contacting agencies, legislation, the senator's record, and so forth. Others are limited to pictures and puffy press releases.

The home page for the U.S. Senate.

You might assume that a senator's own page would also have information about—or at least links to—the senator's campaign committee. That isn't so. Both the Senate and the House of Representatives follow internal rules that prohibit subsidization of a member's campaign by his official budget and a link—however trivial its expense—does just that. (By the way, campaign Web sites cannot provide links to the official Web page, either.)

The Senate home page also has links that lead you to the Senate's schedule, articles about its history, lists of committees and their members, roll call votes, and other useful research information. You can also leap from this page to the system through which you can research specific pieces of legislation. We'll talk about this system, called THOMAS, later in this chapter.

How to Find Your Senators

Finding your senators is easy. Each state's two senators represent the entire state (that is, there are no in-state districts). To find your two senators' names, select your state at the box called Connect with Your Senators on the Senate's home page. Click the down arrow, and scroll to the name of your state. Then click the button labeled Go. The Senate home page will reload, but you will see the names of your senators where you saw the Connect with Your Senators text before.

Email Your Senators

Now that you know the names of your two senators, you can mail their offices with the information, request, or opinion you want them to consider. Click the Senators button to call up the list of senators. Find one of your senators on the alphabetical list, and click on the link to his or her page. That page will often have a button or other link to call up an email form you can use to send your message. At the very least, the page will give you the email address of the senator's office.

You should be aware, however, that the senator will probably never see this message—staff read this material, and probably only after the "snail mail" is done each day.

If you want to make an impact, use clean, decent stationery, a good word processor or pen, and write a neat, clear, and to-the-point letter the old-fashioned way. Because email is convenient, special interest groups often overuse it, and as a result, staff members have learned to tune out much of it.

Think Twice About Email

When you use email to contact your senator, you should realize that the office's inbox is likely stuffed with messages from other constituents—some of whom are probably repetitive or a little off-the-wall. Your note might be lost in the shuffle. Sometimes nothing does the job better than an old-fashioned letter. If you are contacting your senator about problems with an agency (that is, "casework"), a follow-up phone call is also wise.

The House of Representatives

The House of Representatives (sometimes also called *Congress*) is made up of 435 members, each from districts that are roughly equal in population. Hence, California has 52 House members, whereas Montana has one. Each state has at least one House member, so no state is entirely shut out of the House.

The Home Page of the House of Representatives

The House's home page is at *www.house.gov*. Links from this page take you to a directory of House members, a search page to search House sites, members' Web sites, and special pages for committees.

From this page, you can also follow links to schedules and roll call votes on legislation.

If you can't make sense of the various stages of legislation or the technical terminology, click the link to The Legislative Process. This links you to a page titled Tying it All Together. (This page's link is at the bottom of the list. Or, you can enter *www.house.gov/house/Tying_it_all.html* in your browser to go there directly.

Put underlines between the words or the URL will not work.) This summary should answer most of your questions about legislation and legislative procedure.

If you hunger for yet more detail on the legislative process, call up How Our Laws Are Made, which is also linked to this page. You can also go directly to its table of contents at *thomas.loc.gov/home/lawsmade.toc.html*.

The home page of the House of Representatives.

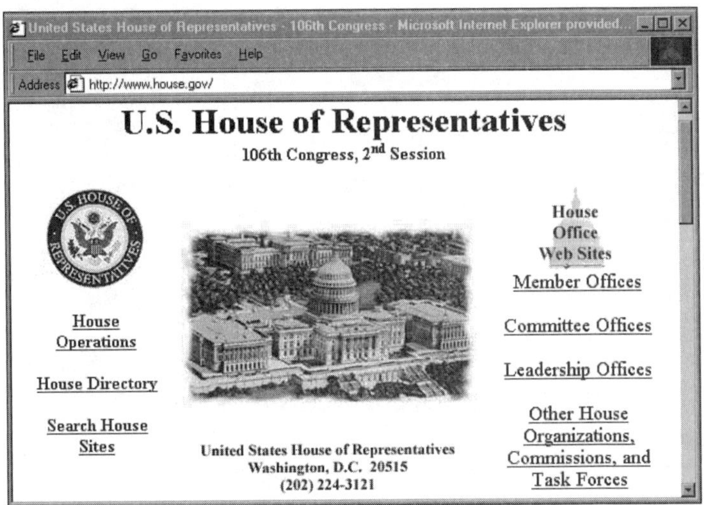

Spacing in URLs

URLs do not use spaces. If you see spaces in between words in a URL, place an underline character (_) between each word. Most URLs will print these, but in cases where the URL address itself is also underlined (that is, when included as a link) you might not be able to see how the spaces are represented.

How to Find and Email Your Congress Member

Finding the name of your representative is a little more difficult than for your senator. Populous states have dozens of congressional districts. Residents of large states rarely know the number of their congressional district. People often mistakenly believe that a local well-known Congress member who gets lots of publicity represents them, when, in fact, they are not in that member's district.

Never fear; the House of Representatives home page provides an easy way to find your representative. At the bottom of the House's home page (*www.house.gov*) you will see the link Write Your Representative. This link takes you to a page that will help you find your House member.

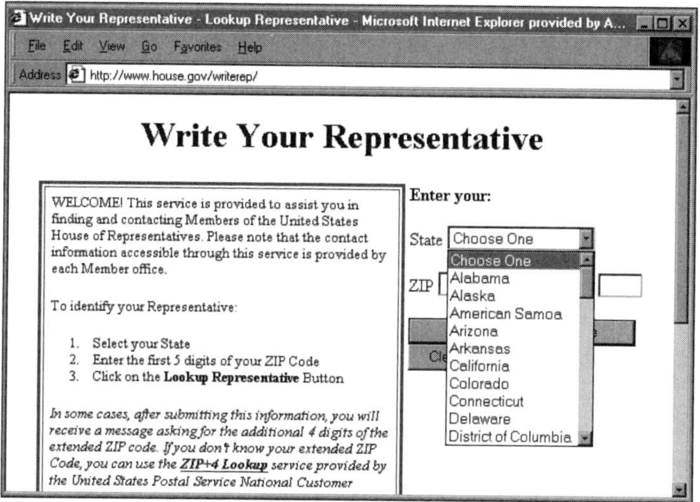

The Write Your Representative lookup page (www.house.gov/writerep/).

▼ Try It Yourself

1. Point your browser to *www.house.gov.*
2. Click the Write Your Representative link in the lower-left corner.
3. Choose your state from the drop-down box on the right.
4. Enter your ZIP Code.
5. A page will load with the name of your House member. If the member uses the Write Your Representative service, the page will have boxes where you can type your name, address, and city, and a button to click to move to a second page where you can type your message to the member's office. If the member does not use the service, you are still given his or her name and district number, as well as an address and phone number to use to contact the congressional office.

▲

Why Would I Write My Representative?

Here are a few common reasons why people contact members' offices. Maybe some apply to you.

- You're having trouble with your federal benefits. You need someone on your side to go up against the Social Security Administration or the Veterans Benefits Administration. Caseworkers on your member's staff are experienced at intervening on behalf of constituents, and can probably help.

continues

continued

- You want change to a federal law or program. Your member's staff can convey your concerns to the member. If the member's committee assignments have jurisdiction over the area you've addressed, your ideas could be part of a new bill!
- Your family is visiting Washington, D.C. and you'd like help with special tours of the Capitol or White House. Again, the member's staff can assist you with these requests.

Just as with many senators, many House members have email links on their own Web pages. You can click these links, and use the form that pops up to compose your message.

The earlier warning regarding email still applies—you might be better off drafting an old-fashioned letter to the member's office than dashing off a quick email.

Monitoring Legislative Activity on THOMAS

Now that you are familiar with your senators and your House member, you might want to see what they've been doing in Washington. A good way to learn about legislative activities is through THOMAS, the Library of Congress's legislative information site. You will find links to THOMAS on the Senate and House home pages, or you can access it directly at *thomas.loc.gov*.

From the THOMAS home page, you can follow links to the House and Senate schedules, find text of legislation, roll call votes, debates as printed in the Congressional record, and other useful information. otice toward the bottom of the page that THOMAS also has links to specific documents of public interest, such as appropriations bills and impeachment documents.

Looking Up Bills in the News by Using THOMAS

Look in the upper-left corner of the THOMAS home page. You'll see a link titled Bills in the News. Clicking this link brings up an alphabetical list by topic of many newsworthy bills. By scrolling through this list, you can find bills covering such hot topics as the patient's bill of rights, gun control, and abortion.

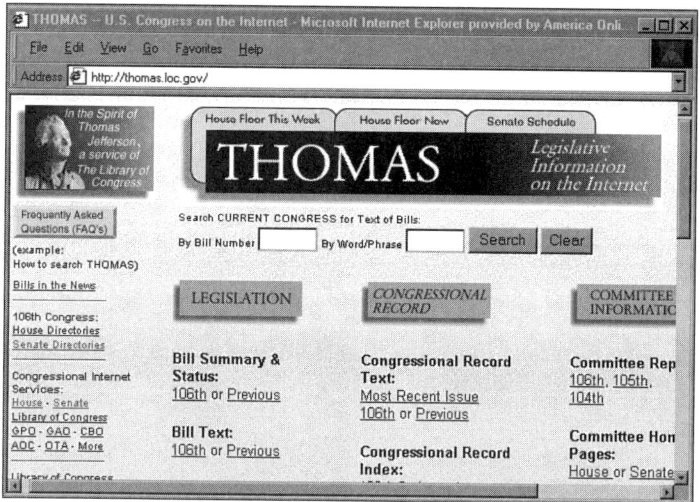

THOMAS: The Legislative Information page of the Library of Congress.

For instance, under Internet Tax you will see a link to H.R. 3252. Click that link and THOMAS will bring up a Bill Summary & Status page.

The links on this page will take you to several useful resources. First, notice that the author's name is also a link. If you click that link, you will see a list of all the other bills sponsored by the member. Under the Bill Status link are the dates and actions taken on the bill as it works its way through Congress. As noted earlier, you should consult Tying it All Together at *www.house.gov/house/Tying_it_all.html* or How Our Laws Are Made at *thomas.loc.gov/home/lawsmade.toc.html* for more information on congressional procedure. The Cosponsors link lists the other members who have signed on to the bill.

Now click Text of Legislation. You will see the text of the measure in plain text format. You will also see another set of links at the top of the page. One link will take you to a PDF version of the bill from the Government Printing Office. This is a better-looking version of the text that you might want to print for your records, show other people, or use for your research because you can cite to page numbers in this format.

Another link takes you to a page where you can review the places in the *Congressional Record* where the bill was mentioned. For

Bills in the News

If you've been following an issue in the news, but don't know the author, title, or bill number of federal legislation on the issue, take a look at the Bills in the News option on THOMAS. There you will find an alphabetized subject index of topical legislation, with links to the texts, summaries, and statuses of these bills. You won't have to wade through a long list of technical bills on a topic to find the big one that everyone's talking about.

controversial bills, there might be a long list of such references, and, unless you know the date of a particular debate you want to find, looking through each item can be time-consuming. So, if you want to see the text of a particular debate, find an account of it in the press first, and then use the date to narrow your search of the *Congressional Record*. You can also use a link to see the bill's text in full display, which makes it easier to review lengthy bills.

The Bill Summary & Status page for H.R. 3252.

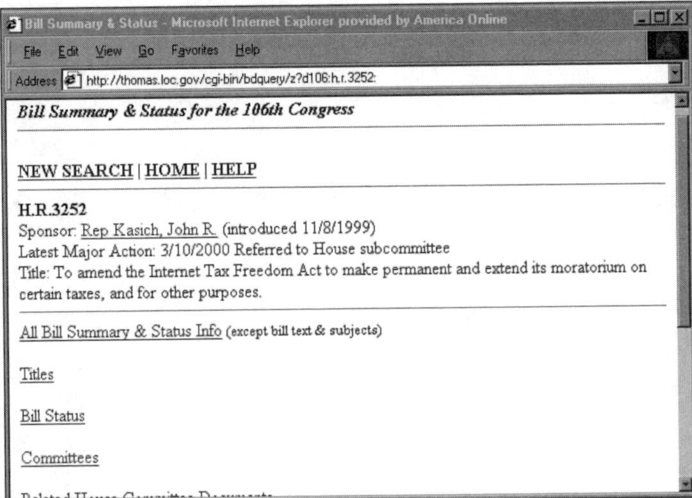

Documents in PDF

You will come across documents in PDF (Portable Document Format) while doing research. To read this format requires Adobe Acrobat Reader. (The Acrobat Reader is available free from Adobe at *www.adobe.com/products/acrobat/readstep.html*.) This format allows documents to be posted on a Web site "as is" and to be read or printed by anyone with the Reader software.

Looking Up Bills by Bill Number

You can also search for bills from the THOMAS home page. This is the most efficient way to obtain the text of a bill if you already know the bill's number. By entering the number in the By Bill Number field and then clicking the Search button, you will pull up the text of the bill with the same links to the PDF version, congressional records, and full display that we saw before. If there is more than one version of the bill, you will see a list with a link to each version.

You might also have seen that you can execute a search by word or phrase from the THOMAS home page. If you don't know a bill's number and the bill relates to a narrow topic, this is another good way to retrieve the bill's text. But if your topic is fairly general (for example, *taxes* or *health care*), chances are high that a number of bills—many of them narrow technical legislation—will be in the system, and it might take a while to sort through them all to find the legislation you want. This is where the Bills in the News feature discussed earlier can be helpful.

Complete Bill Numbers Include "S." or "H.R."

When referencing a bill number, remember to include an "S." before the number for a Senate bill and a "H.R." before bills from the House of Representatives. So, in THOMAS, you would request **H.R. 1** for House Resolution 1, not simply **1**.

Finding Your Senator or House Member's Legislation

Now that you have identified your senators and representative and have reviewed how to research legislation, let's look at how to find the legislation of your particular officials. To get a list of all the bills sponsored by your senator or House member, select the link to 106th under Bill Summary & Status on the THOMAS home page. (The 106th Congress is the current Congress.) On the next page, find Browse and click the link to Sponsors/Cosponsors. You will then see a page listing all the senators and House members, and from here you can link to all bills sponsored and cosponsored by them.

Some Newsworthy Committees

Most of the real work in the Senate and the House of Representatives is done in committees. Here are some powerful committees often in the news. You might want to check their Web pages for recent hearings, upcoming debates, and other information.

- Senate Foreign Relations Committee, *www.senate.gov/~foreign/*. Senator Jesse Helms is the colorful and well-known chairman of this committee. Its jurisdiction includes nuclear weapons proliferation and the United Nations.
- Senate Appropriations Committee, *www.senate.gov/~appropriations/*. Although all appropriations bills originate in the House, the Senate must approve and may amend all appropriations. Both battles with the administration and pet projects for the folks back home are part of this committee's activities. This is the largest Senate committee (with 28 members). A chart showing the subcommittee jurisdiction for each federal spending program can be found by clicking the Jurisdiction button.
- Senate Judiciary Committee, *www.senate.gov/~judiciary/*. Among other things, this committee considers appointments to the Supreme Court and other federal courts. Perhaps the best known witness before this committee is Anita Hill.
- House Ways and Means Committee, *waysandmeans.house.gov/*. This committee writes tax, Social Security, and trade laws, for starters. It is a very powerful committee with broad jurisdiction.
- House Committee in Standards of Official Conduct, *www.house.gov/ethics/*. This committee is also sometimes called the "ethics" committee. On its Web page, you will find the rules governing gifts, conflicts of interest, honoraria, and other ethics-related topics.

continues

Each Session of Congress Has a Number

The Congress serving in 1999–2000 is the 106th Congress. Because each Congress is for a two-year cycle, the 2001–2002 Congress will be the 107th. Likewise, the 1997–98 Congress was the 105th. This detail is important when researching legislation because the bill numbers start over again with each new Congress. So, H.R. 1 from the 105th Congress (which was the Working Family Flexibility Act) is a different bill from H.R. 1 from the 106th Congress (which was about Social Security reform).

continued

- House Commerce Committee, *www.house.gov/commerce*. The Commerce committee reviews energy policy, including competition in electricity. It also has jurisdiction over consumer protection and regulations of communications.
- House Judiciary Committee, *www.house.gov/judiciary*. The Judiciary Committee reviews crime and justice legislation. It is perhaps most famous for the impeachment and trial of President Clinton in early 1999. An exhaustive timeline with links to impeachment-related documents is available at the Impeachment link on this page, or at *www.house.gov/judiciary/icreport.htm*.

Older Legislation

THOMAS can retrieve older legislation, too. In fact, its collection of summaries and enacted legislation (listed by Public Law number) extends to 1973. Full bill text is available back to 1989. Just click Previous under Bill Summary & Status and choose the link for whichever previous session you want to research.

Some Really Interesting Stuff

The research of legislation can be tiring. The procedures are a bit Byzantine, the language is tedious, and the official legislative Web pages can be lacking in the nitty-gritty information you really want. Fear not. There are other Congressional sites to visit for good information on federal legislation; namely, the Congressional Budget Office (CBO), the General Accounting Office (GAO), and the Congressional Research Service (CRS).

The Congressional Budget Office

The CBO is Congress's budgetary and economic research office. Among other tasks, it reviews new legislation to determine its cost to the taxpayers. The CBO's home page is *www.cbo.gov*.

The CBO home page provides a list of links and descriptions of its recently released reports. If a budget issue has hit the news, chances are good that a report on this site covers that topic. In fact, the report itself might be the source of the story. The site also provides data on budget projections, economic projections, and historic information, so you can review the trends yourself.

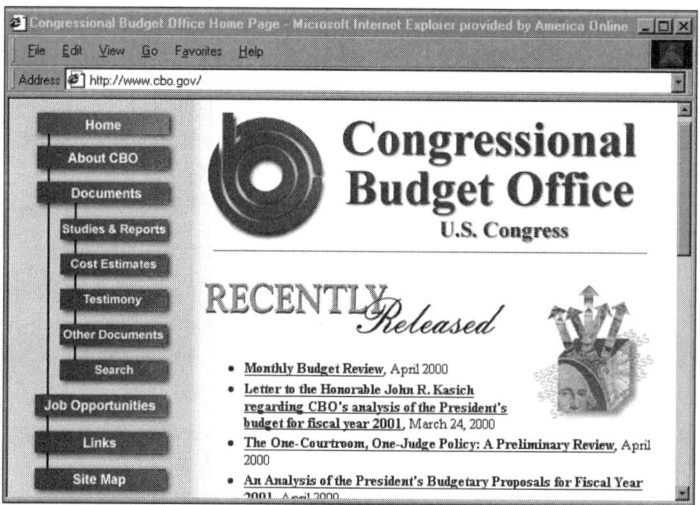

The home page for the Congressional Budget Office, with links to recently released reports.

The General Accounting Office

The GAO provides an important part of Congress's oversight. Not only does Congress pass laws, it also oversees the federal agencies that implement those laws to see whether they are doing so properly and to evaluate whether new laws or amendments are needed. The home page for the GAO is at *www.gao.gov/main.html.*

From this page, you can find copies of GAO reports, Comptroller General decisions, and other information related to governmental accountability. Check the What's New link to see the most recent additions to this site. You can also access FraudNet, which allows you to report waste, abuse, or mismanagement of federal funds you know about.

The Congressional Research Service

The CRS is Congress's research arm. It has been called the "$62-million think tank" and works exclusively for Congress. The CRS does not have a Web page of its own. However, many of the publications issued by the CRS are available on the Web. Try the link provided by the Senate at *www.senate.gov/~dpc/crs/reports/reptsubj.html.* This URL takes you to an index of hundreds of CRS reports, organized by subject.

These reports are provided in both PDF and ASCII. As noted earlier, to read PDF files requires using the Adobe Acrobat Reader program.

Whatever your issue, chances are good that the CRS has written a report addressing it—from privatizing Social Security to nuclear proliferation to global warming. You might want to look under the Reference topic. This lists a number of CRS reports that address legislative research, Internet research, and other guides that readers of this book might find helpful.

Wrapping It Up

In this chapter, you found the home pages of the Senate and the House. You learned how to

- Find the names of your senators and your representative
- Contact those members via email, and reviewed some of the reasons why you might want to contact a member
- Use THOMAS to do research on legislative bills
- Research congressional offices—namely the CBO, GAO, and CRS—with valuable research information

As we saw, Congress considers legislation, and oversees the federal bureaucracy. In fact, two specific offices we found—the CBO and GAO—are important components of Congress's oversight of the executive branch. In Chapter 3, "The Wired White House and Bitmap Bureaucracy," we take a closer look at the executive branch.

CHAPTER 3

The Wired White House and Bitmap Bureaucracy

The next branch of the federal government we look at is the executive branch. It consists of the president, his aides and cabinet, and the agencies of the federal government, sometimes referred to as the *bureaucracy*. The president proposes programs, signs or vetoes legislation, and carries out foreign policy. The agencies run federal programs, and write and implement the regulations that govern these programs. Many agencies also have the power to adjudicate violations of these rules. Although some top agency staff members are political appointments made by the president, many others are career civil servants who are largely protected from changing political winds by the civil service system.

Agencies are interesting animals. They are governed by Congress-passed laws and funded by Congress-appropriated money (of course, only if the president signs these measures), and their upper offices are filled by presidential appointments. But the day-to-day work of agencies is done by permanent civil servants, and they might know more about the minutiae of their programs than anyone else.

What You'll Learn in This Chapter:

- How to contact the White House over the Internet
- Where to find useful presidential documents
- What help and information are available from federal agencies on the Web
- How to research federal rules and regulations

Hail to the Chief

The White House (more formally known as the Executive Office of the President) Web site is found at *www.whitehouse.gov*.

At the White House's site, you can find information about the activities of the president, vice president, first lady, and the vice president's wife. If you click the link The President & Vice-President, a page appears that provides you with links to email forms through which you can email the president, vice president, first lady, and the vice president's wife.

The White House Web site, with links to email, library resources, and agencies.

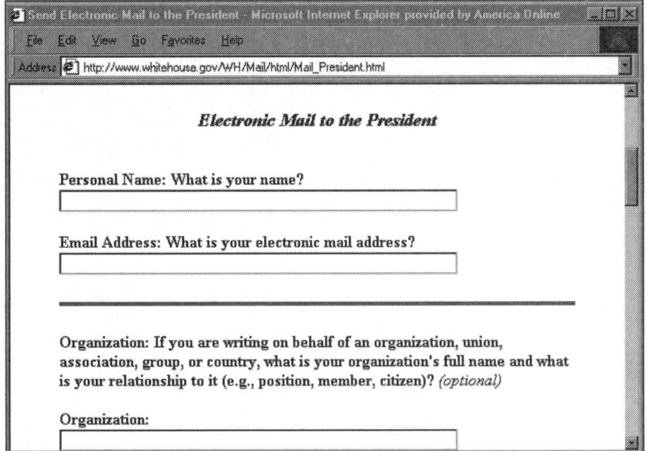

Send email to the president using this form.

This email form is similar to the Write Your Representative form used by the House of Representatives, which we looked at in detail in Chapter 2, "Going Online with the U.S. Senate and the House of Representatives." This form provides you with spaces for your name and address, pull-down menus to describe the purpose and topic of your message, and your affiliation. After you send your message, you will get an electronic acknowledgment from the White House. Any additional communications with you will be made via regular mail.

And, just as I cautioned in Chapter 2, you should remember that the White House receives large amounts of email from all kinds of writers. Depending on the nature of your communication, you might be better off writing an old-fashioned letter to the president or a particular member of his administration.

The White House Web page also links you to a number of useful sites for research information. By clicking The Virtual Library link, you access a list of links to White House documents, such as briefings, radio addresses, and executive orders. The URL for this page is *www.whitehouse.gov/library/*. For current information (less than one week old) as well as interesting statistics, click the link to Briefing Room. The URL for this page is *www.whitehouse.gov/WH/html/briefroom.html*.

Executive Orders

The president can order the federal government to act without Congress's approval by issuing an executive order. Many orders deal with relatively uncontroversial matters; for example, establishing a presidential commission to advise the president on an economic or social issue. But other orders might declare controversial policies, such as regarding affirmative action for federal employees. Still others might address defense or foreign policy questions. An executive order of particular significance is EO 9981, issued by President Truman on July 26, 1948. That executive order desegregated the U.S. armed forces. (You can retrieve more information on this historic document at *www.trumanlibrary.org/9981.htm*.)

The scope of the president's unilateral power is controversial, and a topic beyond the reach of this book. The Virtual Library page has a link to a search page where you can look for executive orders by keyword, or you can reach that page directly at the URL *www.pub.whitehouse.gov/search/executive-orders.html*.

The White House Web page also has a link called Commonly Requested Federal Services. This page contains links to numerous federal agencies. We will talk about several agencies in depth next. If you want to find an agency page I don't discuss here, this link is a good place to start.

You Don't Need to Take a Number: Federal Agency Sites

The day-to-day work of the federal government is usually performed by an executive branch agency. Agencies are large and complicated. Before the Internet, it was difficult for ordinary people to find agency information—even phone numbers. Now, agency publications, phone directories, regulations, how-to manuals, and a host of other useful material can be obtained with the click of your mouse.

This section examines the Web-based information provided by some of the most popular agencies. (Popular in the sense that many people need their assistance at some point in life!)

Social Security Administration

Social Security Online, the SSA's Web site, is at *www.ssa.gov*.

The Social Security Online page.

This page has numerous links for people who need help or information from the SSA. In the top-left corner is a quick search box, so if you have a good idea of what you need, you can type in the keyword, click GO, and you will be taken to the proper page. Just under this feature is a pull-down menu for the SSA's publications.

Try It Yourself ▼

Suppose that you pay someone to help you keep the house clean or watch your children. You want information about the Social Security requirements for employers of household workers. To get a useful guide on this topic, follow these steps:

1. Click the Go To Publications! button.
2. Click the link to What's New - Recently published or revised publications.
3. Under 2000, you will see a link to Household Workers (1/00); (05-10021) (.html)--(.pdf).

4. Decide whether you want the document in HTML (to read using your browser) or PDF (to read using Adobe Acrobat Reader). As discussed in Chapter 2, Adobe Acrobat documents look better, but they can take longer to download.

5. Click the .html or .pdf extension, and the document will be pulled up in that format.

When you read it, you'll see that if you pay a household worker $1,100 or more in cash wages during a year, you must deduct Social Security and Medicare taxes and report the wages once a year.

The Social Security page also offers a retirement benefits calculator at *www.ssa.gov/retire/calculators.htm*. There, you can try three different options: a quick online calculator that uses your age and salary to calculate your benefits; a more-detailed calculator that asks you to provide an earnings history; and a detailed calculator that you can download.

Most of the rest of the Social Security Online home page is devoted to news releases regarding the Social Security system. Notice the row of buttons at the top of the page directly underneath the page's title. The Top Ten Services link is especially handy for most common SSA errands. There, you will find links that help you calculate your Social Security benefits, change your name on your Social Security card, and apply for benefits.

A Taxing Oversight

Social Security and Medicare taxes for domestic help? This tax requirement is often overlooked. If you forget, you could owe back taxes and penalties. For some taxpayers, the oversight proved much worse. This issue arose with nominations for attorney general by President Clinton; first of Zoe Baird, and then of Kimba Wood. Both nominees were found to have neglected the "nanny" tax, after which Clinton withdrew their names. The issue was finally put to rest with the appointment of Janet Reno, who has no children.

The Top Ten Services page also has a link to a page with the most popular given names from 1880 to 1997. The URL for this page is *www.ssa.gov/OACT/NOTES/note139/note139.html*. You might want to bookmark this page for fun. It lists the most common names by year, gender, state, and several other combinations, as disclosed in Social Security applications.

Finally, when you figure out what you need to do, you can retrieve the proper SSA form over the Internet. On the left side of the Social Security Online home page, click the link to Forms. You'll be sent to a page with links to the SSA's most frequently requested forms. Highlight the name of the form you want on the pull-down menu, click the Select the Form button, and you'll obtain the form in PDF. You can then print the form and fill it out.

Taxing Decisions

As more and more of you become self-employed, invest in the stock market, and add complexity to your financial lives, the prospect of completing your taxes yourself becomes more remote. The IRS, to its credit, attempts to make the ordeal easier with interactive features such as Tax Trails, online forms, instructions, manuals, and a wealth of articles and other features. Even so, the tax code is quite complicated, and often only an expert can see how certain transactions interrelate. So, use the Internet for education and planning for the future, but don't be afraid to ask a professional to help you with your taxes.

The Internal Revenue Service's Digital Daily

The IRS's Web page is called the Digital Daily, and it is formatted to resemble a newspaper. Its URL is *www.irs.gov*.

This page features several articles of general interest about taxes. At the bottom are several links you will find helpful. The first link we'll look at is Forms & Pubs. The URL for this page is *www.irs.gov/forms_pubs/index.html*. (Remember to put an underline between the **forms** and **pubs** in the address.) This will take you to an index page with links to current-year forms and publications, "fill-in" versions of some forms, and other information. Clicking the link to Forms and Instructions will take you to a page where you can download current forms and instructions. (The URL for this page is *www.irs.gov/forms_pubs/forms.html*.) You can choose PDF, PCL (printer control language), PostScript (for compatible printers), or SGML text (Standard Generalized Markup Language) as a format. Most ordinary filers print out the forms in PDF using Adobe Acrobat and then fill them out.

Another useful link from the Digital Daily page is called Tax Info For You. This link will take you to a page of links to information commonly requested by individual filers. Links included here are to tax tables, a W-4 withholding calculator, a link to Publication 17 (the IRS's manual for personal tax filers), and many other useful pages.

The IRS's Digital Daily page.

Another link, Tax Trails, leads you through an interactive set of yes and no questions designed to answer many specific tax questions. These "trails" will lead you through the tangle of questions you must answer to determine, for instance, whether you are required to make quarterly estimated tax payments, whether you owe taxes on tip income and how much, and whether you qualify for certain deductions.

The tax code isn't straightforward, so these "trails" can be jargon-laden and confusing. Nevertheless, the IRS has tried to make the convoluted logic of federal taxes easier to wade through, and even if you don't do your own taxes, checking out services such as Tax Trails can be quite an education. But, unless you are already comfortable with most tax concepts, you might want to enlist the help of a tax professional if you are confronted with a complicated tax situation.

The Census Knows the Street Where You Live

The Census Web page is at *www.census.gov*. The Census Bureau does more than just send Americans a long questionnaire each decade. The statistics it compiles are useful for government agencies and private researchers alike. The Census Bureau makes population estimates and projections for cities and regions (which are probably more up-to-date than the highway sign you see when entering your town). It also publishes economic census data, so you can see how a particular business sector has grown (or shrunk) in your area.

Under the Maps link, you can tap the Census Bureau's demographic and mapping services (called TIGER, or Topologically Integrated Geographic Encoding and Referencing System) to draw a map of any locality, specifying features such as census tracks, parks, streets, highways, and even Indian reservations.

For example, if you click the Maps link (or enter the URL *tiger.census.gov*) and then click the TMS 3.1 link (which most anyone can use), you'll reach a page with a default map of the District of Columbia. Click the New Location link, and you'll be asked to provide the name of the town, state, or ZIP Code you want to map. The TIGER system will then provide you with a map, or a list of possible areas if more than one place fits your criteria.

Be a Good Netizen

Death and taxes are inevitable. So is the manipulation of your Social Security benefits and your taxes. Groups are out there to help you keep tabs on the government, and I discuss a number of them in Chapter 11, "Political Interest Groups." Look up a few groups, and see what they have to offer. In particular, the AARP monitors benefits legislation and regulations, and numerous taxpayer groups (such as Americans for Tax Reform) keep an eye on your pocketbook.

Speak your mind directly by contacting your congressman as I discussed in Chapter 2. If you're concerned about an administrative initiative, write to the president and the agency. The most direct way to speak your mind, of course, is to vote. If you aren't registered, do it today.

This is what the page of the map for ZIP Code 10012 (Manhattan) looks like.

The map of Manhattan, courtesy of the Census Bureau. Observe the checklist of items you can specify for your map.

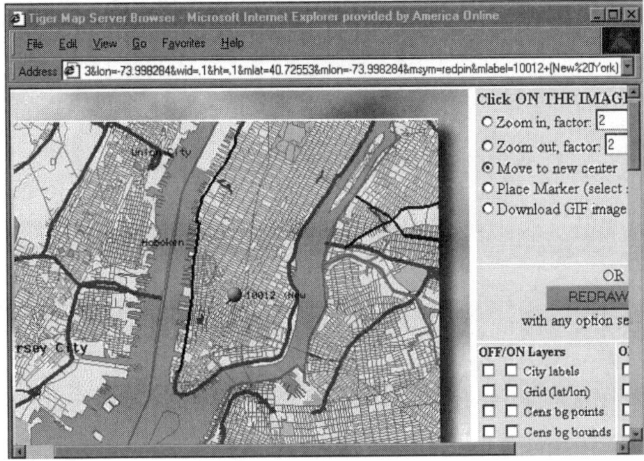

After you draw your map, you can zoom in and out by choosing how you want to rescale the map at the top and then clicking on the image. You can redraw the map with different items marked by selecting those items, and then clicking the Redraw Map button.

The Census Web page also contains portions of the *Statistical Abstract of the United States*, which you can access by clicking Statistical Abstract on the home page or by using the URL *www.census.gov/statab/www/*. This is a very useful reference for any research on economics, land use, growth, environmental issues, labor trends, and a host of other topics.

Other Executive Branch Web Sites

Following is a list of several other agency Web sites that might interest you. These sites contain useful and interesting information.

- The Federal Bureau of Investigation, *www.fbi.gov*: The Bureau's page features the Most Wanted list, as well as a Library link that contains links to bureau crime statistics, reports on internet crime, and the Bureau's newsletter "Cyber Notes," which lists software vulnerabilities to hackers, for example. Click the Major Investigations button and you can read about the FBI espionage investigation of Aldrich Ames.

Under the Freedom of Information Act link (FOIA), you can review the FBI files of a number of famous persons. The direct URL for this page is *foia.fbi.gov/room.htm*. The FBI has included files for such diverse individuals as Lucille Ball, Albert Einstein, Marilyn Monroe, Frank Sinatra, and John Wayne.

- The Department of State, *www.state.gov*: On this site, you can find traveler advisories for various countries, and obtain passport information. At the URL *travel.state.gov/passport_easy.html*, the Department provides advice on how to get a passport in a convenient Q&A format. Click the Regions button at the home page to find links to information about U.S. policies and relations with specific countries.
- The Immigration and Naturalization Service, *www.ins.usdoj.gov*: Here you can obtain INS forms, which are in PDF format and can be read and printed using Adobe Acrobat. The URL for the forms and fees page is *http://www.ins.usdoj.gov/graphics/formsfee/forms/index.htm*. The site also features guidelines, immigration rules, copies of regulations, and up-to-date news articles about changes in immigration policy. Documents related to the Elian Gonzales immigration matter in Florida were recently featured on the page.
- The Food and Drug Administration, *www.fda.gov*: The FDA is the chief regulator of food, drugs, cosmetics, medical devices, and animal drugs. Here you can find the agency's positions and statements about food irradiation, tobacco, and other current issues, as well as recall notifications. The site also features a special page with safety tips for buying drugs online, at the URL *www.fda.gov/oc/buyonline/default.htm*.
- The Department of Education, *www.ed.gov*: This site provides statistics and information on schools nationwide. It also features a page with useful financial aid advice and links at *www.ed.gov/offices/OSFAP/Students/*. Want to consolidate your loans? Check out the Direct Consolidation Loans Information Center at *loanconsolidation.ed.gov*.

One-Stop Agency Shopping

Sure, finding help from federal agencies on the Web is convenient—but digging up the URLs takes time. Want something even faster? Try the Federal Information Center (FIC) Web page at *fic.info.gov*. The FIC has operated a toll-free governmental referral service since 1966, but now its services are accessible through the Internet. Under the link Fed Web Locator, you will find a scrollable menu of topics, which will take you to the governmental Web site where that topic is addressed. The list of links under Popular Subjects can take you to the sites we discuss, as well as numerous others.

Wrapped Up in Red Tape, or How to Research a Regulation

Now that we've seen what a number of agencies offer, we will narrow the focus. The heart of any agency is the rules it enforces. These regulations are enacted (or *promulgated*) according to a strict set of administrative rules. Regulations are published in draft form, and are usually subject to public comment. They are revised, and then printed in the *Code of Federal Regulations* (or *CFR*).

The next section takes you through the process of researching a regulation, to give you an idea of how regulatory law works and where to find a regulation on your own. Of course, that isn't always the end of the story because when regulations go beyond the law, are improperly promulgated, or impinge on constitutional rights, they can be challenged and modified (or stricken) by a court. We will talk more about Internet research of courts in Chapter 4, "A Web Court Appearance."

The *Federal Register*

The *Federal Register* is the official daily publication for rules, proposed rules, and notices of agencies, and executive orders and other presidential documents. The *Federal Register* is published online by the Government Printing Office (GPO) at *www.access.gpo.gov/su_docs/aces/aces140.html.*

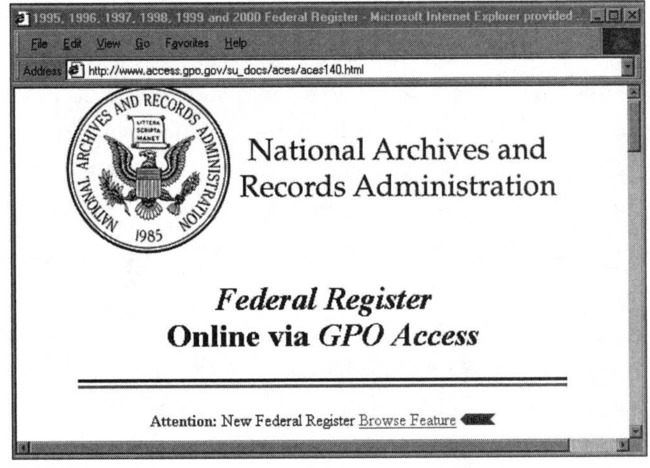

The GPO Federal Register page, which also enables searches of the code of federal regulations, public laws, and weekly compilation of presidential documents.

From this page, you can select the year of the *Register* you want to search (from 1995 to 2000), specify what you are searching for (a proposed rule, a final rule, a notice, or a presidential document) and enter search terms. You can also enter a date or period, if you know the date of publication.

To get a sense of what regulations are currently under consideration, browse the table of contents of today's *Federal Register.* (A link is also provided for the contents of the previous day's *Federal Register.*) This link is featured after the various search options. You can obtain the table of contents in HTML or PDF format. If you are simply perusing it on your computer, you'll probably want the HTML format.

For an example of a proposed rule, let's look at a proposal to add a new grape varietal name. The proposed rule was published on March 9, 2000, in Volume 65 of the *Federal Register*, on page 12,490. If you select 2000 *Federal Register* for your search, and submit a search for **"page 12490"** (including the quotation marks as part of the search term), you should retrieve the proposed rule. The text version is featured here.

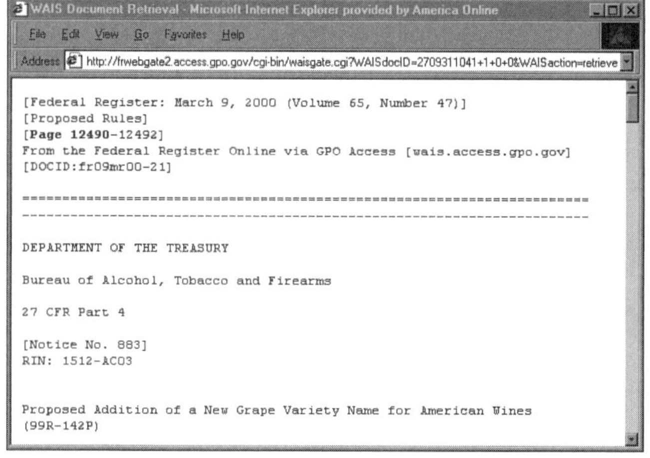
WAIS Document Retrieval - Microsoft Internet Explorer provided by America Online

File Edit View Go Favorites Help

Address http://frwebgate2.access.gpo.gov/cgi-bin/waisgate.cgi?WAISdocID=2709311041+1+0+0&WAISaction=retrieve

[Federal Register: March 9, 2000 (Volume 65, Number 47)]
[Proposed Rules]
[**Page 12490**-12492]
From the Federal Register Online via GPO Access [wais.access.gpo.gov]
[DOCID:fr09mr00-21]

DEPARTMENT OF THE TREASURY

Bureau of Alcohol, Tobacco and Firearms

27 CFR Part 4

[Notice No. 883]
RIN: 1512-AC03

Proposed Addition of a New Grape Variety Name for American Wines
(99R-142P)

The text of the proposed rule to add a new grape varietal name (Dornfelder) to federal regulations.

Proposed rules are an agency's draft of a regulation. They are published so that interested members of the public can comment on them.

Final rules are the text of the final regulation as promulgated by an agency. It will be codified in the *Code of Federal Regulations*, or CFR.

Notices are other agency documents. They might be requests for input from the public mandated by Congress. They might be other ministerial notifications, such as a cost-of-living adjustment made to a regulatory monetary amount, the availability of a new handbook or statistical information, or summaries of information submitted to an agency by the public.

In this proposed rule, you can read the background of the proposal, which explains how and why grape varietal names are regulated, an account of the petition to add this new name, and how you would comment on the proposal to the Bureau of Alcohol, Tobacco and Firearms.

For an example of a final rule, let's look at the final rule on statements made for dietary supplements concerning the effect of the product on the structure or function of the body, which was published January 26, 2000, on page 999. Again, if you enter a search for the 2000 *Federal Register* and insert in the search term box **"page 999"** (with quotation marks), you should pull up this document. As you scroll down the document to the text of the rule, it will look like this figure.

The final rule on statements made for dietary supplements concerning the effect of the product on the structure or function of the body.

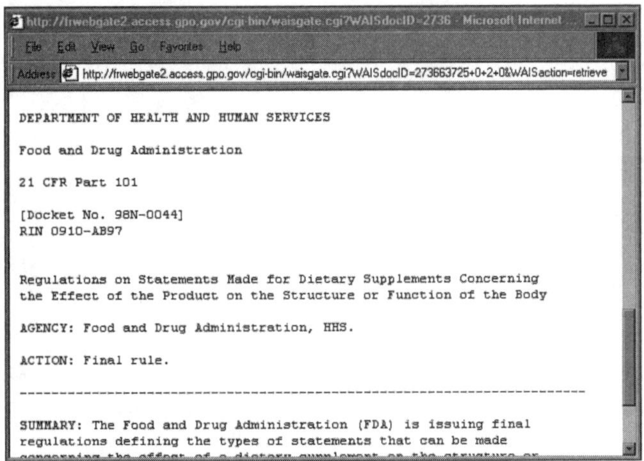

The summary explains what the rule is designed to do. It is followed by the effective date of the rule, and the name of a contact person for additional information. The rule then offers supplemental information on the background of the rule, and explains how the rule came about, what comments were considered, why suggestions were adopted or rejected, and how the rule is intended to work. This has been a controversial rule, so this particular final rule contains a lengthy explanation of its history. The agency is also required to determine the environmental impact and costs of compliance for the new regulation. After this explanation, the actual amendments to the regulation are provided. This is the language that will be codified in the *Code of Federal Regulations.*

The *Code of Federal Regulations*

Researching the *Code of Federal Regulations* (*CFR*) can also be done through the GPO Access page, by clicking on the Code of Federal Regulations link on the GPO Access home page (it's the first link in the top row). You'll pull up the CFR search page, which looks like this.

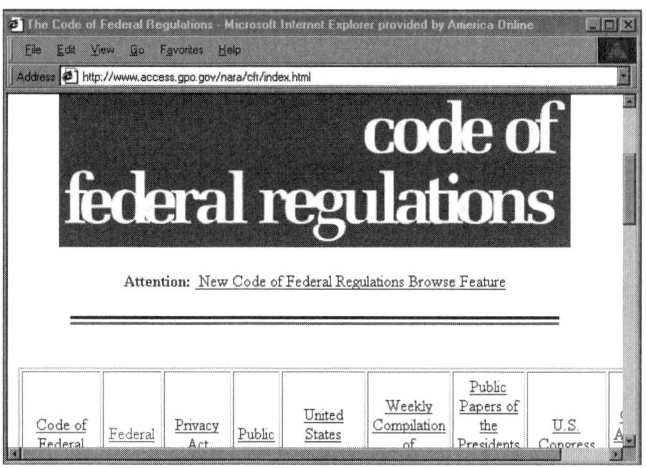

The Code of Federal Regulations search page.

Maybe you know generally what topic you want to research, but you don't have a regulation citation. You can choose the browse feature, which will pull up a chart of available versions of different titles within the *CFR*.

Boolean Logic

Most search engines use Boolean logic. If you want to search for a document containing several terms, link those terms with AND. If you want to retrieve documents that contain any one of several terms, link the terms with OR. So, the keyword search **coffee AND tea** will only retrieve documents that contain both the words *coffee* and *tea*. The search **coffee OR tea** will retrieve all documents with either the word *coffee* or the word *tea*. Not all search engines require you to capitalize the terms AND and OR. The search engine we are using here for the *CFR* does require capitalization.

For example, let's browse through some airport security regulations. In the browse chart you'll see that Title 14 is called Aeronautics and Space. By clicking the January 1, 2000 link in the chart, you will be linked to the current year's posted revisions to these regulations. You'll see in the next chart that a link can take you to the revisions of parts 60–139, which you can browse by clicking that link.

Reviewing the list that comes next, you will see that part 107 is titled Airport Security. By clicking that link, you'll move to a page with all the sections of Part 107 listed, and accessible in either text or PDF format. Reading down this list, you'll see that 107.21 regulates "Carriage of an explosive, incendiary, or deadly or dangerous weapon." Clicking the text version brings up the regulation. This regulation prohibits persons from carrying weapons through airport security. As you would guess, there are a few exceptions, such as for law enforcement officers.

Instead of browsing through the *CFR*, you can also execute a keyword search from the *CFR* search page. This search form works much like the *Federal Register* search we used before. If you want more guidance, you can review the helpful hints for searching the *CFR* by clicking the Helpful Hints link or going directly to the URL *www.access.gpo.gov/nara/cfr/cfrhints.html*.

Maybe our review of the proposed rule regarding varietal names for wine grapes has left you wondering what other wine labeling regulations are on the books. On the *CFR* search page (URL *www.access.gpo.gov/nara/cfr/*), enter **wine AND label**. (Don't use quotation marks here—instead of asking for the search engine to search for the exact phrase, you are asking it to search for documents that contain both words.)

You will retrieve a search result in order of how well the document matches your search terms. You will have retrieved Title 27 *CFR* Part 24, regulating wine; Title 27 *CFR* Part 4, regulating labeling and advertising of wine; and several other results you might find relevant to this topic. From here, click the text, PDF, or summary link to retrieve the version you want to review.

Wrapping It Up

This chapter brought your Web-surfing skills to the executive branch. As you can see, the president and his White House staff are but a part of this branch of government. Now, you should be able to

- Email the president, first lady, vice president, or the vice president's wife.
- Find useful presidential documents, such as executive orders and speeches.
- Get help or information from federal agencies such as the Social Security Administration, the IRS, the Census Bureau, and others. You also saw how to retrieve a map using the Census Bureau's TIGER mapping system.
- Find a federal regulation, not just as codified in the *Code of Federal Regulations*, but also as it was introduced as a proposed rule, and as it was justified in the agency's explanation accompanying the final rule.

CHAPTER 4

A Web Court Appearance

The third branch of the federal government is the judicial branch. It is made up of the Supreme Court and the lower federal courts. The lower courts consist of federal trial courts and federal courts of appeal.

Federal courts are courts of limited jurisdiction. They may hear cases arising under federal law or diversity cases involving parties from different states. They may only hear true cases or controversies presented by parties with standing or a real stake in the outcome. So, for instance, you can't go to federal court for an advisory opinion about how the law would apply to a hypothetical situation, and you can't bring a case to fight someone else's fight.

What You'll Learn in This Chapter:

- Where to find Supreme Court information, including how to retrieve a recent case
- How to find other federal courts on the Internet
- Which courts cover what parts of the country
- What to expect from a court Web site

The Supreme Court Online

The Supreme Court of the United States consists of eight associate justices and one chief justice. The nine justices of the Supreme Court have the final word on legal issues presented to the court. Almost all the cases they hear come to them via petitions for a *writ of certiorari*, which the Court has the discretion to grant or deny. Approximately 7,000 such petitions are filed each term.

The present chief justice is William Rehnquist, who was first appointed as an associate justice in 1972. He was appointed chief justice in 1986. Justices are appointed by the president with the consent of the Senate. Given the power of the Court to revise or overrule laws of the federal and state governments, and the life tenure of justices, appointments to the Court can become controversial. The confirmation hearings of Justice Clarence Thomas before the Senate Judiciary Committee in 1991 were especially bitter because of allegations of harassment made by a former staff member, Anita Hill.

Ordinarily, a justice is appointed to the Supreme Court after serving in a lower federal court. Justices also often have background in the Department of Justice or as law professors. Only one justice on the current court, Sandra Day O'Connor, has served in the past as an elected official.

The Official Supreme Court Site

The Supreme Court has only recently developed a Web site. It is at *www.supremecourtus.gov*.

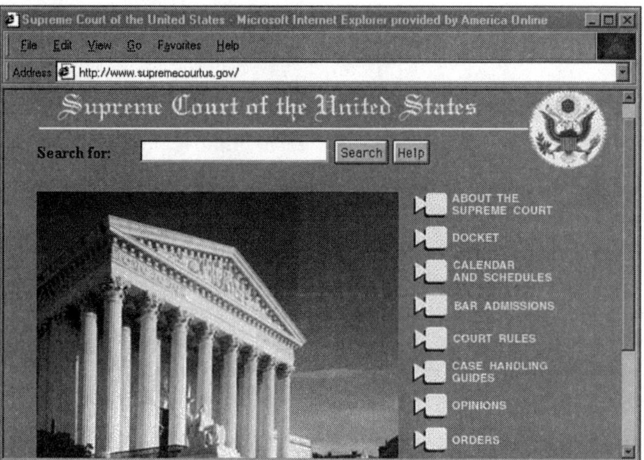

The official site for the United States Supreme Court.

This page contains links to documents about the Court and its activities. The About the Supreme Court link contains several documents about the history and traditions of the Court. The Docket button is not working as of this writing, but in the future, clicking it will take you to the Court's docket. The Court's calendars and schedules, showing the days on which arguments and conferences are held, are at the Calendar and Schedules link. The Court's rules, admissions standards, and case-handling guides of interest to attorneys representing clients before the Court, are under the next two buttons. Slip opinions are found under the Opinions link, and orders such as those denying review, are under the Orders link.

The Supreme Court's sessions are called *terms*. Each term begins the first Monday of October, and continues through summer of the following year.

Certiorari?

A *writ of certiorari* is the primary means for bringing a case before the Supreme Court. When seeking review, a litigant drafts a petition for a *writ of certiorari*. If the petition is granted, the case is heard. If the petition is denied, the lower court's decision stands. Of the petitions seeking *certiorari*, less than 5% are granted. Sometimes news reports say that the Court has approved a lower court's decision by denying *certiorari* in a case. That is inaccurate. Given the small percentage of cases that are granted review, it is inevitable that worthy petitions are not granted. Denial of *certiorari* should not be understood as approval of a lower court's decision.

Each justice approaches *certiorari* petitions differently. In general, the justice's clerks review the petitions and draft a memo to the justice with a summary of the case and a recommendation on the petition. After this review, the justices meet to discuss the cases that seem most worth a hearing. Often, these are cases in which two federal appeals courts have disagreed on a legal standard (called a *split* in the circuit courts).

Almost everything posted on the official site is in PDF, which, as observed before, is more time-consuming to download than a text file. Additionally, the Supreme Court does not provide searchable opinions before those slip opinions released this spring. So, you might find it easier to find what you're looking for using one of the unofficial sites I discuss next.

The Cornell Law School's Legal Information Institute

A useful unofficial site for Supreme Court research is hosted by the Legal Information Institute (LII) at the Cornell Law School. It is found at the URL *supct.law.cornell.edu/supct*.

You can find almost everything about the Court at this site. Links on the right side of the page will take you to decisions and order lists from the month (where you will find the names of cases denied review and other administrative decisions of the Court). Other links will take you to decisions, orders, calendars, oral argument schedules, and a list of the questions presented in cases for the term.

How is this site useful? You might need a copy of the Supreme Court's rules because out of the blue your neighbor asks you to handle his appeal to the Supreme Court. You might also be interested in perusing the opinions of your favorite justice. More likely, you probably just want to see the opinion in a recent case because you've read about it and the opinion concerns a topic of interest to you, or maybe it deals with an issue of importance to your family or your business. We'll now see how easy it is to find a recent Court opinion on this site.

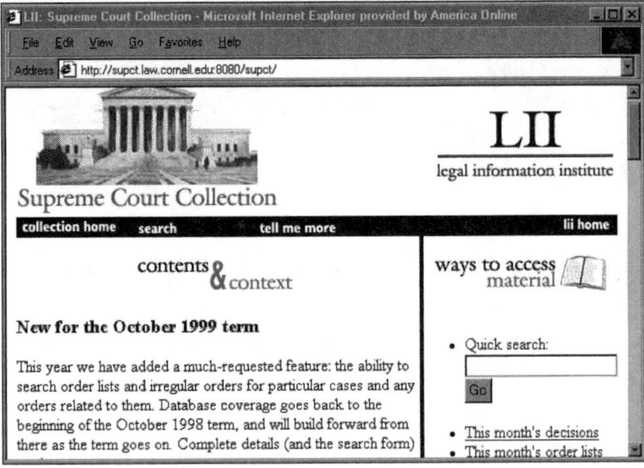

The Legal Information Institute's Supreme Court Collection page.

Try It Yourself ▼

You've just read in the newspaper that the Supreme Court has handed down an important decision. You want to read the decision. This is how you can easily retrieve most recent decisions.

1. Go to the Legal Information Institute Supreme Court page, at *http://supct.law.cornell.edu/supct/*.
2. Click the This Month's Decisions link on the right.
3. You will retrieve a list of case names, followed by the case number, date of argument, and date of decision.

4. Click the link to the case you want to read. The newspaper will probably give you a good idea of the date of decision or the names of the parties.

5. The next page enables you to choose what part of the decision to read (the syllabus, which is a summary; the opinion; or any concurring or dissenting opinions) and what format (HTML or PDF) you want to use.

You can also search decisions since 1990 by topic (and even earlier, if you desire). The links are on the right side of the LII Supreme Court page. The direct URL to the topic search page for decisions from 1990 to the present is *supct.law.cornell.edu/supct/topiclist.html.*

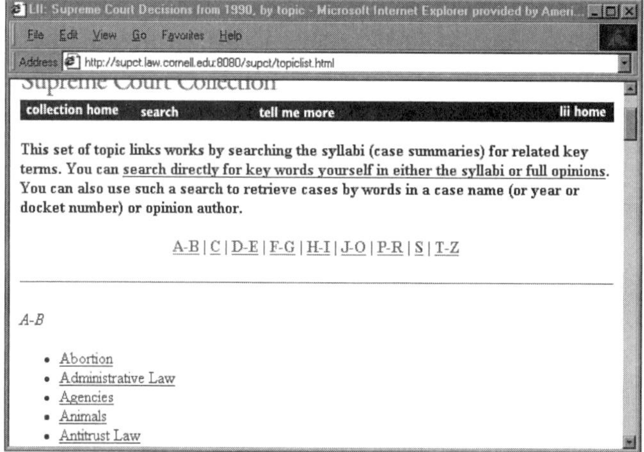

The LII Search by Topic page.

If you are looking for a recent decision on a particular subject, but don't know its name or its date, a topic search might help. You will, however, retrieve a list of case names, and might have to review several case links before finding what you want. Let's look at the list of opinions that is retrieved under the topic "animals." (Remember, this is just since 1990.)

Depending on how long a list you want to retrieve for your topic, you might prefer to use your own keyword to search. If your topic is narrow, you might find you get a more manageable result this way.

A topic search often retrieves a number of different cases.

Legal Terms

Suppose that you found the opinion and read it, but are put off by the legal terms used in it. You don't need to find a lawyer. At the bottom of the Legal Information Institute page is a link to a glossary. Under the headings provided in the glossary, the Institute has posted helpful explanations of some of the arcane terms used in Supreme Court opinions. Still stumped? Try *dictionary.findlaw.com.* This URL takes you to a search page where you can enter the term and retrieve a definition from the 1996 edition of the Merriam-Webster *Dictionary of Law.*

The Oyez Project

Northwestern University hosts a site called The Oyez Project. Oyez, pronounced "o-yay," translates into "Hear Ye" in Law French, a language used in English courts after the Norman Conquest until the 18th century. The Marshal of the Supreme Court opens a Court session with the cry, "Oyez, oyez, oyez."

On the home page at *oyez.nwu.edu*, find the Cases link. This will take you to links for events on this date in Supreme Court history, and search options to search cases by title, subject, citation, and date.

For subject searches, the Oyez site provides a list of subjects. You can choose a subject by highlighting it, or more than one by holding down the Shift key while you click multiple subjects.

Some of the opinions on the Oyez site are linked to recordings of the oral arguments at the Court, which you can hear through RealAudio's RealPlayer. If you don't have it, you can download a free copy of RealPlayer from *www.real.com.* I will talk more about sound files in Chapter 10, "Is There a Ministry of Silly Walks? Iconoclastic, Humorous, and Hard-To-Describe Political Sites"

For example, if you retrieve *Buckley v. Valeo* (citation 424 *U.S.* 1) and have RealPlayer, you can hear the oral argument in this landmark election law case.

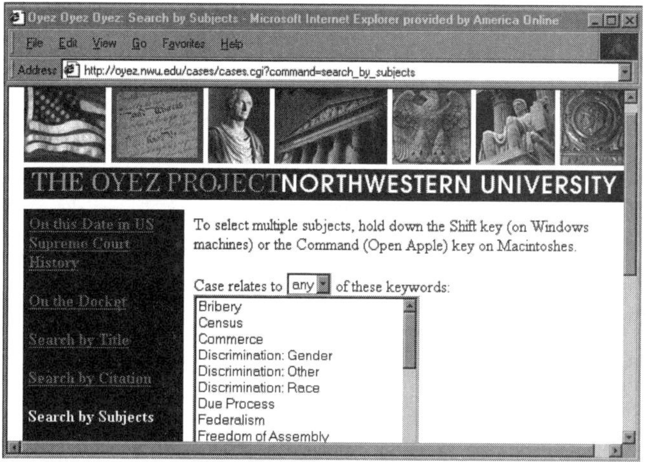

The Search by Subject Menu on The Oyez Project site.

The Oyez Project site also features a virtual tour of the Supreme Court building.

FindLaw's Constitutional Law Center

FindLaw, a Web portal with a vast and growing law library, has a specific page for Supreme Court materials, found at the URL *supreme.findlaw.com/supreme_court/resources.html.*

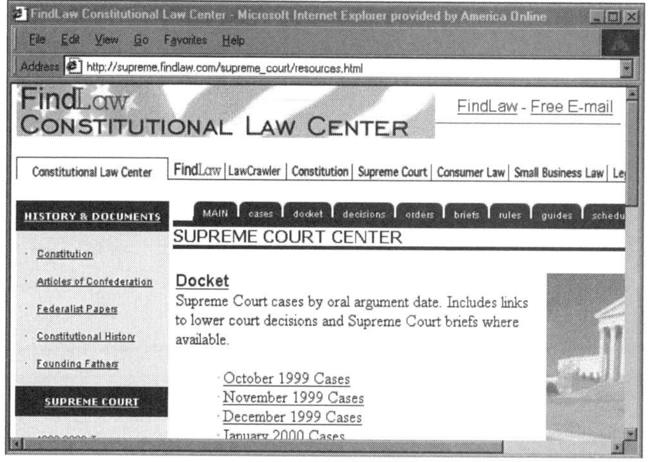

The FindLaw Supreme Court page.

On FindLaw, you will find materials similar to those provided at the LII site, but organized differently. The Docket link lists cases by date of hearing (not date of decision), and it also provides copies of briefs filed by parties to cases. Here, you can read what the attorneys for each side had to say about the issues in the case. Amicus briefs, filed by others with the permission of the Court (usually to emphasize a point that might not otherwise be made), are also provided.

FindLaw also offers links to articles on hot constitutional law topics and message boards. You can also subscribe to email update lists and have notices regarding developments in specific legal areas sent automatically to your email address. These links are found at the lower left of the FindLaw Constitutional Law Center's page.

Historical Society

The Supreme Court Historical Society hosts a Web page, found at the URL *www.supremecourthistory.org*.

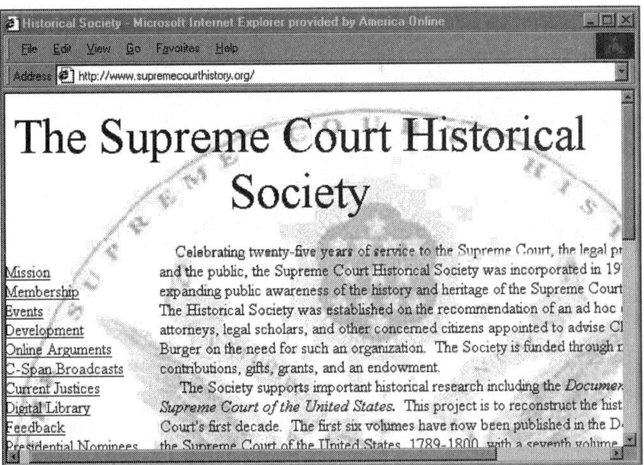

The Supreme Court Historical Society.

Links from this page can lead you to biographies of the justices, articles about the Court's history, and a chart of all the justices through history and which president appointed them.

Additional Sites with Supreme Court Information

As you have seen, several sites provide comprehensive, accurate, and up-to-date information from the Supreme Court, such as recent opinions, orders, rules, and biographical information on justices. What follows are URLs to sites with more background information about the Supreme Court, its decisions, and its influence on politics and government:

- The New York Times Guide to the Supreme Court: *www.nytimes.com/library/politics/scotus/index-scotus.html*
- Court TV's "A Journey Through Time," a multimedia presentation of the Court through history: *www.courttv.com/multimedia/supremecourt/index.html*
- The USAToday Supreme Court page: *www.usatoday.com/news/court/nscot000.htm*
- Washingtonpost.com's Supreme Court page: *www.washingtonpost.com/wp-srv/national/longterm/supcourt/supcourt.htm*
- The Law News Network's Supreme Court Report: *www.lawnewsnetwork.com/supremecourt/*

Legal Citations

Each decision is referenced by a legal citation. Supreme Court decisions are published in a book series called *U.S. Reports*. In citations, this is abbreviated *U.S.* So, a Supreme Court citation is of the form [Volume Number] *U.S.* [Page number] (year). Therefore, *Buckley v. Valeo's* citation is 424 *U.S.* 1 (1976) because it was published in Volume 424 of the *U.S. Reports* at page 1, and decided in 1976. Lower-court opinions work the same way, only the name of the book series will change. Even though much legal research is today done electronically, lawyers and courts continue to reference these specific publication citations because they provide a uniform unique reference for each case, and, frankly, because lawyers and judges are accustomed to them.

Other Federal Courts

The federal court system consists of a number of different court below the Supreme Court; namely, the district courts and special courts such as bankruptcy courts, the Court of Federal Claims, the Court of International Trade, and appellate courts.

First Stop: The Federal Judiciary Home Page

The Federal Judiciary Home Page is maintained by the Administrative Office of the Courts. The URL is *http://www.uscourts.gov/*. As the name suggests, you can find administrative information here about the federal judiciary, including budgets and statistics. On this home page, click the link to Frequently Asked Questions (also referred to as the FAQ).

As you can see, most questions about the structure and function of the federal courts are answered here.

Federal District Courts

Cases enter the court system usually through trial courts. This is the stage where litigants present their facts, fight about documents, cross-examine the opponent's witnesses, and give the jury (or oftentimes the judge) the best arguments they can. Most cases go through federal district courts. Some cases fall under the jurisdiction of special federal courts, which are discussed in the next section. Federal bankruptcy courts also serve in the federal circuits.

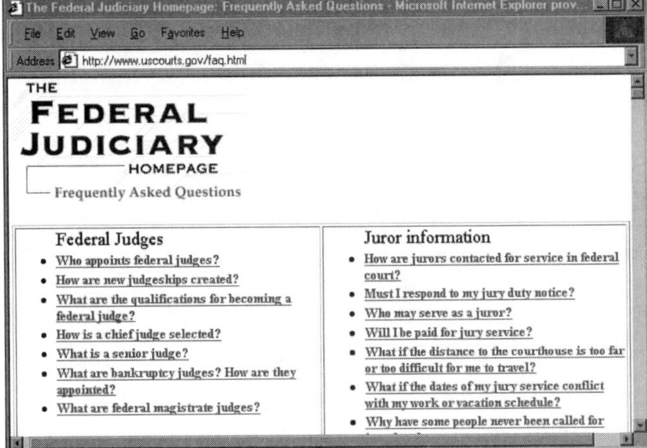

The FAQ available on the Federal Judiciary Home Page, at http://www.uscourts.gov/faq.html

The best source for links to these court pages is, again, a page hosted by the Administrative Office of the Courts. At *http://www.uscourts.gov/links.html*, you will view a national map, from which you can select the circuit of interest to you. Within each circuit's page, you will view a list of links to the district courts and bankruptcy courts within that district.

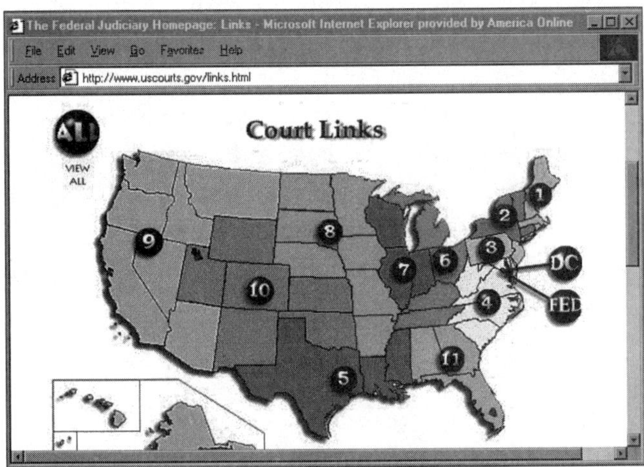

The Federal Judiciary Links page. Click the number of the circuit of the case, and you will retrieve the list of Web pages for the courts in that circuit.

Be warned that not all courts have made it to the 21st century; not all offer Internet connections to their files and information. As of this writing, Connecticut's federal courts, for example, do not have Web pages that you can use to get information about the opinions, rules, or cases before the court.

You should also be aware that docket information on live cases — including the status of the case, the papers that have been filed, deadlines, and so on—is usually obtained through a subscription service called PACER. The federal courts also offer a subscription call-in service through PACER that enables individuals to search for a name to see whether that person is involved as a party in litigation in the federal courts anywhere in the nation. These services, and additional electronic access information, are available at *pacer.psc.uscourts.gov/pubaccess.html*. The direct link to PACER's registration page is *pacer.psc.uscourts.gov/register.html*. (If you foresee the need to check federal case dockets frequently, this might be of use to you.)

Case in the News

A decision in the news you might want to see contains the conclusions of law in the Microsoft antitrust case. It is available from the Washington, D.C. district court's Web page. The URL from which you can retrieve it in PDF or HTML is *www.dcd.uscourts.gov/microsoft-conclusions.html*.

Other Federal Trial Courts

Cases involving trade, money claims against the U.S. government, and tax appeals are handled by special courts, which have national jurisdiction. The following are links you can use to get information about these courts:

- The United States Court of Federal Claims Web page is hosted by The George Washington University School of Law: *http://www.law.gwu.edu/fedcl*. This court hears cases involving claims for compensation against the United States, such as tax refund suits, contests over federal government contracts, and compensation for seizure of property under federal laws and regulations.
- The United States Court of International Trade page is at *www.uscit.gov*. This court's jurisdiction is over import/export and other trade cases.
- The United States Tax Court, at *www.ustaxcourt.gov/ustcweb.htm*, is the court that hears appeals by taxpayers of deficiency findings by the IRS.

Federal Appeals Courts

Federal appeals courts hear appeals from the federal trial courts. Links to the individual courts can be found, as you saw earlier, through the federal judiciary home page. The U.S. Federal Courts Finder, provided by the Emory University School of Law, is available at *http://www.law.emory.edu/FEDCTS/*. If you do not see a link in the official list, try the Emory list, which includes governmental and academic links.

Here is a list of the U.S. Courts of Appeal, and their jurisdictions:

First Circuit (Maine, Massachusetts, New Hampshire, Puerto Rico and Rhode Island): *www.law.emory.edu/1circuit* (Opinions only through Emory.)

Second Circuit (Connecticut, New York, Vermont): *www.tourolaw.edu/2ndCircuit*

Third Circuit (Delaware, New Jersey, Pennsylvania, Virgin Islands): *www.law.vill.edu/Fed-Ct/ca03.html*

Fourth Circuit (Maryland, North Carolina, South Carolina, Virginia, West Virginia): *www.law.emory.edu/4circuit*

Fifth Circuit (Canal Zone, Louisiana, Mississippi, Texas): *www.ca5.uscourts.gov*

Sixth Circuit (Kentucky, Michigan, Ohio, Tennessee): *www.ca6.uscourts.gov*

Seventh Circuit (Illinois, Indiana, Wisconsin): *www.ca7.uscourts.gov*

Eighth Circuit (Arkansas, Iowa, Minnesota, Missouri, Nebraska, North Dakota, South Dakota): *ls.wustl.edu/8th.cir*

Ninth Circuit (Alaska, Arizona, California, Idaho, Montana, Nevada, Oregon, Washington, Guam, Hawaii): *www.ce9.uscourts.gov*

Tenth Circuit (Colorado, Kansas, New Mexico, Oklahoma, Utah, Wyoming): *www.ck10.uscourts.gov*

Eleventh Circuit (Alabama, Florida, Georgia): *www.ca11.uscourts.gov/opinions.htm*

D.C. Circuit (District of Columbia): *www.cadc.uscourts.gov* (Many cases involving federal agencies must be heard here.)

Federal Circuit: *www.fedcir.gov*. All Federal judicial districts. This is the court that generally hears appeals from the Court of International Trade or the Tax Court, for example.

Wrapping It Up

In this chapter, you looked at the judicial branch of the federal government. Although often thought to be the exclusive territory of lawyers, with the help of the Internet, the courts are becoming more accessible to ordinary people, too. In this chapter, you learned

- Where to find all kinds of information on the Supreme Court, including case information, rules, dockets, and a glossary of terms.
- How the lower federal courts fit into the system, and where to find them on the Internet.
- How to retrieve an opinion that interests you. For certain important Supreme Court decisions, you found audio records of the oral argument, too.

PART II

Beyond Washington: State, Local, and International Governments Online

CHAPTER 5

State Sites on the Web

Now that we've looked at the federal government, we will examine state governments on the Web. Although the federal government governs many important aspects of our lives, so do the states. Information about state government and politics can be especially important when dealing with environmental and land use issues, law enforcement, education, and infrastructure issues such as roads. These kinds of programs are still largely under state authority, and the agencies and legislative initiatives that affect them will probably be found on the Internet in state sites.

Because one chapter can't cover every state in detail, this chapter will instead give you a sample from different states of the kinds of features that many states provide to an online researcher. I've featured six sites that provide good examples of state Web-based research. Then it is up to you to go exploring!

What You'll Learn in This Chapter:

- How to find a state's home page on the World Wide Web
- Where to find useful state agency information, such as driver's license information and tax forms
- What you'll find on a state legislative page, and why you might want to contact a legislator
- How to access state court pages, and what information you'll find there

State Government on the Web

The quality of state sites varies, but they usually feature some introductory message about the state, and links to government, tourism, and business development sites. Here is an example of a state home page, from the Commonwealth of Massachusetts, at *www.state.ma.us*.

On this page, you see a number of links that will take you to a page about almost any aspect of state government you could want. A useful characteristic of this site is that it places a number of links up front for easy identification. It also sorts state information by area (for example, Children and Health) as well as by kind of publication (for instance, Maps and Laws).

Several organizations have posted lists of links to state sites. Try GovSpot, at the URL *www.govspot.com/categories/stategovernment.htm*. This page has a State Home Pages link that will take you to a list of states. Just click the name of a state and you'll be taken to the appropriate home page.

Also try *http://www.piperinfo.com/state/index.cfm* for links to state home pages and state agencies on the Web.

The Massachusetts home page.

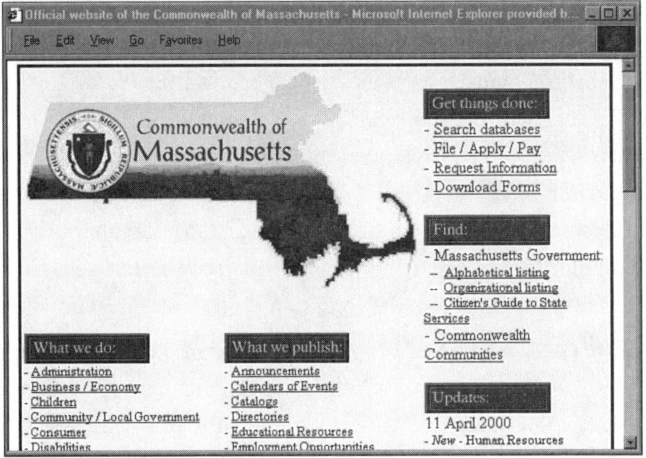

Address Under Duress

In a hurry and don't know the URL of the state's page you want? State home pages usually follow a set formula, which is *www.state.___.us*, where the blank is filled in with the two-letter postal abbreviation of the state. So, the Massachusetts URL is *www.state.ma.us*. Not every state uses this formula, so if you get an error message instead of the page that you want, check one of the links lists, or put the state's name in your browser.

State Executive Branch Agencies

Just as in the federal government, the state executive branch agencies provide a wealth of useful information on the Internet. This makes it much easier for ordinary citizens to get the information they need to complete necessary transactions with the state, and to obtain copies of state regulations. We will take a look at a couple of different state agency Web pages to see what they offer.

California's Department of Motor Vehicles

Perhaps no encounter with a state agency is more widely shared (or lamented) than the trip to the agency that regulates motor vehicles. Almost everyone, at some point, has had to take a driving test, register a vehicle, obtain a new driver's license, or sort out a problem with this agency.

The California Department of Motor Vehicles, like many of its sister agencies in other states, has made the process easier by posting its information on its Web page.

The home page of the California Department of Motor Vehicles, at www.dmv.ca.gov.

Here, you can obtain the information you need about when and how to register a vehicle. You can also learn how to obtain a driver's license, and find information about the different classes of licenses, copies of the state's driver handbooks, and even copies of written driver's tests for practice. You can learn the rules for smog checks, and the registration procedures for boats and motorcycles.

Eligible California drivers can also renew their registration online. Just follow the Vehicle Registration link from the home page or use the URL *www.dmv.ca.gov/online/vrir/vr_top2.htm.*

Virginia's Department of Taxation

The Virginia Department of Taxation site provides information about who must file tax returns in Virginia, and Virginia's exemptions, deductions, and credits.

The home page also links you to forms that you can download and use to file your taxes. Virginia also accepts electronic filing of tax returns, and a link from the home page will take you to a copy of the online filing handbook as well as to a list of approved software developers.

Where's the Line Between the State and the Federal Governments?

Both your state and the federal governments have environmental, transportation, and education bureaucracies. Both have prisons. Both charge you for taxes. Why this redundancy? Where does one government start and the other end?

The answer, and it is never very clear, falls under the name *federalism*. We have separate state and federal governments because under the Constitution, the federal government is limited to certain enumerated powers. All other powers are left to the states, or to the people. Of course, as the federal government has grown, the overlap between federal and state governments has become broader. But that discussion is a topic for a term paper, not a note in an e-politics manual.

The home page of the Virginia Department of Taxation, at www.tax.state.va.us.

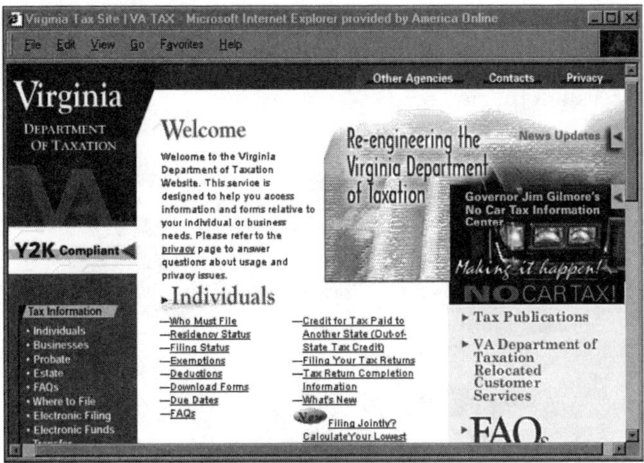

But before you become too depressed, you should realize that state agency sites aren't all about taxes and fees. Some can even make you rich…maybe. The New Jersey Division of Taxation has a page where you can search for unclaimed property in New Jersey, at *www.state.nj.us/treasury/taxation/updiscl.htm.*

Finding abandoned property in New Jersey.

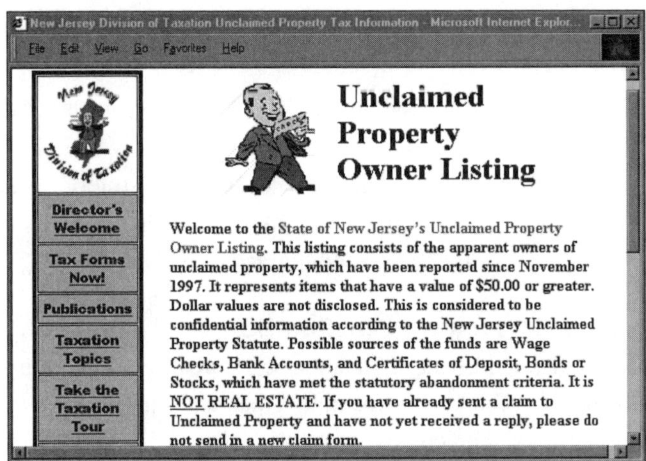

Taxes in Two States?

Maybe you worked in more than one state in the tax year, and owe income taxes to both. Check out the links to all state tax sites at *www.lib.lsu.edu/govdocs/taxes.html.* This site, hosted by Louisiana State University, can save you time when you need to retrieve tax forms from several states.

If you find your name listed as an apparent owner of unclaimed property (usually abandoned stocks, bonds, or bank accounts), you can file a claim with the state and retrieve your assets. Claim forms are also available through the site.

Other states with similar searchable sites include

- Texas: *www.cpa.state.tx.us/comptrol/unclprop/upsearch.html*
- California: *www.sco.ca.gov/col/ucp*
- Florida: *up.dbf.state.fl.us*

Many states are beginning to provide searchable databases of abandoned property through the Internet. If you want to search a different state, go to the state's home page, find a state agency index, and then look for *abandoned property* or *unclaimed property*. Chances are you'll find a searchable database for that state.

You can also use a national service, at the URL *www.missingmoney.com/main/index.cfm*. Although this service is free, you must register before you search this database.

State Legislative Sites

State legislatures host their own sites. These sites are usually linked to the state home page. They feature information about the legislature, committees, and schedules, and links to member's and committees pages, and legislative information. These sites are roughly analogous to the congressional sites I reviewed in Chapter 2, "Going Online with the U.S. Senate and the House of Representatives."

An example of a state legislative site is this one, hosted by the Texas House of Representatives, at *www.house.state.tx.us*.

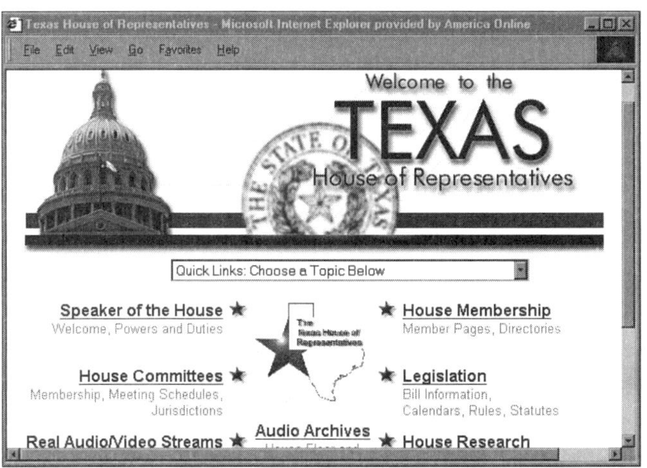

The home page of the Texas House of Representatives.

Why Write My Legislator?

You might want to contact your legislator to express your view of a piece of legislation you've read about. You might also be having trouble with a state agency and need the assistance of the legislator's staff to untangle the problem. You might be interested in a tour of the state capitol. You might want to invite your legislator to a community event. And many state legislators have email addresses to make contact with the office convenient. But, just as I cautioned in connection with congressional contacts, sometimes email isn't treated as well as a good, old-fashioned letter. So, before you type up that missive and send it through cyberspace, consider whether email is the best way to handle your request. A letter or phone call might get better results.

As you can see, this page provides links to members' own pages, legislation, calendars, rules, bill analyses, journals, and committee information.

Under the House Membership link, you will find links that enable you to identify your Texas house representative (if you're a Texan) by your ZIP Code, address, or county, as well as looking up representatives by name and district number. Many state legislative sites have such "finder" features because few of us know what legislative district number we live in, or the names of our state legislators.

Under the Legislation link, you can access the Texas Constitution and Code.

If you want to review Texas's regulations, they are at *www.sos.state.tx.us/tac/index.html*. Just as in the federal government, regulations are written by state executive branch agencies. Links to regulations are usually presented through the agency sites, not the legislative sites.

Links and legislative information about state legislatures is available at the Web page of the National Conference of State Legislatures, at the URL *www.ncsl.org*. This page has information about meetings, model legislation, and news aimed primarily at state legislators and their staffs. Nevertheless, in your research you might want to see what legislators are being told by this support organization. Another page that offers news and programs aimed at state officials is *www.states.org*, sponsored by the Council of State Governments.

State Judicial Sites

The judiciary of each state consists of a state supreme court or another high court (for instance, the highest court in New York is called the Court of Appeal). Lower courts include trial courts and state appellate courts. These courts hear matters arising under state law and regulation, and common law claims. If you are involved in, or want to know more about, an adoption, divorce, personal injury, criminal, or contract suit, chances are that the records are with the state courts.

An example of a state judicial Web page is the Colorado courts Web site, at *www.courts.state.co.us/ct-index.htm*.

The home page for the Colorado state courts.

The Colorado courts provide researchers with links to recent opinions. The link from the home page states, "Click here to view current and upcoming Colorado Supreme Court Decisions online." From here, you are taken to a list of links for each date that the court handed down decisions. Click the link for the relevant day in either HTML or PDF format, and you'll pull up announcements of each case, with the name of the case, name of the judge, and disposition. From here, click the case number, which is a link to the opinion in the case (in Word).

The home page offers several other useful features. A map (accessed by using the Map link on the left side of the page or the URL *www.courts.state.co.us/colomap.htm*) shows you each of the 22 judicial districts for Colorado's trial courts. Click a district, and you are taken to that court's page, from which you can get information about that trial court. The proper court, or venue, for a case is usually where the defendant lives or the act at issue in the case took place.

Venue

Venue refers to the locality where a case may be heard. For instance, a state trial involving a slip-and-fall at an amusement park would probably be heard in the trial court for the region (city, county, district, or whatever division the state uses to assign venue to courts) where the amusement park is located. If you want to look at records from a trial, you need to know where it was held, and venue rules will usually point you to the proper courthouse.

continues

continued

In some famous trials, especially criminal trials, you'll read about the defendant seeking a change of venue. That is because defendants may claim the people of the area where a crime took place are too biased to be fair jurors. Accordingly, judges will sometimes change venue to another court.

This page also links you to a form index, from which you can download Colorado's legal forms in PDF. The URL for this page is *www.courts.state.co.us/scao/Forms.htm*. This page also contains links to pamphlets on common topics, such as marriage dissolution, child support, sealing criminal records, and traffic court.

As you can see, plenty of useful legal information is provided at the Colorado courts Web page. Here are some links to other state court pages:

- New York: *www.courts.state.ny.us*
- Illinois: links to judicial offices, including courts, are listed at *www.state.il.us/judicial.htm*
- Georgia: *www2.state.ga.us/courts/supreme*
- Arizona: *www.supreme.state.az.us*

If you want to research a different state court, use the links to state court Web sites provided by the National Center for State Courts, at *www.ncsc.dni.us/COURT/SITES/Courts.htm*. You can also try accessing a state's home page by using the *www.state.__.us* formula, and then looking for a link to Courts, Supreme Court, or Judiciary.

Wrapping It Up

This chapter provided you with an overview of the many state services and information sources available on the Internet. Although every state has some information available on the Web, the formats vary. Still, generally you will be able to find the same kinds of information from state to state.

Now, you should be able to

- Find a state on the Web, even when you don't have the URL at hand, and understand the type of information that states can provide via the Internet
- Obtain information about motor vehicle regulation, state taxation, and unclaimed property using state agency sites
- Identify your state legislator, and know how to contact him or her
- Find the state judiciary's page, identify different trial court districts, and know where to start to find the proper court for a particular matter

CHAPTER 6

All Politics Is Local—And Online

Much of the everyday contact people have with government is through their local governments. Parking tickets, garbage collection, schools, noisy neighbors, and construction permits usually involve interaction with city or county officials (or people under contract to the city or county government). Have a complaint about these services? You call the local government staff, or attend a board or council meeting.

Every region's governmental organization differs. Nevertheless, I have found some samples from throughout the nation to demonstrate the kinds of information provided by local governments on the Internet, and how to find and use that information.

What You'll Learn in This Chapter:

- How to find your city on the Internet and what you'll find on a city Web site
- How to obtain county information on the Web
- Where to find your school's Web sites, and how to obtain other education information
- What information other local governments might have for you online

Cities on the Web

More and more cities are establishing a presence on the Web. City home pages, like those for the states we saw in Chapter 5, "State Sites on the Web," are part information and part advertising. Cities use their sites to encourage businesses and individuals to relocate to the city, so expect to find pretty pictures and reports about the great character of the place. But many cities also take their public information responsibilities seriously, and incorporate important information into their pages.

Examples of City Web Sites

A good example of a basic, yet informative, city Web site is hosted by the city of Tumwater, Washington, at *www.tumwater.wa.us*.

The city of Tumwater provides easy links to city information.

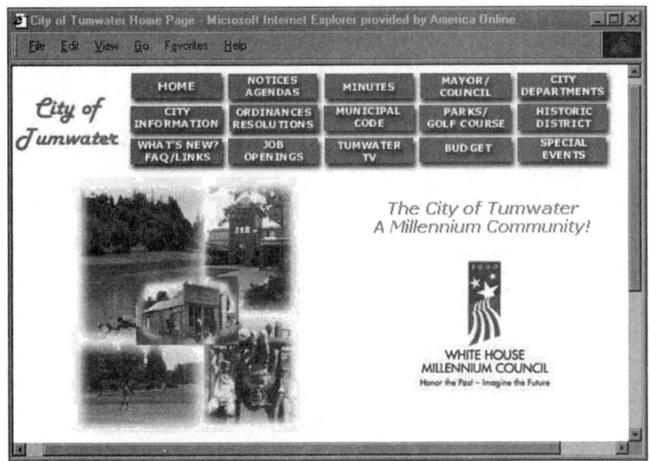

From this home page, you can click to the city's code, agendas for city council meetings and meetings of various city commissions, minutes from meetings, information on the history of Tumwater, and announcements of job openings. This is a good, clean, basic site that enables you to find the information you need easily.

Another city with an informative, but flashier site, is the city of Las Vegas, Nevada, at *www.ci.las-vegas.nv.us*.

The city of Las Vegas features information for tourists and locals.

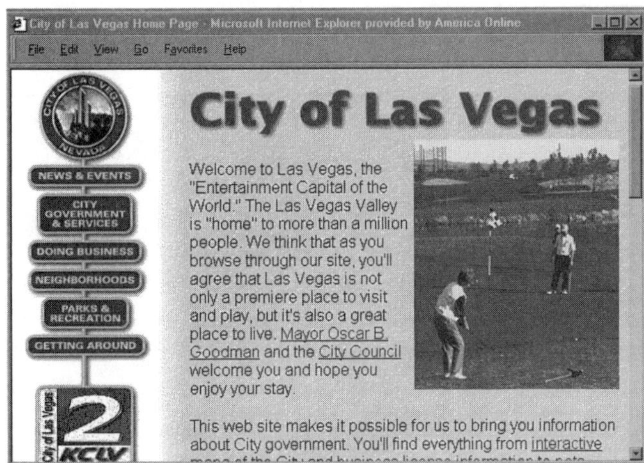

The Las Vegas page provides a city description with a link to City Government & Services. From there, a narrative about the city contains links to the city budget, demographic information and maps about the city, schedules and agendas for the city council, planning and zoning commissions, the municipal code, information about paying bills and fines owed the city, and even a link to the animal shelter. The city also offers a fax back service that provides city forms by fax.

Other links from the home page take you to a business license server, at the URL *arachnid.ci.las-vegas.nv.us/bus-license/*, from which you can search for existing licenses or apply for a Las Vegas business license. All the information you need to obtain a building permit is at *www.ci.las-vegas.nv.us/building_and_permits.htm*.

Almost anything that once justified a trip to city hall can be found on this city site. The Las Vegas site is a good example of how the Internet can make interaction with local government more convenient.

▼ **Try It Yourself**

You might need information from the city of Las Vegas if, while visiting, you received a parking ticket. This is how you'd find the information you needed to resolve that little problem:

1. Go to the Las Vegas page at *www.ci.las-vegas.nv.us*. You could find this either through one of the city portals, or by entering *"Las Vegas"* in your search engine.
2. Click the link to City Government & Services. Or, click the Search button and enter a search for **parking and ticket**—this search engine uses Boolean logic. The list of documents you receive will include a link to one called Parking Tickets.
3. Click the Parking Tickets link, and you are taken to a page with information on where to pay or contest a Las Vegas–issued ticket, as well as the applicable deadlines. The URL for this page is *www.ci.las-vegas.nv.us/parking_tickets .htm*.

▲

Finding Your City on the Internet

You can use several methods to find the URL for a city page. You can enter the name of the city in the search engine of your Web browser. If you want to research information from several cities and find this process time-consuming, you might want to check out a portal that lists links to city Web pages.

A portal especially for local government sites is at *officialcitysites .org/usa.htm.*

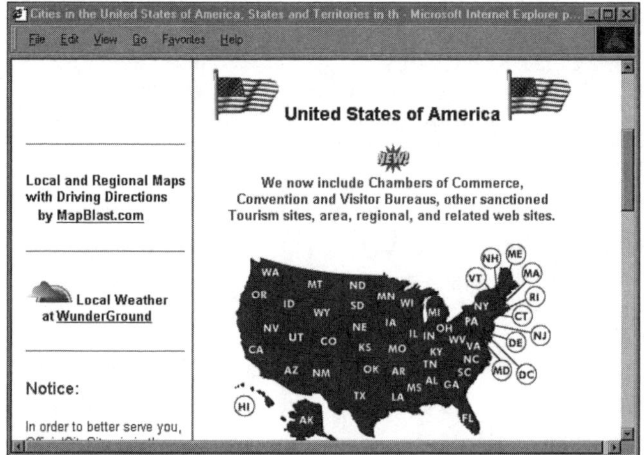

The Official City Sites page, with a map linking you to city and regional Web pages.

This page provides a map of the nation. When you select a state, you retrieve a page with facts about the state (population, state motto, state flower, and so on) and two links: one for county and regional governments and another for cities and towns. Clicking the Cities and Towns link takes you to a list of the alphabet. To reach the city you want, click the letter corresponding to the name of the city. This site also provides links for convention and visitors bureaus, chambers of commerce, and other civic boosters.

After you find the city's site, you'll probably be able to link to local newspapers and other media, other government agencies, schools, higher education, calendars of events, and a variety of other local information. With a small investment of time, you can gather quite a bit of information about a place from the Web.

City Portals

Here are URLs for other city portals you might want to try:

- *www.piperinfo.com/state/states.html*: This portal lists the states in alphabetical order, with links to cities, counties, and regions within each state.
- *www.pti.nw.dc/links.index.html*: This page contains a list of regions, within which are links to state and local governments in each region.

Counties on the Web

As you might have noticed, many of the portals that provide information and links to cities on the Web provide that information for counties, too. Chances are that when you find your county Web site, you'll find similar kinds of information there: links to ordinances, meeting information, property assessment and taxation information and other details that in the past required you to take a trip to the county's administrative center.

Nevertheless, a useful site especially for county-related research is the National Association of Counties site at *www.naco.org/counties/index.cfm.*

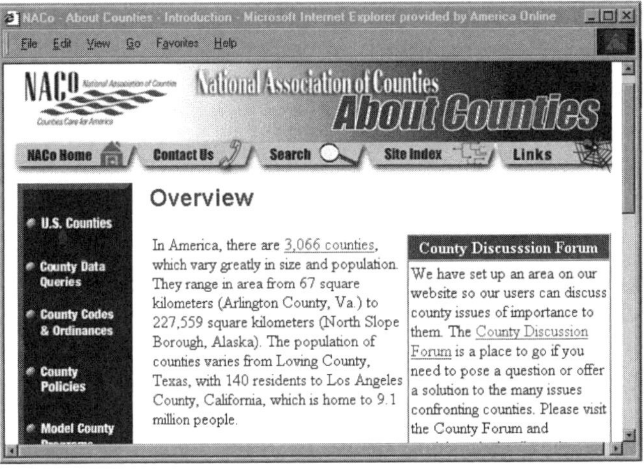

The National Association of Counties page has information on counties from across the nation.

From this one page, you can research counties across the nation. For instance, the Codes and Ordinances link enables you to search county laws by keyword. You can also link to a list of county ordinance links.

Be advised that not every county participates in this database. If you are interested in a specific county—for instance, you need to know your own county's rules—you would do best using the various portals I discussed earlier. Or, you could enter the name of your county in your browser, and see what comes up. Many counties in different states have the same names, so you might have to do some sifting if you choose this route.

One of the specific services provided at the county level in many states is the small claims court. If you have a dispute of a relatively small financial value (this threshold differs from state to state), you might want to settle it in small claims court.

In most cases, you can to obtain small claims information on the Internet. Here is a small claims information page that provides the rules information for California small claims courts, at *www.courtinfo.ca.gov/courts/trial/smallclaims/*.

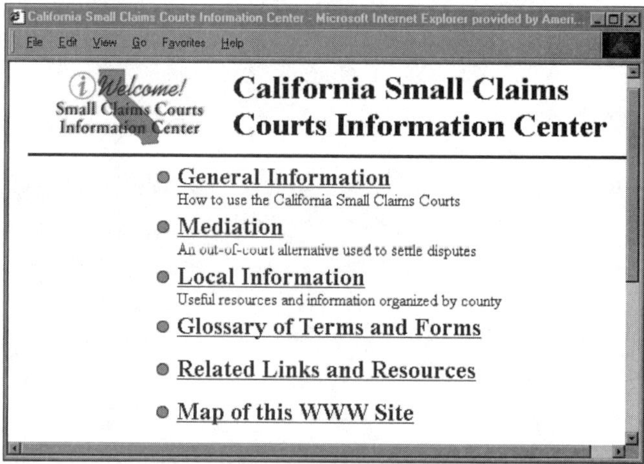

The statewide California Small Claims Court Information Center page provides general information on the small claims process.

On this one site, you can obtain general rules for filing or defending a case in small claims court, specific information about county courts, a glossary, and useful links to other books and materials.

Schools on the Web

Many school districts and individual schools are taking advantage of the easy communications provided by the Web. At many sites you can retrieve forms, review policies, and see what the cafeteria is serving for lunch.

How do you find your school or school district on the Web? Here are a couple of ideas:

- Type the name of the school or district in your Web browser. It might come right up.
- Go to your state's home page, and look for the agency that regulates education. Its page might offer links to individual districts and schools. For instance, the Missouri Department of Elementary and Secondary Education provides links for its schools at *www.dese.state.mo.us/schdistrictsweb.htm*.
- Try Yahoo (which is more of an index than a search engine). From *www.yahoo.com*, find the Education heading and click the K–12 link. On the next page, click Schools and review the headings that come up to see which might fit the school you're looking for.

Home Schooling

As parents grow increasingly concerned about the quality and safety of their local schools, more and more are investigating the home schooling option. The Web contains numerous sites on home schooling from every part of the political spectrum, and every level of professionalism, from formal to folksy. You can obtain curriculum guides, book lists, legal information, and ask advice from home schoolers on most of these sites.

If you are interested in this subject, here are a few sites you might want to review:

www.home-ed-magazine.com: Hosted by *Home Education* magazine.

Homeschool.crosswalk.com/learnathome: This is a link to Crosswalk.com's HomeSchool channel. It has good general information, as well as information aimed toward Christian home schoolers.

www.gomilpitas.com/homeschooling: This site is maintained by Ann Zeise, a home schooling parent in Milpitas, California. It contains links to articles, directories, guides, and other helpful information.

Other Regional Governments on the Web

Some civic issues are regional in character. Accordingly, some areas have developed regional governments to address those issues. These regional bodies do not fit neatly into the traditional city/county/state division of authority. Their members are cities and counties, but they often have autonomous authority to plan and execute programs, pass rules, and even levy fines.

Accountability is different for these bodies, too—rarely are the decisionmakers elected directly to the body by the people they govern, as is the case with a city councilmember, for example.

The first example of a regional government is the South Coast Air Quality Management District. It is the smog control agency for the southern California air basin, which includes several counties and many cities. The home page for the district is *www.aqmd.gov.*

The Web page for California's South Coast Air Quality Management District.

This page provides links to a myriad of informative pages, including information about permits, rules and regulations, air quality plans, as well as meeting agendas and minutes. From the link Smog Levels, you pull up a page where, among other things, you can see what the day's smog levels are in different subregions of the area. By clicking the Current Hourly Reading (Clickable Map) link (URL: *www.aqmd.gov/smog/areamap.html*), you retrieve a map of the southern California air basin. And, by clicking on a place in the map, you can get that location's current air quality readings. This might come in handy for people with respiratory ailments, and in any case makes diverting reading.

Another regional government is the Twin Cities Metropolitan Council of the Minneapolis-St. Paul region. Its URL is *www.metrocouncil.org*. This regional government operates bus lines, wastewater treatment, and is the regional planning organization for the seven counties in the Twin Cities region. On the home page, there are links to several development, transportation, and housing plans.

Along the left side of the page are links to regional parks, public transit information, housing assistance, planning documents, information about the region, and meetings and agendas. Clicking the Meetings & Agendas link takes you to links for the Metropolitan Council as well as the various commissions underneath it.

Wrapping It Up

Although the structure of local government varies from place to place, you've seen the type of information generally available from local governments on the Web. Now you can

- Find your city or any other on the Internet, and follow links to local laws, permitting information, agendas, and parking ticket requirements
- Find your county or any other on the Internet, and follow links to county ordinances and information on local courts such as small claims court
- Find schools and school districts on the Internet, and learn about home schooling
- Find other regional governments on the Internet, and learn what activities they regulate

CHAPTER 7

The Web IS Worldwide: International Political Research on the WWW

The Internet provides an unprecedented forum for people from all countries to communicate about the issues that concern them. The Web is truly worldwide and, fortunately for most Americans who lack a second language, English is becoming the language of choice for international communications.

But how do you wade through all the various sites? This chapter simplifies the information available so that you can launch your research on a foreign nation or issue with confidence. Of course, new information is added all the time, and a productive researcher should also follow links and make additional searches to see what new efforts are on the Web. Moreover, research on a specific issue might involve sites from far-flung hosts. This chapter can provide only an overview—the rest is up to you.

What You'll Learn in This Chapter:

- How to find the Web sites for a country, and its institutions and political parties
- Where to go for reliable information on a country's political system
- What other sites can provide useful information on international politics; namely, embassies, media, and international organizations

Foreign Governments on the Web

Several excellent sites are available to assist you in finding a foreign government on the Web. You may be interested in obtaining governmental information to help you plan a trip overseas, or you may be working on a school research project that requires foreign political information, or a nation may have just piqued your interest. Using these sites is quicker and easier than simply using a browser to search the Web because they focus specifically on foreign governments. Therefore, you'll find more of what you want and less of what you don't want using these specialty pages.

Worldwide Governments on the WWW

Worldwide Governments on the WWW is a good starting point. At its English-language page, *www.gksoft.com/govt/en/world.html*, you receive an alphabetical list of countries.

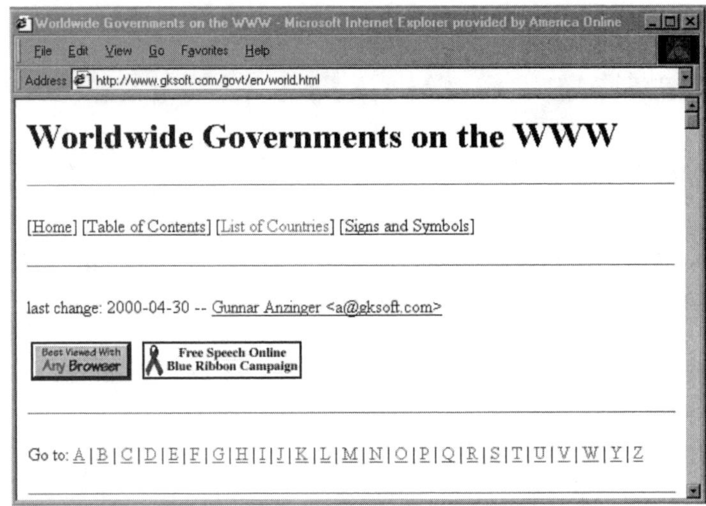

A fast and easy page for finding foreign information is the World-wide Governments on the WWW site, at www.gksoft.com/govt/en/world.html.

The Queen's English

How can you find an English-language version of a country's Web page if you can't read the language? Look for the union jack flag on a foreign language site—it often designates an English-language link.

This page is especially useful for researchers who are using older computers or slower modem connections. The Webmaster of this site uses a minimum of graphics, so the pages load quickly, giving you more time for research.

Each country name in the alphabetical list is also a link, which pulls up several entries for that country. Typically, an entry includes the official government site (if any), often in English or with an English option. It also provides links to encyclopedia entries for the country, travelogue entries, and a link to the CIA Factbook (which I will discuss later in this chapter).

Try It Yourself

Suppose that you need basic information about Chile's political system. Let's use the Worldwide Governments on the WWW site to find that information.

1. Enter *www.gksoft.com/govt/en/world.html* in your Web browser's address line. Scroll down the list of countries to the link to Chile. That link will take you to the 107 entries on Chile.

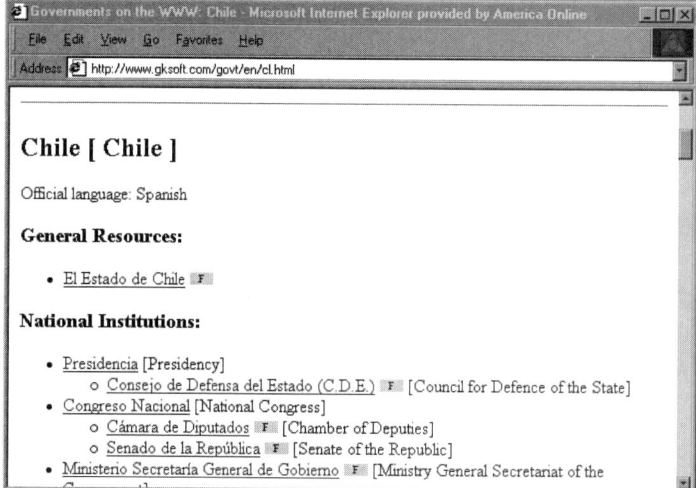

The entries for Chile on the Worldwide Governments on the WWW site.

2. As you scan the list, note the F icon beside many pages. This means the page is presented in frames. You will see that the Chilean government offers numerous Web sites in Spanish. If you scroll to the Representations in Foreign Countries heading, you can click a link to the Chilean embassy in the U.S. (It is at the end of the list.) This site contains basic political, economic, and travel information about Chile for Americans. Follow the Political link for information on Chile's political system. (The URL for the page explaining Chile's political structure is *www.chile-usa.org/documents/political/institutions.htm*.)

3. Under the Additional Information link on the Worldwide Governments on the WWW site are other good links for information about Chile's political system, including The Almanac of Politics and Government (URL for Chile *www.polisci.com/world/nation/CI.htm*) and Elections Around the World (URL for Chile: *www.agora.it/elections/election/chile.htm*). There's also a link to the CIA World Factbook entry on Chile. ▲

WWW Virtual Library: International Affairs Resources

Another good site for beginning a research project on a foreign nation or issue is the WWW Virtual Library: International Affairs Resources page, at *www.etown.edu/vl/*.

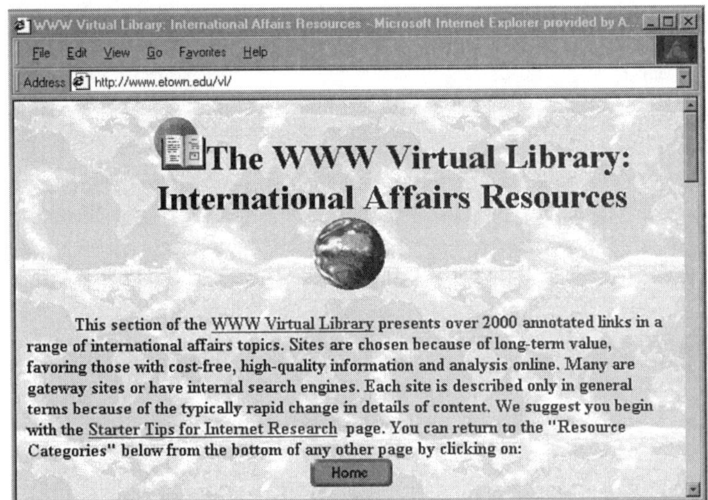

The WWW Virtual Library: International Affairs Resources page

This page contains links to media, international organizations, specific countries grouped by region, and topics. These links are sorted by categories.

To demonstrate: If you are interested in Chile, you would click the Latin America link. You would then see a page of links to country-specific search engines (many in Spanish). Below that are listed other links, providing more sophisticated analysis for researchers. The links to the Handbook of Latin American Studies and the Hispanic Reading Room (both hosted by the Library of Congress) both lead to good articles, analyses, and information in English about Chile and other South American countries.

You should also check out the Starter Tips for Internet Research link at the top of the WWW Virtual Library page. It contains a large number of links to guides for refining Internet research skills. These tips are useful not just for international research, but for any Internet research you might do.

The CIA World Factbook

You might want to review the CIA's account about a country directly. For that, point your browser to *www.odci.gov/cia/publications/factbook/*, the direct link to the CIA World Factbook online.

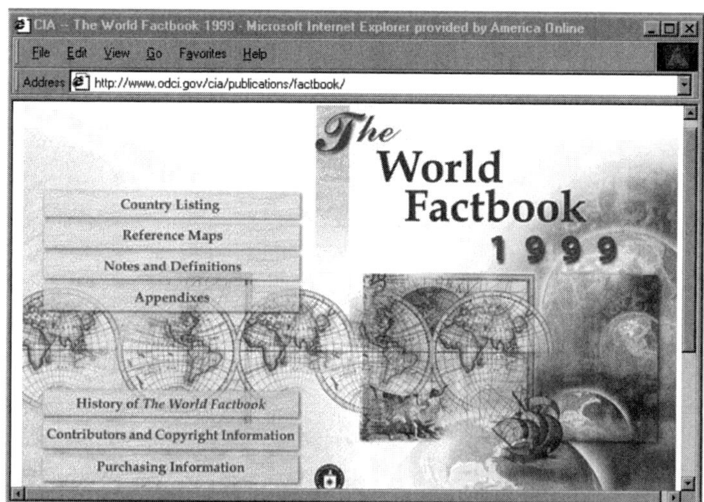

The CIA provides a comprehensive profile of each country in the World Factbook.

The Factbook isn't classified, and you won't find sensitive intelligence or weapons secrets here. The Factbook is revised each year, and has been sold to the public since 1975. In it, you will find a broad and comprehensive summary of every country in the world. This is the Joe Friday–approach to information ("Just the facts, ma'am,") and it can make for dry reading. You shouldn't let that deter you from using this wonderful source for information about other countries.

The Factbook provides details about a country's economy, political system, infrastructure, culture, demographics, crime rates, and much more. The information is set forth in a list of topics for easy reference. The format for each country's entry is the same, so you can easily compare one country with another.

To look up a country, click the Country Listing link. You are taken to an alphabetical list of the countries in the Factbook, with each country's name working as a link to the country's listing.

There is even a World link that contains the cumulative statistics and relevant information for the entire world.

You might also want to look at the Library of Congress Country Studies for a specific country. They are found at *lcweb2.loc.gov/frd/cs/cshome.html*. These pages are online versions of handbooks researched from 1988–98, and do not cover every nation. So, you might not find the country you want in the collection, or you might find that the information is outdated. Nevertheless, the series is worth a look. If the handbook on a country is reasonably up-to-date, you can gain useful insights into the history, culture, and international position of a nation. Many of these handbooks also make pleasant reading in their own right.

Political Resources on the Net

For international political information, another good resource is Political Resources on the Net, at *www.politicalresources.net*.

Political Resources on the Net provides political links via its world map.

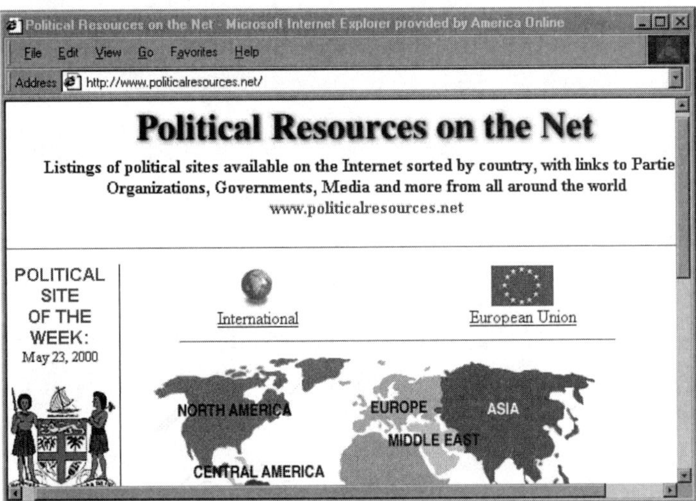

You can access Political Resources' country information by clicking a continent on the map. A list of countries in that continent appears, with links denoted by each country's flag (as well as its name). Click the flag, and you receive a list of links relevant to that country's politics. Usually the list includes the government's own Web sites, those of the country's political parties, and links to media, independent analysts, statistics, and other information.

You can also reach a country's link by selecting its initial from the alphabet list below the map.

The Political Resources on the Net site also selects a Political Site of the Week. This link is on the left side of the home page. Usually these are interesting sites, even when they are not directly related to a topic you might be researching. An archive of the Political Sites of the Week is also available, if you want to review what other sites the hosts of this site have selected.

A Country's Own Site

You might just be interested in what a country has to say about itself. For that, you might want to review the country's own Web site. As an example, look at the site from the country of Trinidad and Tobago, at *www.gov.tt/home.html*.

The home page for the Caribbean nation of Trinidad and Tobago.

Trinidad gained its independence from Great Britain in 1962 and, therefore, English is the language of the nation and of this Web site. From this home page, you can access information about the government, directories to agencies with Web pages, and media information such as speeches, press releases, and calendar information. It also includes two links to newspapers, Trinidad Express at *http://www.trinidadexpress.com* and the Trinidad Guardian at *http://www.guardian.co.tt/*, and links to banks and other investment services.

You might wonder why there is a relatively large number of investment-related links on this site. A quick check of the World Factbook indicates that Trinidad and Tobago is a popular country for foreign investors.

Embassy and Diplomatic Information

You might be interested in traveling to a country and need information about visas or restrictions, or you might need immigration information about that nation. Or perhaps you want information on business opportunities, culture, or history. Embassy and diplomatic sites can help answer these kinds of questions.

Many of the questions you have as a potential traveler are answered in the U.S. State Department's Travel Warnings and Consular Information Sheets at *travel.state.gov/travel_warnings.html*. As an example, here is the State Department's advisory for travel to Russia.

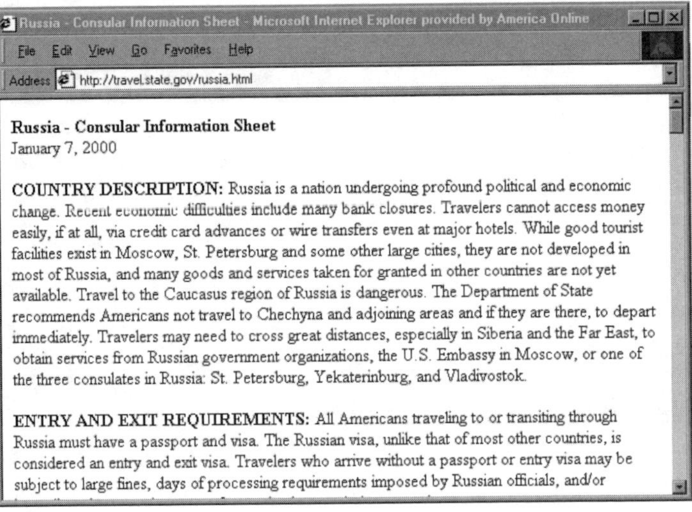
Russia - Consular Information Sheet - Microsoft Internet Explorer provided by America Online
File Edit View Go Favorites Help
Address http://travel.state.gov/russia.html

Russia - Consular Information Sheet
January 7, 2000

COUNTRY DESCRIPTION: Russia is a nation undergoing profound political and economic change. Recent economic difficulties include many bank closures. Travelers cannot access money easily, if at all, via credit card advances or wire transfers even at major hotels. While good tourist facilities exist in Moscow, St. Petersburg and some other large cities, they are not developed in most of Russia, and many goods and services taken for granted in other countries are not yet available. Travel to the Caucasus region of Russia is dangerous. The Department of State recommends Americans not travel to Chechyna and adjoining areas and if they are there, to depart immediately. Travelers may need to cross great distances, especially in Siberia and the Far East, to obtain services from Russian government organizations, the U.S. Embassy in Moscow, or one of the three consulates in Russia: St. Petersburg, Yekaterinburg, and Vladivostok.

ENTRY AND EXIT REQUIREMENTS: All Americans traveling to or transiting through Russia must have a passport and visa. The Russian visa, unlike that of most other countries, is considered an entry and exit visa. Travelers who arrive without a passport or entry visa may be subject to large fines, days of processing requirements imposed by Russian officials, and/or

The State Department provides travelers with advisories and recommendations for travel to Russia at travel.state.gov/russia.html.

This Consular Information Sheet advises travelers about visa requirements, crime, and areas to avoid when traveling to Russia. Other information might also be available. If you look under the country listing for Russia, you will find that the State Department has also posted an information sheet on the use of global positioning systems (GPS), cellular phones, and computers in Russia, at *travel.state.gov/gps.html*. This information sheet informs travelers that use of a GPS device in Russia has been punished with heavy fines and imprisonment because the Russians believe such use jeopardizes state secrets.

If you are traveling and need the location of an American embassy, the State Department's list of embassies and consular offices overseas is at *www.state.gov/www/regions_missions.html.*

If you need to contact the embassy of a foreign country here in the United States, the foreign embassies in Washington DC host a joint site at *www.embassy.org*. From this site, you can follow links to the sites of particular embassies.

Another site that enables you to find embassies both here and abroad for most all countries is EmbassyWeb.com at *www. embpage .org*. This commercial site has links to embassies, as well as other international sites, and a knowledge base archive of email questions about travel overseas. In addition, the Open Forum link leads to a bulletin board where an individual's questions are answered by other users, with the links maintained so that any visitor can read the exchange.

Embassy and consular sites are useful for more than travel information. As you saw before, embassy sites can be good sources of links to media, history, and governmental information. Sites of U.S. embassy sites and foreign embassies in the U.S. can provide a wealth of English-language resources. So, if you are trying to track down information about a specific country, it is probably worth your time to check that country's embassy site, and the site of the U.S. embassy in that country.

Can You Believe Your Eyes?

In many cases, you can expect that a country's own site—especially if it is an English-language site for a country where the native language is not English—will be written to appeal to visitors and investors. You might be able to add to your perspective of a country by reviewing the sites of its major newspapers, but even then the English-language press might be tailored to put the nation's best face forward. Even the native-language offerings are stilted in countries where criticism of the government is punished. So, what information can you rely on? Perhaps the best answer is to gather information from a variety of sources—American press, national press, international organizations, independent analysts—and sift it yourself. After that, you will see what seems credible and what seems incredible.

News from Around the Globe

Perhaps you aren't as interested in a specific country as you are in an issue or trend. Or maybe you just want to see what's going on in a region.

A good place to start for a general news inquiry is the Web site of a major news media provider. Here are a few sites that might be worth a look:

- The Internet edition of the *Times* of London at *www. sunday-times.co.uk/news/pages/Times/frontpage.html*

Is There an Embassy in Cyberspace?

From embassies, you can get visa information and other travel requirements, regulations, as well as useful cultural information. But embassies are usually not equipped to handle your requests online. You will, in most cases, need to obtain a visa application and other paperwork in hard copy, complete them by hand, and mail them to the embassy along with applicable fees (and your passport).

- The International News page of the *New York Times* on the Web at *www.nytimes.com/yr/mo/day/world* (registration required)
- The International Herald Tribune at *www.iht.com*
- The BBC at *news.bbc.co.uk*
- The Nation & World page of the LATimes.com site at *www.latimes.com/news/nation*

There are also sites that specialize in providing links to media from around the world. Two sites you might want to try are

- News and Newspapers Online, by the Walter Clinton Jackson Library at The University of North Carolina at Greensboro, at *library.uncg.edu/news*. This site enables you to browse an alphabetical list of nations and regions, and then pulls links for you with descriptions of the online media for that place.
- The E&P Online Media Links page at *emedia1.mediainfo.com/emedia*.

International Organizations

International organizations can also be a good source for information about nations and global issues. Two of the most prominent in the news are the United Nations, located in New York, and the North Atlantic Treaty Organization, located in Brussels, Belgium.

The United Nations

The biggest fish in the world of international organizations is the United Nations. Its home page is at *www.un.org*.

The home page contains a number of links. Buttons are provided that link you to maps, publications, and various topics. Links in the page's center can take you to five main areas of UN jurisdiction:

- The International Law link leads to information on the Law of the Sea, information on the UN's subscription service for treaties, international trade law, and the decisions and documents of the International Court of Justice.

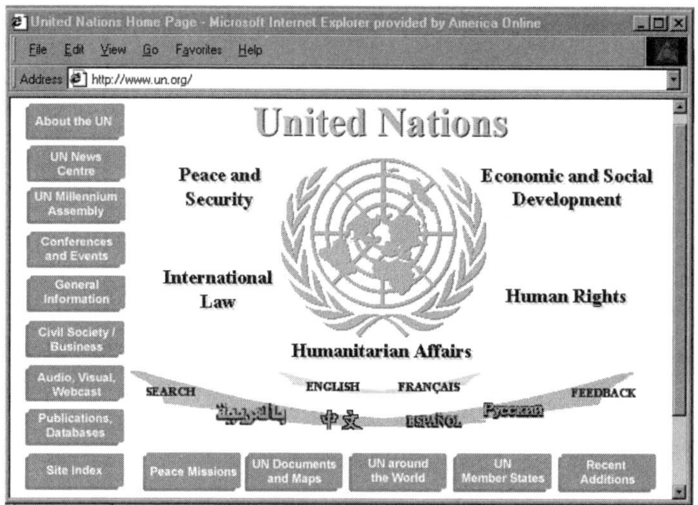

The Home Page for the United Nations.

- The Human Rights link leads to the Universal Declaration of Human Rights and related information, and the UN's human rights briefing papers.
- The Humanitarian Affairs link leads to information on relief projects, including UNICEF.
- The Economic and Social Development link leads to information on meetings, statistics, trade, crime, drugs, environment, and population.
- The Peace and Security Link leads to information on peacekeeping missions, and links to the Security Council and General Assembly, as well as related documents.

The UN has 188 member nations. A list of member nations, with Web links to their UN representatives where available, is at *www.un.org/overview/unmember.html*. The United States representative to the United Nations has its own Web page, at *www.un.int/usa*.

The UN's General Assembly (comprised of all members) and the Security Council (comprised of the United States, Great Britain, Russia, China, and France, as well as several other nations by election) both act through Resolutions. You can browse through General Assembly and Security Council Resolutions at *www.un.org/documents*. If a vote was taken on the Resolution (many are adopted by acclamation), that information will also be provided. The Resolutions are in PDF, and will require Adobe Acrobat Reader to read.

The North Atlantic Treaty Organization, or NATO

Another prominent international organization is NATO. There are 19 members in NATO, eighteen European nations and the United States. Its home page is found at *www.nato.int.*

The NATO home page features links to the alliance's history, current events, and library.

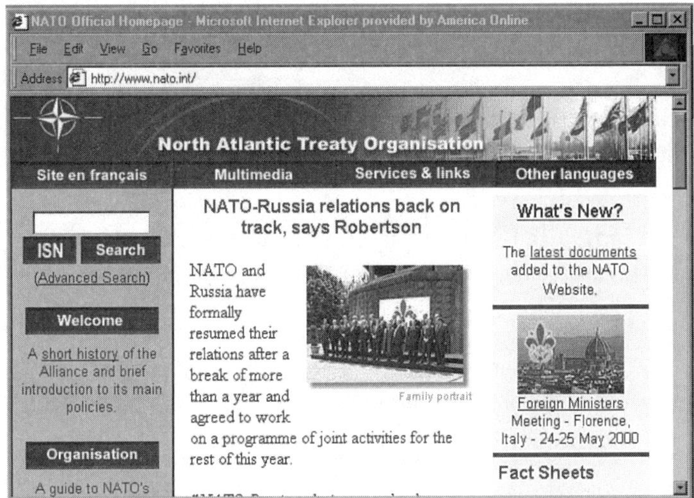

From the NATO home page, you can link to its online library by clicking a button on the left side of the page. The library contains documents, newsletters, and reports about the activities of NATO. It also provides a link to the basic texts of the alliance, such as The NATO Treaty, and The NATO Handbook (in HTML and PDF) reference manual. Basic fact sheet are also posted, in both English and French. These sheets provide basic information about specific NATO activities and issues of concern. The NATO online library is a good place to find more detailed information about many issues relating to the NATO alliance, European security, and the former Soviet Union.

Finding an International Organization on the Web

You might want to find the Web page for an organization, but you don't know its official name. Or maybe you are interested in finding an organization that deals with a specific issue, but you aren't sure an organization even exists.

A resource you can try is GIANT (Global Information Access Net), hosted by the University Center for International Studies at the University of Pittsburgh at *www.ucis.pitt.edu/dbinfo*. This is a database of governmental, educational, political, and similar groups.

Try locating international information using GIANT.

From the search page, you can search by keyword or by subject (a long list of subjects includes topics such as arms control and deforestation). Your search result will include the name and address of the group, as well as a Web link to the group's Web site.

Foreign Legal Sites

You might find it necessary to review the laws—or at least articles about the legal system—of a foreign country. Here are several good links for you to try:

- *www.findlaw.com/search/list.html* (FindLaw's International and foreign law search page)
- *www.waslaw.edu/forint* (a foreign and international law page hosted by Washburn University School of Law)

- *http://www.uni-wuerzburg.de/law/* (This German university site provides an index with links to the constitutional documents and laws of over 100 nations)

Some Specific International Political Issues

Some groups have an interest in a particular issue. If you are researching that issue, you'll want to check out the offerings of such groups. Below is just a sample of the sites available on a few specific international political issues.

- Nuclear proliferation: The Nuclear Files at *www.nuclearfiles.org/prolif/index.html*
- Human rights: Human Rights Watch at *www.hrw.org* and Amnesty International at *www.amnesty.org*
- International crime: Interpol at *www.interpol.int/Default.asp*, or the U.S. site for Interpol at *www.usdoj.gov/usncb*.
- International environmental protection: The library at the National Council for Science and the Environment page at *www.cnie.org*.

Wrapping It Up

This chapter provided an overview of the international political sites you can use to find what you need. Now you should be able to

- Find a government's Web site, and well as reliable independent information sites about that country
- Find an embassy site, and know what an embassy can provide
- Review the news and information relevant to a country or region, and evaluate the credibility of what you find
- Find the international organizations active in the areas you want to research

PART III

Sites with Attitude

CHAPTER 8

Left-Brain Activity: Progressives and Liberals on the Web

This chapter shows you where on the Web to find information from the left-of-center ideological perspective. Certainly this designation is something readers can debate—some readers might find these sites unacceptably mainstream, whereas others would include numerous other sites in the "left" or "liberal" category.

This chapter provides you with pointers on those sites that provide views from the left of the political spectrum on a variety of topics in one place. These sites promote themselves as "left," "liberal," or "progressive." Single-issue sites or groups are specifically featured in Chapter 11, "Political Interest Groups," which discusses interest groups. Overtly campaign or political party–related sites are in Chapters 13–15, which cover political parties and candidates.

What You'll Learn in This Chapter:

- Where to find progressive and liberal sites and information on the Web
- What variety of issues and methods for connecting with like-minded visitors you will find on these sites
- How to find and use a Web ring
- What basic rules should be followed in online forums, chat rooms, and Usenet newsgroups
- Where to find additional sources for news and information from a left-of-center perspective

What's on the Left?

Left-of-center ideology is generally understood as including views favoring social or political change. For example, feminists, gay rights advocates, racial justice proponents, death-penalty opponents, labor organizers, and drug normalization activists are usually classified as *left wing*. But not all issues fit discretely into a left-or-right view. For instance, groups on both the left and right oppose liberalizing international trade, although for different reasons.

Macrocosm USA

The Macrocosm USA site is maintained by a nonprofit corporation of the same name. Its home page is at the URL *www.macronet.org*.

Macrocosm USA provides an extensive directory for left-of-center groups, causes, and issues. From the home page, you can search for sites via a keyword search. You can also use one of several directories listed on the left side of the page. The MacroNet Directories link page contains about 7,000 separate listings by category and in alphabetical order. The Central Links Station has even more links, and other databases can be found under Activist Directories. Macrocosm USA also provides a link to a page where you can participate in discussion forums on various topics.

Macrocosm USA provides one stop for progressive political information and activists.

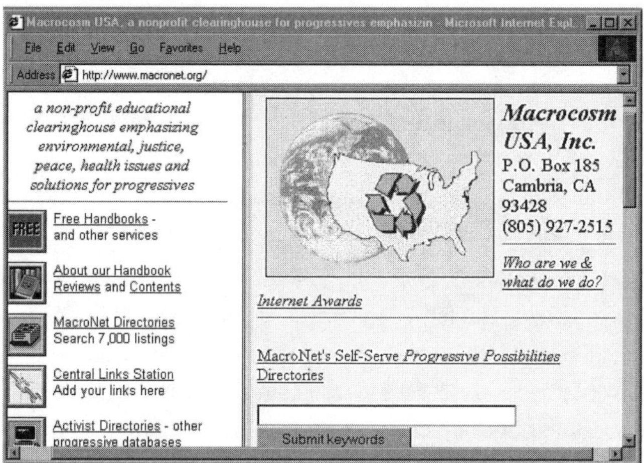

ZNet

ZNet describes itself as "A community of people concerned about social change." It is at the URL *www.lbbs.org/weluser.htm.*

From the ZNet home page, you can review the top stories on protests, global economics, and the other issues followed here. You can also subscribe to a free email update by submitting your email address in the designated box. The interests represented on ZNet are wide ranging, and include animal rights, labor, international economic disparities, self-determination, gender issues, and multiculturalism.

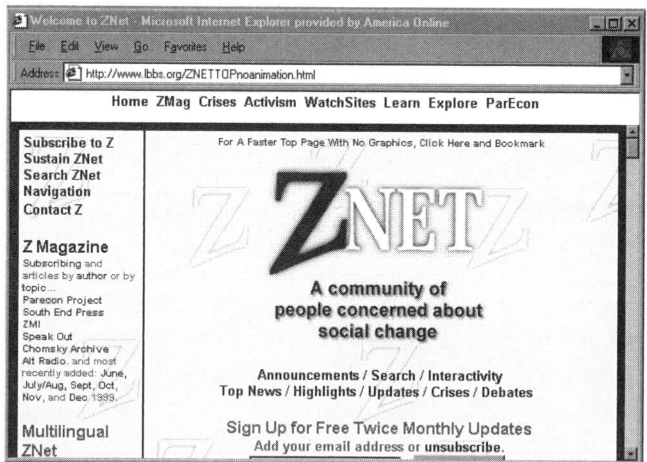

ZNet provides links, news, and email updates on numerous issues.

What Does Liberal Mean?

Liberal is a world used in politics worldwide. Note that here it is given the meaning it has in American politics, where it is applied to people with left-of-center views regarding regulation, social welfare, crime, economic regulation, and foreign policy. A Czech liberal or a Taiwanese liberal might hold very different views than a modern American liberal. That's because the term *liberal* is usually used with reference to the status quo. A Czech liberal or a nineteenth-century American liberal might favor free markets as a liberalization of governmental control over the economy, but in the U.S. in the twenty-first century, a free market–oriented person is generally deemed *conservative*.

Turn Left

Turn Left bills itself as "the home for liberalism on the Web." It is at *www.turnleft.com/liberal.html*.

From the Turn Left home page, you can link to its most popular features. The Liberal/Conservative Places link takes you to a list produced by Turn Left visitors of the most liberal-friendly, and most liberal-unfriendly, places to live in the U.S. As places are nominated, visitors can comment on why they agree or disagree with the designation. You might want to review the messages posted about your hometown, or about a place you might live in the future.

The bar along the left side contains links to Turn Left's other pages. About Liberalism provides a glossary, list of liberal periodicals, and essays on aspects of liberalism. The Politics page has

Different Kinds of Organizations Follow Different Rules

On the left, you'll find nonprofit charities, lobbying groups, and (later in the book) political committees. These different legal forms restrict what a group can do. A nonprofit charity—also known as a 501(c)(3)—can perform research on policy issues and disseminate its analyses, but it shouldn't lobby for legislation or campaign for politicians. A lobbying group can do anything a charity can do, plus lobby for legislation, but not electioneer for candidates or parties. A political committee can engage in partisan politics.

Under these rules, why would anyone organize a charity? Because contributions to a charity are tax-deductible. It is much easier to raise funds if you can offer your donors a tax deduction.

links to political parties and campaigns. The Culture page has links to sites related to cultural matters, including another link to the Liberal/Conservative Places page. Fight the Right has links to groups that monitor activities of the Right and argue against conservative views. The Interactive page provides discussion groups on issues, and a link to receive regular email from Turn Left. In the discussion groups, be aware that conservatives as well as liberals weigh in on these issues.

The Turn Left home page with links to its most popular features.

Jay's Leftist and 'Progressive' Internet Resources Directory

This site has a folksier name than the others, but packs a lot of information and news in one place. Jay's is found at *www.neravt.com/left/frontpage.html.*

The Jay's Directory home page alone provides a list of new links and articles, a Web Site of the Week, featured articles, and an extensive feature on Today in Radical History. A scrollable box titled Current Issues at the bottom of this page enables you to select a slogan, and link to news, information, and links relevant to that cause.

You will also see at the end of the page a box designating the site as a member of the Class Struggle Web Ring. This means the site is linked to sites of similar interest in a daisy chain or "ring." You can move to the next site in the ring by clicking Next, the previous site by clicking Previous, or a random site in the ring by clicking Random. You can also view links to all sites in the ring by clicking All Sites.

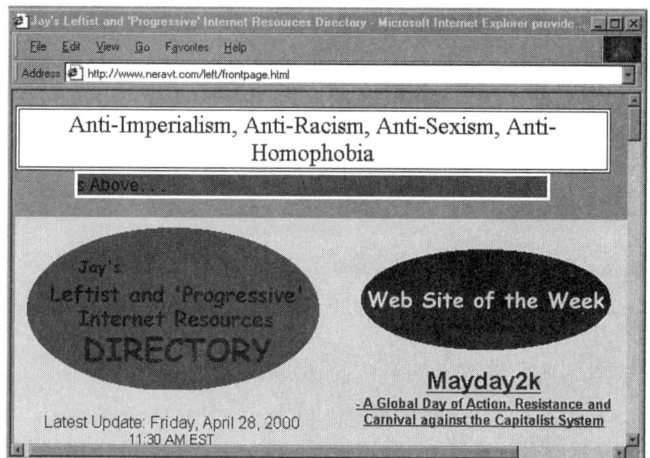

Jay's directory provides articles, news, and information from the left.

Web rings enable you to scan related sites quickly and easily, without recalling them from your Favorites bookmark list, and without jumping back to a common directory or browser result. You might also discover a new favorite site in the ring. Rings provide an alternative way to surf from site to site, if you're interested in grazing rather than researching a specific topic.

Finding Web Rings

As you peruse Web sites, you will find some that are included in Web rings. Is there a less haphazard way to find Web rings? Yes. An index of Web rings is at *www.webring.org/index.html#ringworld*. It supports a browsing function by topic, or you can search by keyword to find the Web ring you want. Web rings have been formed for liberal and conservative politics, as well as on a variety of other issues.

Institute for Global Communications (IGC) Internet Progressive Gateway

The IGC Internet Progressive Gateway provides news and information about its members, which are a collection of liberal and progressive groups. The Gateway is at *www.igc.org/igc/gateway/index.html.*

The Gateway home page contains an overview of the site, with a featured article from its PeaceNet, EcoNet, WomensNet, and Anti-RacismNet networks. From the home page, you can sign up for a weekly newsletter by submitting your email address in the box provided. This site also maintains a directory of progressive sites, which is accessed through the Browse Sites by Category link at the top of the page.

The IGC Internet Progressive Gateway features PeaceNet, EcoNet, WomensNet, and Anti-RacismNet.

If you are interested in one specific network—for example, PeaceNet—you click PeaceNet at the top of the page and go to the PeaceNet page. There you can browse for links to other sites relevant to peace issues, join a discussion group on a peace issue, or check the PeaceNet calendar. Each of the other three network pages offers the same features.

Liberal? Progressive? What's the Difference?

Often the terms *liberal* and *progressive* are used interchangeably, especially by sites that want to attract a number of visitors. Standard definitions are not much help in differentiating the two terms, either. A *liberal* is defined in one dictionary as a person who believes it is the duty of government to ameliorate social conditions and create a more equitable society, and a *progressive* is defined as a person favoring progress toward better conditions or new policies, ideas, or methods. In the United States, *liberal* has been used successfully to marginalize left-of-center candidates, whereas *progressive* has not acquired the same baggage.

Try It Yourself ▼

Because your research will probably focus on an issue, rather than liberalism in the abstract, let's see what issue-specific information we can obtain about feminism by using the IGC Internet Progressive Gateway.

1. Call up the home page for the Internet Progressive Gateway at *www.igc.org/igc/gateway/index.html.*

2. Click the link to WomensNet at the top of the page. This takes you to the WomensNet home page at *www.igc.org/igc/gateway/wnindex.html.*

3. This page features the lead article from WomensNet, and links to other headlines and action alerts along the left. After you've looked at these, click on the Browse WomensNet Sites link. You'll see a list of organizations with a feminist or women's perspective. Depending on your specific interests, you might want to look at a few of these other sites. Some of the listed sites you might want to try are the American Association of University Women at *www.aauw.org/home.html*, New Moon Publishing at *www.newmoon.org*, and Off Our Backs at *www.igc.org/oob.*

4. The WomensNet home page also has a link to WomensNet Discussion Forums at the top of the page. Click this link and you will see a list of topics for discussion. The moderator has also provided a Guided Tour link for you to read before participating in the forums. Registration (at no cost) is required before browsing or participating in the WomensNet forums. ▲

Yahoo's Directory of Liberal Opinion

Another directory to use when looking for liberal sites is the Yahoo directory Liberal Opinion. You can reach it by calling up Yahoo (*www.yahoo.com*), and then following the links to Government, Politics, Political Opinion, Liberal. Or you can reach it directly by using the URL *dir.yahoo.com/Government/Politics/Political_Opinion/Liberal.*

This directory contains a lengthy list of sites, with some brief descriptions. In the list, you might find the address of a Usenet newsgroup, such as *alt.politics.radical-left*. Depending upon how your computer is configured, you might be able to click the Usenet link and pull up the messages posted there.

Usenet newsgroups provide another way for people to communicate, express views, and organize and exchange information over the Internet. You might just want to flip through the messages and read selectively, or you might want to participate in the conversa-

Courtesy and Respect

When you participate in chat rooms, bulletin boards, and newsgroups, you might sometimes find courtesy in short supply. The visitors who take the time to communicate this way are usually passionate about their beliefs. All too often, tempers flare and posted messages become angry and personal. Such a message is sometimes referred to as a *flame*. Resist the temptation to respond in kind. Nothing is gained by flaming others, and the momentary satisfaction you feel does not compensate for the tone such correspondence creates in a forum or chat room. Remember that there are hundreds, perhaps thousands, of other people reading these messages, and they will appreciate a robust but civil conversation.

tion. It is always a good idea to read the posted messages thoroughly before posting your own so that you do not make an observation or ask a question that has already been covered. Just as when you join any conversation, you should listen awhile before offering your views.

If you become a regular and want to see the newsgroup everyday, you can usually have its messages sent directly to your email address. Check the folder in the newsgroup for a FAQ folder to learn how to subscribe.

Usenet

Usenet is a series of messages posted to computers. It is divided by topic into newsgroups. You might think of a newsgroup as a repository for an email conversation. When you call up the newsgroup, you can see all the messages posted by all other visitors on that subject. Most browsers support Usenet, but depending upon how yours is configured, you might need to use a newsreader or simply read the messages through your browser program.

If you want to find a Usenet newsgroup on a topic, or want to learn more about Usenet, go to Deja.com's Usenet archive and information site at *www.deja.com/usenet* or the Usenet Information Center at the University of North Carolina's Sunsite at *metalab.unc.edu/usenet-i/*.

Cafe Progressive

Cafe Progressive provides an online community coffeehouse for visitors interested in progressive political issues. It is found at *www.cafeprogressive.com.*

Cafe Progressive's WebGuide lists the URLs of progressive Web sites by category. It also provides a search function for you to search for a site by keyword. Its NewsWire link provides headlines and links to the mainstream press and links to alternative news sites.

The Cafe also provides progressive forums where you can read and send messages to bulletin boards on progressive issues, and a chat room where you can correspond in real time over the Internet with other visitors. You should follow the advice regarding Usenet newsgroups when participating in bulletin boards and chat rooms. Read what others have written before jumping into the fray so that you have a good sense of the territory already covered.

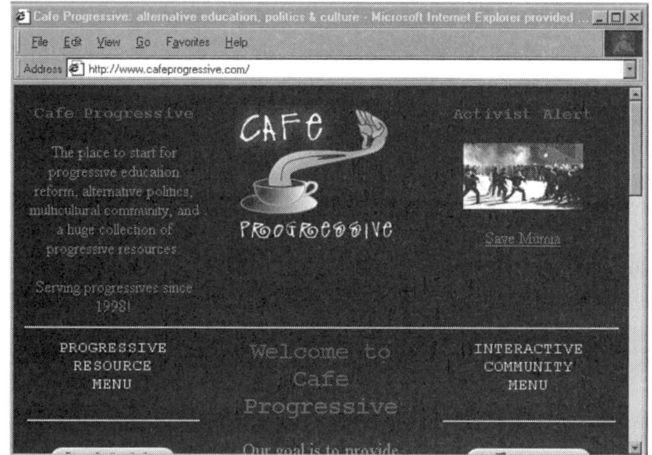

Cafe Progressive's online coffeehouse for news, information, and networking.

Other Sites on Your Left

Here are the names and URLs of some other liberal sites of interest. They offer links to other sites, Web rings, news and information, discussion groups, opinions, photos, and other items of interest:

- Communications for a Sustainable Future, at *csf.colorado.edu*
- ProActivist.com, at *www.proactivist.com*
- Essential Information (founded by Ralph Nader in 1982) at *www.essential.org*
- The Direct Action Network, at *www.directactionnetwork.org*
- AdBusters (The Culture Jammers Network), at *adbusters.org/home*

Sources for News and Current Events from the Left

As you review the news items and groups on these sites, you might want to see what liberal publications are saying. Here are several available online, with some information about each one:

- *Mother Jones*'s The MOJO Wire: *www.motherjones.com.* Launched in 1976, *Mother Jones* magazine was named after labor organizer Mary Harris Jones. The Web version offers articles from the print magazine as well as original Web content.

- *The Nation*: *www.thenation.com*. *The Nation* was founded in 1865 by abolitionists, and today is a weekly magazine of liberal politics and current events.
- *The Progressive*: *www.progressive.org*. *The Progressive* has been published since 1909, and is a monthly magazine focused on peace and social justice.
- *The American Prospect*: *www.prospect.org*. *The American Prospect* was founded in 1990 as a magazine of liberal philosophy, politics, and public life. The Web version contains magazine and Web-only content.
- *Dissent*: *www.dissentmagazine.org*. *Dissent* is a quarterly focused on progressive culture and politics.
- *Utne Reader*: *www.utne.com*. Founded in 1984, *Utne Reader* selects articles from the alternative press for republication. It also offers reviews and original content on its Web site.
- *Ms. Magazine*: *www.msmagazine.com*. *Ms. Magazine* began regular publication in 1972, and offers news, commentary, and articles from a feminist perspective.
- Pacific News Service: *www.pacificnews.org*. Based in San Francisco, this wire service provides a liberal alternative to mainstream news wires.
- *Bad Subjects*: *eserver.org/bs*. This is the electronic version of a magazine dedicated to "political education for everyday life." *Bad Subjects* was founded at the University of California at Berkeley in 1992.

If you don't see a periodical you're looking for in this list of liberal publications, you should try the Alternative Press Center's Alternative Press Index, at *www.altpress.org*. It provides listings of alternative and independent publications, with editorial information, street addresses, subscription information, and email or Web addresses.

Wrapping It Up

Web surfers have a wealth of information about liberal and progressive issues, groups, and causes at their fingertips. This chapter provided you with an overview of that information, by focusing on sites offering a variety of different liberal issues and ways of spreading the word. From these sites, you can find more specific sites on particular issues, or sites focused on particular activities (such as protests or letter writing). Let your curiosity take you beyond this sampling to the multitude of other Web sites on the left side of the Web.

Now you should be able to

- Find sites with a general liberal perspective and directories of liberal and progressive Web sites
- Appreciate the wide variety of issues and perspectives provided in these left-of-center sites
- Find and use a Web ring
- Participate appropriately in forums and chat rooms sponsored by liberal and progressive sites
- Navigate Usenet and find newsgroups on liberal and progressive issues
- Find and retrieve news and information from liberal periodicals

CHAPTER 9

Place Your Right Hand over Your Keyboard: Conservative Web Sites

This chapter provides a variety of useful sites for conservatives and people researching conservative political views. As in the previous chapter, the sites discussed here are general in character. Sites for specific groups or issues are discussed in Chapter 11, "Political Interest Groups," and sites for political parties or candidates are featured in Chapter 13, "Democrats Online," through Chapter 15, "Other Parties Online."

As with the term *liberal*, the term *conservative* means different things to different people. Included here are sites that refer to their own views as conservative, and that reflect at least some part of modern American conservative political opinion.

Some readers will have a broader view, and some readers might disagree on the conservative credentials of one or another site included here. And, of course, any research should move beyond the necessarily incomplete sampling here to find other conservative views and opinions on the Web.

What You'll Learn in This Chapter:

- Where to find general information from a conservative perspective
- How to register for a registration-only message board or chat room
- What cookies are and what they do
- Where to go for conservative analyses of public policy problems
- Where to find a conservative take on the news of the day

Town Hall

The Heritage Foundation, a conservative think-tank, sponsors the general-interest conservative site Town Hall. Its URL is *www.townhall.com*.

Town Hall incorporates a number of useful features. Its home page provides descriptions and links to articles by conservative writers and news from conservative groups. It also provides a pull-down menu with links to groups that are members of Town Hall, and an issue library that also works with a pull-down menu.

Members of Town Hall include many conservative groups, such as Americans for Tax Reform, Accuracy in Academia, Citizens Against Government Waste, the Family Research Council, and the Media Research Center.

The Town Hall home page links visitors with current events, other groups, and government sites.

Conservative

What's a conservative? Conservatives tend to favor the status quo and advocate change only in moderation. Conservatives often support free market economic policies, and oppose "big government" intervention in social and economic areas. Conservatives are socially pro-family, anti-abortion, and favor traditional moral values and religion. They also support a strong military.

From the Town Hall home page, you can also write your congressman or the editor of your local paper using the convenient links. (But keep in mind the attention paid to email as compared to regular mail.)

Town Hall also features message boards and chat rooms. For instance, the Rush Room is a real-time chat room for people to discuss the Rush Limbaugh radio show. You must register and open an account with Town Hall before participating in the Rush Room or the other chat rooms.

Town Hall provides a conservative Web directory called RightPages that you can reach by clicking the RightPages Internet Guide button on the home page. RightPages has a search engine, features a Right100 directory of popular conservative sites, and a site index by topic. The topics included are Books & Publishing, Elections & Campaigns, Government, News & Media, Business & Marketing, Entertainment & Arts, Issues & Advocacy, and Research & Resources.

> **Other Conservative Web Directories**
>
> Another conservative Web directory you might want to try is RightBot at *rightbot.com.* As with RightPages (and other directories you might have used), RightBot combines a search function with a directory of sites sorted by topic. It has headlines and links to current news articles on the right side of the page, and headlines and links to humorous articles below the real news links.
>
> RightGuide.com also provides a directory of conservative organizations at *www.rightguide.com/conservative.htm.* You can review entries on a large number of organizations alphabetically and by subject, as well as through the RightGuide search option. Each entry provides an address, contact information, and brief description of the group.

Free Republic

Free Republic provides news and information for conservatives, and a forum area with a number of topics to choose from. It is at the URL *www.freerepublic.com.*

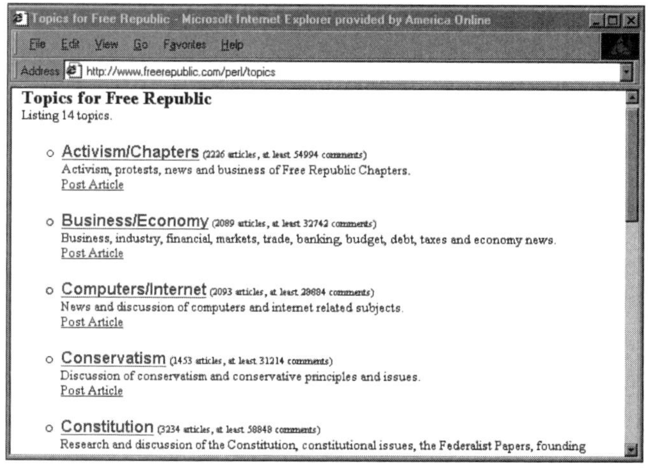

Here is a partial list of the forum topics at Free Republic that also gives the numbers of posted messages for each topic.

The Free Republic home page links you to a list of topic descriptions as well as to each forum. To post a message, you should register first, which you can do easily by clicking the Register to post link. According to Free Republic, it has over 20,000 registered posters to its forum area. But, if your email account is with a free email provider (such as Yahoo! Or Hotmail), as of this writing, Free Republic will not accept your registration.

Try It Yourself

Free Republic manages its forum area by requiring users to register first, and by monitoring posts for acceptable content. Here is a step-by-step guide on how to register at this site. Many of these steps can be followed at similar sites that host message boards.

1. Click the Register to post link on the Free Republic home page, *www.freerepublic.com.*
2. You will see the Registration and User Agreement page. To register, enter your screen name (the name you want other forum visitors to see—it can be your real name or an alias such as RightWinger). You also must provide your real email address (which is revealed to other Free Republic visitors only if you want it to be) and a password.
3. You will also review the site's guidelines. They follow the basic rules of civil Internet discourse. By registering with Free Republic, you agree to abide by these rules. Free Republic can pull a post from you and suspend or revoke your account if you violate these rules.
4. You will receive an email message from Free Republic with an activation URL and an authorization code. Go to the URL, and enter your screen name, password, and email address.
5. After your account is activated, you can log in to Free Republic. When you log in, you'll be prompted for your screen name, password, and email address. Include your email address at the login stage only if you want other Free Republic visitors to see it. You must have cookies enabled in your browser for the login program to work.
6. Posting requires basic HTML coding in the text of the message form to designate paragraphs, bold, or centered text. You can preview your post by clicking the Preview button (always take this extra step). Click the Post button to send your message to Free Republic.

7. Need more help or guidance on how to post to the forum? The Free Republic help page is at *www.freerepublic.com/help.htm.*

Free Republic also provides links to a number of other sites, under Resources. Quick Links lists links to news sites of interest to conservatives. Free Republic also has chapters across the nation. You can obtain more information about them under the Chapters link at the top of the home page.

Cookie Monster?

Cookies aren't just sweet things from the bakery. *Cookie* also refers to information that a Web site has stored on your computer's hard drive so that the site can recognize you in the future. Often, the cookie records personal preferences that you've provided in the past—for instance, if you've customized a page with specific stock or news preferences. You must enable your browser to accept cookies, or they won't be saved on your computer. Cookies can be found on your computer's hard drive in a file or subdirectory usually named Cookies.

Some users object to cookies, because they can potentially reveal information about the sites you visit and your activities online. You can learn more about cookies at *www.cookiecentral.com.*

Rightgrrl

Rightgrrl refers to its site as "A Meeting Ground for Conservative and Prolife Women." Its address is *www.rightgrrl.com.*

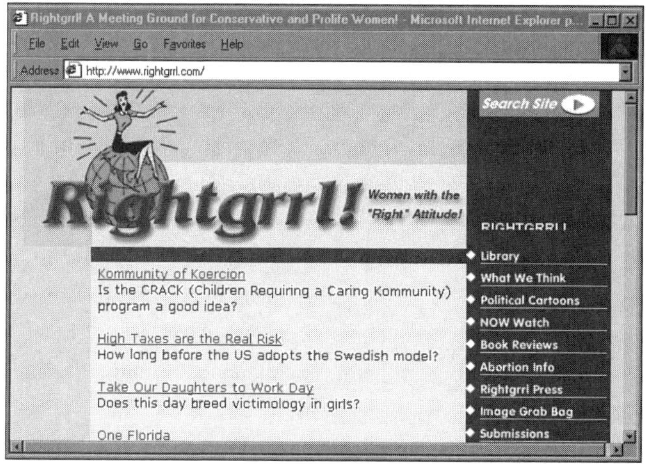

The Rightgrrl page with issues and information for conservative women.

From the home page, you can link to a list of commentaries, cartoons, and an option to join the Rightgrrl email list. The Rightgrrl page also has specific links to a NOW (National Organization of Women) Watch, abortion information, Linda Tripp information, Bill Clinton information (viewed with a critical eye), photos, and a chat room.

Rightgrrl belongs to a Web ring called The Ring of Conservative Sites and the Pro-Life Web Ring. You might want to try the other sites in these rings. Web rings were discussed in Chapter 8, "Left-Brain Activity: Progressives and Liberals on the Web."

Enter Stage Right

Enter Stage Right describes itself as a "Journal of modern Conservatism." It can be found at *www.enterstageright.com.*

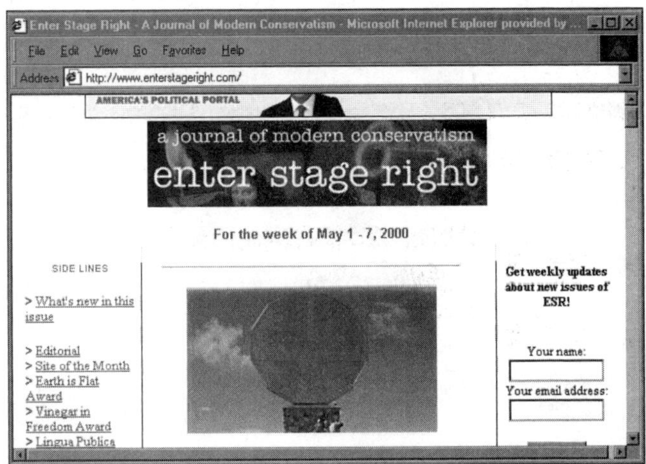

Enter Stage Right provides original commentary and awards to sites and figures in the news. Its features should be of interest to American and Canadian conservatives.

Enter Stage Right offers visitors articles from each weekly issue. It also features awards for conservative sites, criticism of figures in the news (under the Earth is Flat Award link), and favorable news developments (under the Vinegar in Freedom Award link). The Lingua Publica link lists quotes from public figures on a current topic of interest. You can receive a weekly update from Enter Stage Right by signing up with your name and email address using the designated form on the home page.

Conservative Institutes ("Think Tanks") on the WWW

Think tanks are non-profit organizations funded by donations. They write policy analyses, hold conferences, publish books, and engage in similar activities to publicize their views on issues and events. Several conservative public policy institutes host Web pages that provide good general conservative information and links. These can be useful in your research on conservative views and issues.

The Heartland Institute

The Heartland Institute's site is at *www.heartland.org*.

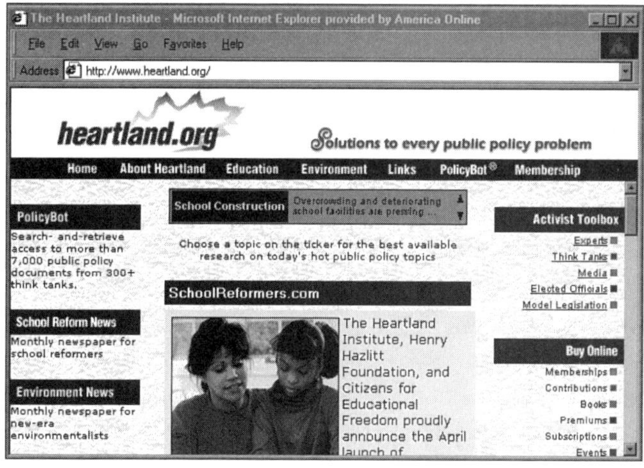

The Heartland Institute can link you to reports and analysis from hundreds of other organizations through PolicyBot.

Through this site, you can find articles from the institute's publications on the environment, school reform, and other current events. The Heartland Institute also provides a service called PolicyBot that enables you to find thousands of documents from more than 300 other public policy institutes. This service requires a free one-time registration.

The American Enterprise Institute

This moderately conservative think tank was founded in 1943. Its Web page address is *www.aei.org*. The American Enterprise Institute (AEI) examines foreign and domestic policy issues. This site provides links to articles by AEI scholars and information about AEI events.

Claremont.org

This is the Web site for The Claremont Institute, a conservative organization in southern California. Its address is *www.claremont.org*. Claremont.org offers analyses from its own scholars and writers on a wide variety of topics of interest to conservatives.

Other Conservative Sites

You might also want to try these sites on the Right side of the World Wide Web:

- The Conservative Caucus, at *www.conservativeusa.org*
- The Common Conservative, at *www.commonconservative.com/index.html*
- ConservativeHQ.com, at *www.conservativehq.com/chq/home* (registration required)

Conservative News Services

Many of the most informative conservative sites are focused on reporting and commenting on news. The following are several sites that you might want to review. Each site offers up-to-date articles on current events, and many also offer the features of general-purpose sites, such as chats and forums. Visit them for yourself and see where you find the best match with your personal interests.

- The Drudge Report, at *www.drudgereport.com*. This is perhaps the best-known news service site on the Internet. In addition to its original reporting, the site features links to other news sites, columnists, and similar information.
- WorldNet Daily, at *www.worldnetdaily.com*.
- National Review Online, at *www.nationalreview.com*.
- American Vibe, at *www.americanvibe.com*.
- Conservative News Service, at *www.cnsnews.com*.

Wrapping It Up

This chapter showed you some places you can find news, information, chats rooms, message boards, and other information sources with a conservative point of view. Now you should be able to

- Find several general-interest sites for conservatives, and follow links to specific conservative groups
- Use a Web directory to find other conservative sites on various topics
- Register to participate in a chat room or message board
- Retrieve conservative public policy analyses and reports from conservative think tanks
- Find the conservative perspective on the news of the day

CHAPTER 10

Is There a Ministry of Silly Walks? Iconoclastic, Humorous, and Hard-To-Describe Political Sites

You've seen the federal government online. You've worked your way through regulations, local ordinances, and international intrigue. Maybe you've chatted with liberals and conservatives. Now is the time to have some fun.

This chapter looks at some of the political humor, parodies, and fun sites on the Web. Of course, political issues are ultimately serious. What is a poke in the ribs to one person might be offensive to another. Some advice: Don't take yourself too seriously, and laugh a little.

What You'll Learn in This Chapter:

- Where to find Web political humor
- How to listen to audio files over the Internet
- What stranger-than-fiction news might have happened near you
- How to find sites that let you warp a politician for free and support a tree for Congress

Not the Real White House

Our first stop is at a parody page of the White House's Web site. The real White House site is *www.whitehouse.gov*. The parody site is *www.whitehouse.net*.

This home page is designed to look like the real White House Web page. You'll notice some differences when you look closely. Several different versions of the page are accessible, so when you pull up the page it might not look like the page I feature here. In some versions, you can see a figure running along the top of the White House in the photo. In another version, the page solicits advertising as a way to offset the cost of the White House. The links might also change from visit to visit. And some of the links take you to the official White House pages. For instance, clicking the library link takes you to the real White House library page.

The site also links to letters from visitors, some of whom were unclear that the site was a parody and not the genuine White House Web page.

It looks like the White House site, but it's not.

Dave Barry for President

Columnist Dave Barry, known for his humorous takes on politics and life, is running for president. Not really, but his campaign Web site, at *www.herald.com/content/archive/living/barry/dave2k/main.htm*, might encourage you to support him anyway.

Don't like the others? Consider Dave Barry for president.

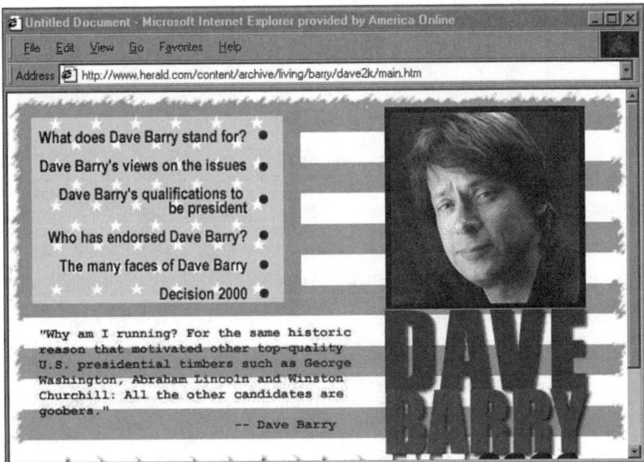

Barry's site contains a brief but perfunctory platform, endorsements from the likes of Robert Goulet, and pictures of well-known figures holding Dave's campaign bumper sticker. The campaign claims that these pictures don't indicate endorsements, but I haven't seen Steve Martin or Kurt Vonnegut holding any other candidate's propaganda. Maybe Barry's just a little too modest.

Doonesbury Electronic Town Hall

For almost 30 years, *Doonesbury* has been following the travails of the folks from Walden College as they comment on and experience the news of the day. You can visit them at *www.doonesbury.com/ieindex.html.*

The Doonesbury Electronic Town Hall with news briefings, chat rooms, and archives of the strip.

The Doonesbury home page contains links in the form of pictures of characters from the strip. The Flashbacks link enables you to search the archives of the strip from its beginning by date, and by character or topic from the mid-1980s. The Daily Briefing link is a page providing pithy summaries of the day's news. The link to The Cast enables you to sort out the tangled history of the *Doonesbury* family and friends, and the GBT's FAQs gives you the same information about the strip's author.

Soundbytes leads to the Doonesbury chat rooms. After you are registered, you can converse with other Doonesbury Electronic Town Hall visitors about the strip, the site, or the news. The

Dbury@Sbucks and The Sellout links both contain *Doonesbury*-related merchandise. Under the Get Involved link, you can learn what charities benefit from the proceeds from sale of all these knickknacks.

Radio Satire Online with *The Daily Feed*

The Daily Feed is a satirical daily radio program available at *www.dailyfeed.com/washingtonpost.html.*

The Daily Feed satirizes current events.

The Daily Feed provides 90-second audio satires, and is now on the Web. From *The Daily Feed*'s page within the Washingtonpost.com site, you can select from a list of the most recent broadcasts.

How do you listen to an audio file on your computer? Usually, it is quite simple after you obtain the proper software. As with many other Web sites, the audio files on *The Daily Feed*'s site are in RealAudio format. You need to acquire the RealAudio software before you can listen to them.

Try It Yourself ▼

Many Web sites have integrated audio files into their offerings. To listen to those files, you usually need to download the appropriate software. In this lesson, you walk through the steps required to obtain RealAudio software, which is required to listen to a broadcast of *The Daily Feed* and other sites.

1. From *The Daily Feed*'s page at *www.dailyfeed.com/washingtonpost.html*, click the Download the plug-in link or go directly to *www.real.com/products/player/index.html*. This page asks you whether you want to download the basic RealAudio player for free, or purchase the Plus version. As of this writing, the latest RealPlayer version is version 7.
2. After you choose the version you want to download, you are asked your name and email address, what operating system you use (Windows or Mac, for example), what CPU you have, your language, and your connection speed. You are also asked to consider what features you want, and are advised how long the download should take.
3. You then should pick a download location near you from a list. You are asked to designate where on your hard drive you want the file to be saved. Often, saving it to the desktop is easiest. (You'll be able to see the file when the download is over without opening any other folders.)
4. When downloading starts, don't be alarmed if your file download window initially estimates the download time at 4 hours. The download should take about the amount of time indicated by Real.
5. After the program has been downloaded, log off the Internet. Open the RealPlayer setup folder and follow the prompts in the setup box. It only takes a minute or so for the setup program to install RealPlayer. If you change your system settings in the course of the installation, you should restart your computer.
6. Now that you have RealPlayer, log back on to the Internet, and listen to a file or two from *The Daily Feed*, or another site with files in RealAudio format.

The Capitol Steps

The steps of the U.S. Capitol are a popular site for press interviews and protests. The Capitol Steps, by contrast, are a D.C.-based singing group of seasoned political staffers with their own twist to the news of the day. They are found at *www.capsteps.com*.

The Capitol Steps package beltway barbs with Cole Porter melodies.

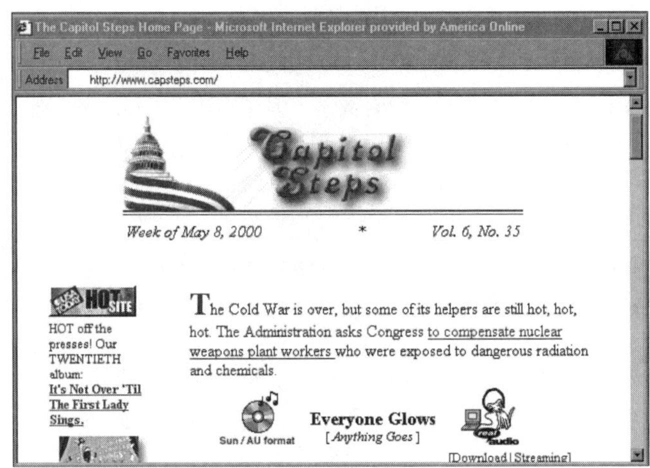

You can hear the Capitol Steps through the RealAudio files available on their site, either by downloading the song or streaming it through your computer directly from the site. MP3 files of their songs are also available for downloading. You can listen to those files on one of a number of programs that handle MP3 files. If, after listening to these songs, you want more, the Steps have released 20 CDs over the years. You can purchase the Capitol Steps' most recent CDs on their Web site, too.

What Is an MP3 File?

MP3 is a storage format for compressed sound files that would otherwise take a great deal of computer memory. MP3 uses a formula to remove the sound data that most people cannot hear, so audio files can be moved and stored electronically without long download times and large storage requirements. Some operating systems come with a built-in MP3 player, or a player can be downloaded from several sites.

Remember that some MP3 files offered for download might be protected by copyright. Taking a sound file without the owner's permission is no better than walking out of a store with that artist's CD. Be careful when you download audio files to select only those files that aren't pirated. You can be confident when you download a file from the artist's own site—such as an MP3 file from the Capitol Steps site—that copyright restrictions aren't a problem.

Want to know more about MP3? Check out the definition and links at *www.whatis.com/mp3.htm*.

The Onion Is "America's Finest News Source"

The Onion is a weekly newspaper published each Wednesday. It features humorous and satirical articles on politics and middle-American life. Its URL is *www.theonion.com*.

When something stings your eyes, it might just be The Onion, bringing the news to you...after a fashion.

On *The Onion*'s home page, you can read its News in Brief, with its strange and, usually, fictitious accounts from around the nation. The home page also has a teaser of the top story of the day, with a link to the whole story—unlike some major papers, *The Onion* doesn't charge you to read the rest of the story, either. The In the News section contains links to the other stories in the issue.

Along the left side of the page is a link to *The Onion*'s horoscope section, by Lloyd Schumner, Sr., Retired Machinist. If you are looking for an excuse to avoid the world, stay home, and watch television, this horoscope is for you. Along the right of the page are links to The Onion AV Club with features, reviews, and even some interviews with real people.

News of the Weird

If *The Onion* isn't off-the-wall enough for you, check out the real-life accounts at News of the Weird, *www.newsoftheweird.com*. This site contains the latest version of Chuck Shepherd's syndicated column, and archives of past articles.

The home page contains a link that enables you to send tips on weird stories to Chuck. It also has a search engine allowing you to search the archives for weird stories on a particular topic. The Weird Map link

continues

continued

provides a national map, from which you can pull News of the Weird stories from a specific state. The "Backstage at News of the Weird" link takes you to a page with Shepherd's behind-the-scenes stories on news items, follow-ups on stories, and other observations. You can also subscribe to a weekly News of the Weird email update.

Both Sides Are Fair Game at Slick Times

The Web version of the political humor magazine *Slick Times* is at *www.slick.com.*

Slick.com has political humor to arm Democrats, Republicans, and "Neithers" for the 2000 race. Its home page has links to jokes, articles, fake photos, and merchandise.

The home page for Slick Times with links to political jokes, satirical articles, and the Slick Times catalog.

Warp Speed Ahead

Maybe you want a more creative flight of fancy with your political humor. Try *www.msintergate.com/warped/warp.html.* This page enables you to warp and distort the faces of famous politicians and celebrities.

The site's list of warpable pictures is at *www.msintergate.com/warped/warp_2nd.html.* After you have selected a picture, just click and drag on the photo to warp it. You might find this a satisfying activity after nine chapters of online political research.

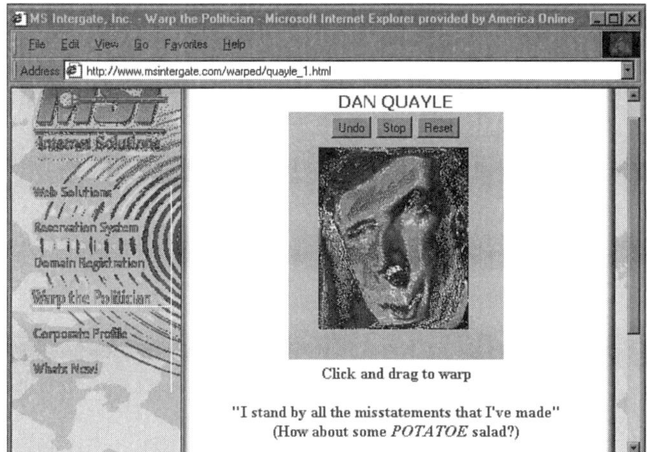

Vice President Dan Quayle after a session with the warper.

Other Sites

Here are links to some other sites you might enjoy:

- *www.ficus2000.com*: Yes, they *are* the potted plants. Is a ficus running for office in your area? Check this site, brought to you by Michael Moore, to find out.
- *www.dumblaws.com*: This site includes dumb laws from international, federal, state, and local jurisdictions. Think twice before you take that elephant on a walk.
- *www.europa.com/~bknotts/speechmaker.html*: Think all politicians' speeches bear an eerie resemblance to one another? Write a speech yourself with these easy steps.
- *www.paunchmagazine.com*: A modern take on the classic magazine *Punch*.
- *www.humorisdead.com/news/index.html*: Another humorous look at current events, with a more international focus. Be careful—some of these stories are real.

Wrapping It Up

Political humor is a popular topic for Web pages, so you should consider this tour just a taste of what's available. Most sites are meant in good fun, but not every site you find will hit your funny bone. Also, some Webmasters might use popular topics, such as political jokes, to pull you to a site where you'll be inundated with annoying—and maybe offensive—advertisements. So, you might find some surprises along with the laughs.

Now you should be able to

- Pull up several humor sites on the Web
- Download the RealPlayer plug-in software and listen to an audio file
- Find and download an MP3 file, and understand when it is wrong to do so
- Enjoy reshaping an important public figure—or at least that public figure's face

CHAPTER 11

Surfing for the Cause: Interest Groups on the World Wide Web

For many people, political involvement starts with an issue. And there are sites on the Web for almost any issue you can imagine. There are also Usenet groups, bulletin boards, and chat rooms to enable you to learn about an issue or say your piece. In addition, there are letter-writing campaigns and rallies. In fact, all the traditional tools of political organizations have Internet counterparts.

This chapter can cover only a small sample of the groups on the Internet. Depending on your interests, you might find an organization here that you want to know more about, or you might need to do your own digging. This chapter is designed so that as you move around various sites, you understand better what you will find on similar sites and how to use that information for your own interests.

What You'll Learn in This Chapter:

- How to find a number of different issue groups on the Web
- What some of the legal and organizational differences are among these groups, and how those differences might limit their activities
- How to contribute online to a group you support, and when that contribution may be tax-deductible
- How to learn more about a group by reviewing certain publicly available IRS forms
- How you can track down both sides of an issue

Technology Issues

As more and more people incorporate the Internet and other technological advances into their lives, issues are raised about privacy, taxation, indecency, access, and a host of other concerns. A site to check about these issues is the Electronic Frontier Foundation (EFF), at *www.eff.org*.

The EFF supports free expression and privacy on the Internet. From the EFF home page, you can learn more about the EFF's views on these issues, and read news about recent developments in these areas. You can also join the EFF, or sign on to one of its campaigns such as the Online Free Speech & Press campaign. You can sign up for the EFFector newsletter, too. A link on the home page also allows you to contribute to EFF.

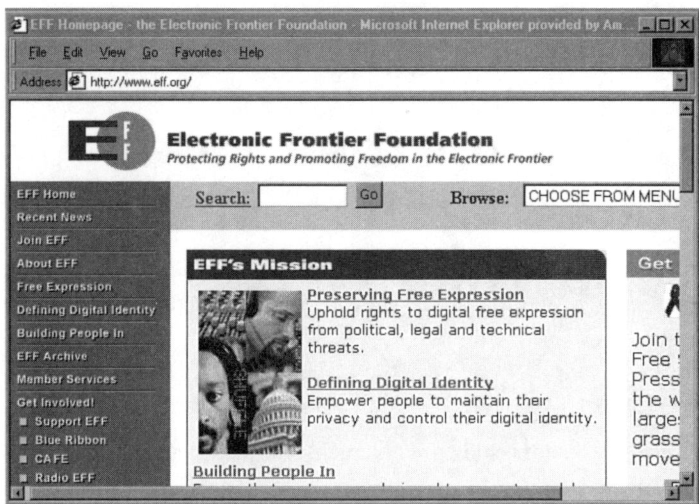

The Electronic Frontier Foundation home page with links to issues, news, and recruitment pages.

Another group interested in this area is the Center for Democracy and Technology (CDT), at *www.cdt.org*. Like the EFF, the CDT seeks to secure free expression and privacy on the Internet. Along with Common Cause (at *www.commoncause.org*), the CDT has worked on issues relating to domain names, including reforms of the Internet Corporation on Assigned Names and Numbers (ICANN—the policy board that governs domain names).

Both the EFF and CDT are good places to go for information on Internet privacy initiatives, encryption policy, Internet censorship, and other similar issues.

Different Kinds of Groups

Here's a brief rundown of the kinds of organizations you might find on the Internet. This is meant as an overview, and some groups might combine features of more than one category.

Research foundations or "think tanks": These groups research issues, analyze problems, and debate solutions. They are political in the sense that policy and politics inevitably overlap. Such groups do not endorse candidates or lobby for legislation.

Grass-roots groups: Organizations with a broad membership base, usually consisting of people who already know how they view a particular issue. They lobby for laws and regulations, monitor governmental action, and promote letter-writing campaigns and other kinds of broad-based activities, as well as offer other services of interest to their members.

Lobbying organizations: These groups focus on legislative and regulatory advocacy. They distribute research (sometimes their own, sometimes from other groups), employ lobbyists, and place advertisements advocating their views. They may engage in a minimal amount of election activity.

Political action committees (PACs): PACs are explicitly election-oriented. They raise money under the rules of the jurisdiction in which they are active. (So, PACs that participate in federal elections are governed by federal laws.) They raise contributions under legal restrictions, make contributions to candidates, parties, and other PACs, advertise independently for or against candidates, and organize political rallies.

Mothers Against Drunk Driving

Mothers Against Drunk Driving, or MADD, is well known for its campaign to stop drunk driving, lower DUI blood-alcohol levels, and prevent underage drinking. Its home on the Web is *www.madd.org*.

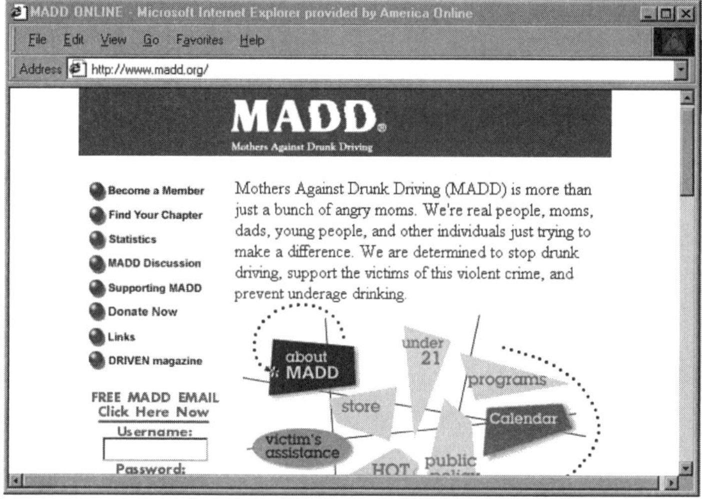

The MADD home page with links to news, information, chapters, bulletin boards, and contribution information.

The MADD home page provides links to news and information, statistics about drinking and driving, and membership information. MADD also provides free email to members—a sign-in space for that service is also part of the home page. The home page also links to MADD's victim's assistance programs, a youth page for visitors under 21, and a calendar of upcoming events. The Donate Now link leads to a page for making a financial donation.

Try It Yourself

Increasingly, groups are soliciting contributions online. Most of the forms work the same way, so we will use the MADD contribution process as an example of how to contribute online.

1. From the MADD home page, click the Donate Now link on the left.
2. You will now view the MADD donations page (URL *www.madd.org/donations/default.shtml*). It contains links to information about MADD's corporate sponsors, how to get a MADD Visa card, and planned giving to MADD. (Essentially, how to remember MADD in your will or other estate-planning devices.) Other groups might also offer similar programs.
3. To make an online donation from this page, complete the form. Check the box indicating the amount of your donation. Fill in the boxes with your name, address, phone number, email, and any other information required for memorial donations or honorary donations. Then click the Proceed to Secure Server button at the bottom of the form.
4. Although you don't need to enter information in every space on the form, if you do not fill in at least your name and email address, you will not be able to proceed to the secure server.
5. The secure server form will take your credit card (Visa or MasterCard) number and expiration date. This particular secure server processes the order in real-time. You will receive an email certification of the payment from your card to MADD.
6. If you would rather mail a contribution to MADD, you can choose that option from the donations page, and receive a form to print, fill out, and mail with your check.

Tax Deductions to Nonprofit Organizations

On the MADD donations page, it states that MADD is a 501(c)(3) nonprofit organization. What does that mean? As we discussed briefly in Chapter 8, "Left-Brain Activity: Progressives and Liberals on the Web," for the donor, it signifies that contributions to MADD are deductible from her taxes as a charitable contribution. 501(c)(3) groups are charitable in character and can offer such deductions to donors. Lobbying groups and advocacy groups are usually exempt from taxes themselves under section 501(c)(4), but this section does not allow donors to these groups to deduct their donations. Contributions to political committees, such as candidates, parties, or PACs, also are not deductible.

Consumer Protection

An example of an organization that contains both an advocacy group and a foundation charity is Public Citizen. It can be found at *www.citizen.org*.

Public Citizen was founded in 1971 by Ralph Nader. Its general mission is to advocate health, safety, and government reform. Its six divisions include health research, congress watch, global trade watch, the Critical Mass Energy and Environment Program, and a litigation group that pursues cases on these and related issues.

Because Public Citizen pursues a wide variety of issues, you might want to obtain a more specific explanation of its activities. You can do this by clicking the More About Public Citizen link at the bottom of the home page. This page (URL *www.citizen.org/newweb/more_about.htm*) provides a more detailed description of the group.

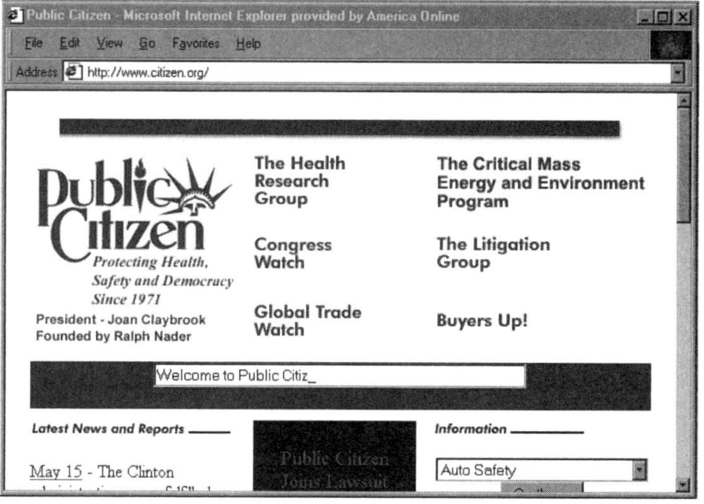

The Public Citizen home page with links to its projects.

At the bottom of the More About Public Citizen page, you will see a link to Public Citizen's Form 990s. These are the forms that exempt groups file with the IRS. If you want more information about the support Public Citizen receives, or how it budgets its funds, you can look at the Public Citizen form or the form of its related foundation. These forms are in PDF, readable using Adobe Acrobat Reader, and might take some time to download.

Form 990

This is the IRS form that tax-exempt groups file with the IRS. Almost all such groups must provide copies of these forms to the public on request. Groups are not required to release the schedules of donations they also file with the IRS, to respect the privacy of their donors.

More and more groups find it convenient—and good public relations—to post their Form 990 on the Web.

If you don't see the Form 990 for a group you care about on their Web site, drop the group an email and ask for it! Better yet, ask the group to post the information on its Web site.

The Environment

There are dozens of organizations that focus on the environment. One of the better-known environmental groups is the Sierra Club. It can be found at *www.sierraclub.org*.

The Sierra Club's page features a Take Action site for online activism that gives you an easy way to write public figures and express your views on the issues. From this link, you can send your Representative (via email) a predrafted message. As of this writing, the letters include one to Congress on behalf of bond legislation before Congress, a letter to the editor praising President Clinton's wilderness policies, and a half-dozen other customizable letters.

The Sierra Club site also has daily news updates on relevant news, and information about the Sierra Club and its activities.

In addition, a Sierra Club–related Usenet group you might want to check out is at *alt.org.sierra-club*.

Another environmental organization of national prominence is Greenpeace. Its U.S. site is at *www.greenpeaceusa.org*.

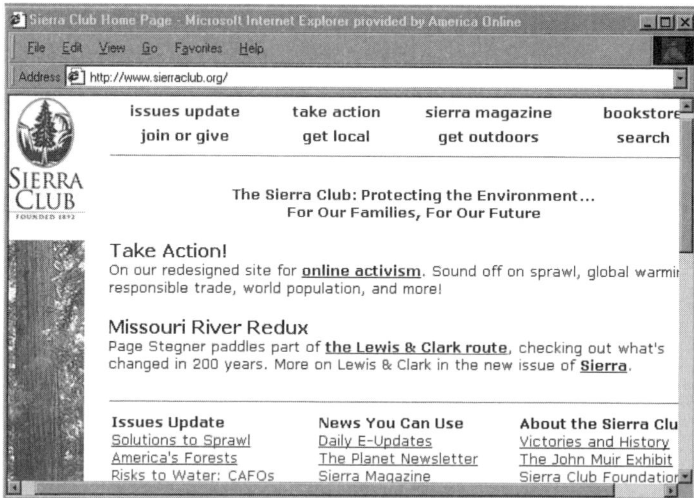

The Sierra Club home page with news and information about the environment.

Greenpeace has offices around the world and is headquartered in Amsterdam. Its activities reach across the globe, and among the many issues it tackles are nuclear testing, protection of endangered species, and opposition to genetically modified foods. Its approach tends to emphasize creative nonviolent confrontation rather than lobbying and letter writing, but if you're itching to send a missive to someone, check the Save link on the home page, and then click the Action Center link. Greenpeace suggests a few places to write.

Numerous other environmental groups have Web sites and Usenet discussion groups—more than I can address here. A good directory can be found at *www.yahoo.com*, by clicking Society & Culture, and then Environment and Nature. You can then choose from a sizable list of additional headings, or scroll through the list of links.

Retirement and Elder Issues

For issues related to aging, retirement, Social Security, Medicare, or similar matters, you might try the home page for the AARP, at *www.aarp.org*.

The AARP provides a wide range of services for people older than 50. From its home page, you can click the Member Services and Discounts button to link to a membership form (dues are a whopping $10!), and check out the travel, insurance, investment, and pharmacy services provided to members. The Computers and Technology button leads to articles about using your computer, including an Internet expedition at *www.aarp.org/expedition* that provides the basics of Web use.

The AARP offers many services on its Web page.

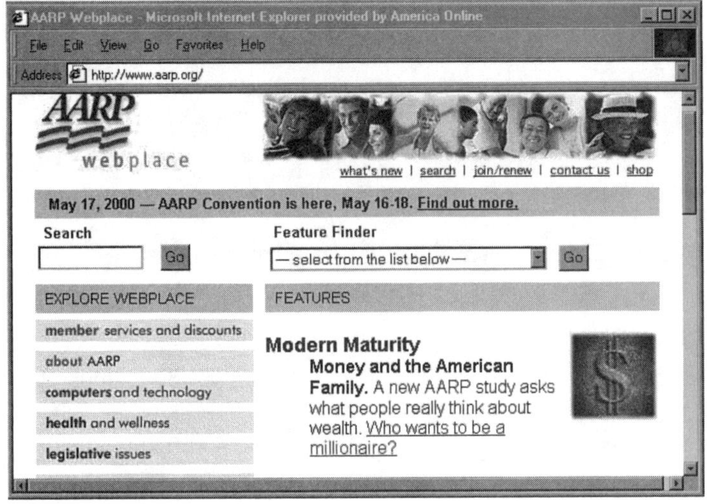

Register to Vote

Voter registration has never been easier. Because of changes in federal law, you can register through the mail easily in every state in the nation. With BeAVoter.org, the process becomes even simpler. From this home page at *www.beavoter.org*, select the Register to Vote link. You are asked to select a state, and a form comes up for you to fill out. You will receive a copy of your form in about two weeks to review and mail to your local voter registration office. The form will come with an envelope already addressed to your registrar. Unfortunately, if you live in New Hampshire, North Dakota, or Wyoming you can't use the BeAVoter form, and should obtain a registration form from a local government building or post office.

BeAVoter is not a government site. It is sponsored by the AARP, AOL, and MCI WorldCom.

Of more direct political interest, the Legislative Issues button provides a link to online voter registration services through BeAVoter.org, as well as AARP voter guides, hot legislative topics, and a candidate database. You can access the AARP/Vote program by selecting its title from the Feature Finder on the home page (or by using the URL *www.aarp.org/aarpvote*). This is the AARP's voter education and issue advocacy program, with information on AARP's voter guides, candidate forums, letter-writing campaigns, and volunteering.

Under the AARP's Research and Reference button, you will find a link to a Web resource guide for seniors, with links to numerous sites. The direct URL for this Web directory is *www.aarp.org/cyber/general.htm*.

Issue Advocacy

The phrase *issue advocacy* is almost self-defining—it is advocacy about issues. Issue advocacy has become a loaded term because of the use of issues as an indirect method of influencing elections. Elections are necessarily about issues, so some issue advocacy by independent groups during the election is to be expected and, in fact, is protected by the First Amendment.

But, because issue-advocacy groups do not operate under the same limits as political committees and candidates, issue advocacy has become a popular device for people who want to help (or hurt) a candidate, but don't want to play by the restrictive rules applied to candidates. For example, if a lobbying group ran an advertisement against Congressman Jones demanding that people vote against him, it would be a regulated "independent expenditure" or even an in-kind contribution if Jones's opponent helped with the spot. If the same group ran an advertisement criticizing Congressman Jones's bad voting record on an issue, that would be "issue advocacy," protected from regulation.

Tax Reform

No one likes to pay taxes. But you might be surprised at the magnitude of the average person's tax burden. A place to go for this kind of information is the Americans for Tax Reform (ATR) page, at *www.atr.org/main.htm.*

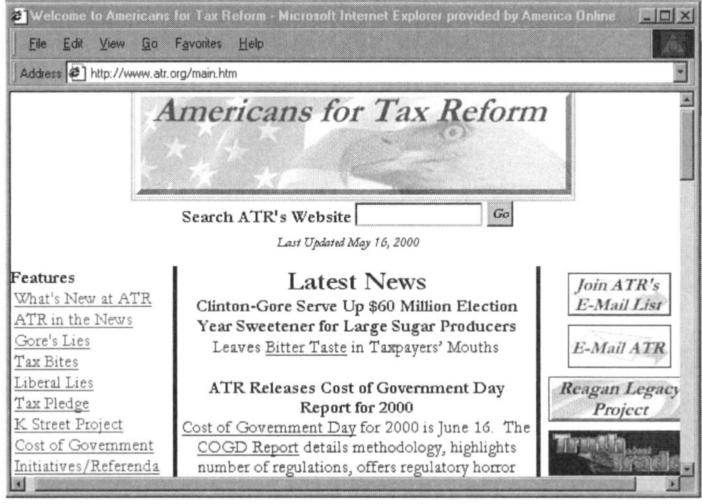

Americans for Tax Reform fights tax increases.

From the ATR home page, you can read tax news updates with links to the full articles, as well as the group's own commentary about legislation, public officials, and tax policy. ATR rates congressmen and senators, and from this home page you can check whether ATR thinks one of your representatives is an "enemy of the taxpayer."

Along the left side of the page are other links to taxpayer-related news, ratings, awards, copies of ATR's Tax Alert column, policy briefs, editorials, and press releases, and links to a contribution form and information on becoming a member.

Want more information or a different view of tax reform? Try one of the listings provided by About.com on tax reform. The URL to the About.com list of tax-reform links is *law.about.com/newsissues/law/msub30.htm.*

Civil Rights, Race, and Ethnicity

There are many excellent places to go for information on race relations, civil rights, and affirmative action. One site you might want to try is hosted by the Leadership Conference on Civil Rights at *www.civilrights.org*.

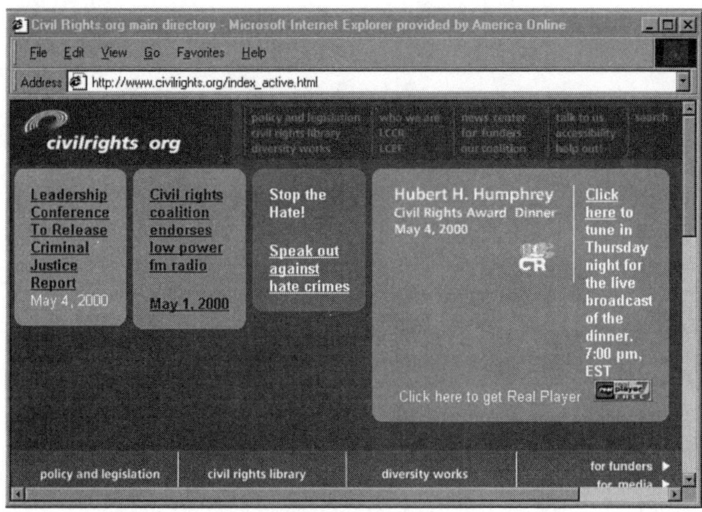

The Leadership Conference on Civil Rights hosts the civilrights.org page.

This page has links to a variety of resources. By following the Policy and Legislation link, you can find information on legislation and policy proposals at the federal and state levels. The Civil Rights Library link takes you to a growing collection of civil rights materials. The This Week in Civil Rights link takes you to a calendar, where you can specify a date period and see what events are coming up. You can also read the Leadership Conference's report on criminal justice. The Help Out link takes you to a form that you can use to make a contribution online.

Because many civil rights victories come about through litigation, another good source for information in this area is the Lawyers' Committee for Civil Rights Under Law. This group's page is at *www.lawyerscommittee.org/index2.html*. It provides legislative alerts, as well as current information on civil-rights–related cases.

The concern over race-based hostility on the Internet has prompted the formation of HateWatch, found at *hatewatch.org/frames.html*. This group monitors racist and other hate groups on the Internet, and provides many other services.

A number of civil rights groups address the concerns of specific communities. Perhaps one of the best known is the National Association for the Advancement of Colored People (NAACP). The NAACP's home page can be found at *www.naacp.org*. Here you can learn the latest about the group's rallies, boycotts, litigation, and other activities.

A few other community-specific groups are

- National Council of La Raza, at *www.nclr.org*
- Japanese American Citizens League at *www.jacl.org*
- Anti-Defamation League at *www.adl.org*
- Native American Rights Fund at *www.narf.org*

As civil rights laws have moved from general colorblind reforms to preferences, groups have organized to respond to concerns raised by reverse discrimination. For information on this topic, you might want to look up Adversity Net at *www.adversity.net*. A foundation that does research and analyses critical of racial preferences is the Center for Equal Opportunity at *www.ceousa.org*.

Hate and Bigotry: Limits to Online Speech?

The HateWatch site defines a hate site as one that advocates violence against or unreasonable hostility toward a person or group based on race, religion, ethnicity, gender, sexual orientation, or disability. Although the Web has been celebrated as an open forum for views of all kinds, in the eyes of many Internet service providers and Web providers (not to mention Web users), such speech is not a legitimate part of cybersociety. Moreover, in many cases, it violates the provider's use agreements. If you come across hate speech on the Web (either on a site or in email), drop a note to HateWatch. Also, if the site or communication involves a big ISP or Web host, you can report it to them for appropriate action.

Hearth and Home: Really Personal Issues

Some of the most controversial (and lively) political issues revolve around the most personal aspects of life. Abortion, contra-

Why Aren't More PACs on the Web?

When you read the paper, PACs seem to be big political business. Why don't more PACs have Web sites? Out of the roughly 3,800 federal PACs registered with the FEC, only about one-quarter can legally talk to the general public about making contributions and supporting the PAC. (And an unknown percentage of these are dormant.) Why? The majority of PACs are business or labor PACs, and under law, they can solicit contributions only from certain corporate employees or union members. Soliciting outside these groups is illegal, and solicitation is interpreted quite broadly to cover almost anything positive about the PAC. And, if you can't say something nice about yourself on a Web site, why say anything at all?

ception, sexual preference, religion in public life, and "traditional values" are all parts of the policy and political map that I lump into this category.

As with the sites we reviewed earlier, these sites provide news, legislative records, research, and similar information. They also provide forms you can use to join and contribute to the cause. Many of these sites are quite well known, so this list of Web addresses should enable you to check out their activities and provide your support, if you so decide.

- The Christian Coalition of America, at *www.cc.org*.
- The Human Rights Campaign, at *www.hrcusa.org*.
- The National Organization for Women, at *www.now.org*. (From this site, you can also reach NOW's charitable foundation at *www.nowfoundation.org*, and the NOW political action committee at *www.nowpacs.org*.)
- National Right to Life Committee, at *www.nrlc.org*.
- People For the American Way, at *www.pfaw.org*.
- The Gay and Lesbian Victory Fund, at *www.victoryfund.org/templates/victoryfund/index.html*.
- Eagle Forum, at *www.eagleforum.org*.
- The National Abortion Rights Action League, at *www.naral.org*.

Business Groups

Taxes and regulations hit business squarely in the bank account. To obtain the business perspective on politics and policy, you might review the U.S. Chamber of Commerce's site at *www.uschamber.org*.

The U.S. Chamber of Commerce was formed in 1912 to provide one group that could speak for business in Washington. Now, of course, there are many such groups, but the Chamber of Commerce is still very influential. Its membership is nearly three million companies. It is divided into state and local chapters, and those groups monitor developments in state and local government as well.

Under the Policy & Issues link, you will find a list of links. Under Index of Issues is a list of issues by topic and an alphabetical list. In addition to a Chamber of Commerce summary of its position on the issue, you can obtain other related documents from here.

▼ **Try It Yourself**

We will now use the U.S. Chamber's Policy & Issues link, and links from that page, to gather information and perspective on an issue. Here, for an example, I chose ergonomics.

1. From the Chamber of Commerce's Policy & Issues page, choose the Index of Issues link. From the alphabetical list, choose Ergonomics.
2. You will pull up a page with a Chamber of Commerce summary of its views. In brief, the Chamber is opposed to an OSHA rule on standards for ergonomics in the workplace, because of its expense and because it is not based on adequate research or comments from regulated parties. The summary contains a link to the Chamber's OSHA Alert on the rule regarding ergonomics.
3. When you click the OSHA Alert link, you are taken to the Chamber of Commerce's summary of the scope and requirements of the proposed OSHA rule. At the bottom of the Alert, you can link to the text of the standard posted on the OSHA Web page at *www.osha-slc.gov/ergonomics-standard*.
4. From the OSHA link, you can pull up information on hearings about the proposed rule, the text, a FAQ about the rulemaking, guides for the media, and other information.
5. Got an opinion about the rulemaking? By clicking your browser's Back button, you will return to the Chamber's page. In the box along the left of the Alert is a link that says, "Give OSHA a Piece of Your Mind Send a Message Now!" This links you to a page with information on how to fax a message to OSHA about the rulemaking.
6. As you were reading the Chamber's summary of the OSHA proposal, you might have seen a mention that the AFL-CIO supports the rulemaking. To complete your review, pull up the American Federation of Labor-Congress of Industrial Organizations (AFL-CIO) page at *www.aflcio.org*.

7. From the AFL-CIO page, click the link called Safety & Health on the Job. This page features a number of links to items about the ergonomic regulation, including AFL-CIO testimony in favor of the rule under the page's Stop the Pain Updates. If you prefer this perspective, the page provides a link so that you can contact Congress (not OSHA, you might notice) about your support of the rulemaking.

The U.S. Chamber of Commerce site provides news updates and information on laws affecting business.

Organized Labor

Because I mentioned unions, you might be interested in finding organized labor on the Web. Here are some politically newsworthy organizations that you might want to look up:

- Service Employees International Union (SEIU) at *www.seiu.org*
- United Farm Workers (UFW) at *www.ufw.org*
- International Brotherhood of Teamsters at *www.teamster.org*
- Laborers' International Union of North America at *www.liuna.org*

Wrapping It Up

In this chapter, you sampled a number of sites from interest groups. Now you should be able to

- Find a group that interests you, and check up on its activities and positions
- Understand the forms and restrictions of different kinds of groups
- Make an online contribution
- Obtain a voter registration form online
- Compare the policy views of different groups, and decide for yourself what to think

CHAPTER 12

The Cyber-Swiss Army Knife: Sites That Put It All Together

In the previous chapters, we looked at legislation, opinions, views, and agencies. Now, you should have a good idea how to find these items on various sites and the information you'll see when there.

But a number of sites have been developed to consolidate this process for you. These nonpartisan Web pages enable you to catch up on news, legislation, issues, and political races, as well as (in many cases) register to vote and write your representative. Polls, humor, and discussion forums are also often provided. Some are standalone sites, but others provide a family of related sites. You can use the policy pages of these sites to study an issue, and then move to their activism pages to learn what you can do.

What you gain in breadth you might sacrifice in depth. An all-purpose site's treatment of an issue will likely not be as penetrating as the treatment offered by a group that specializes in that issue. But if what you're after is a place that provides an overview and variety of services, one of these sites might be a good choice.

What You'll Learn in This Chapter:

- Where to find a variety of nonpartisan political information and links in one place
- How to register with a site to customize the site's pages for your interests
- Where to find campaign advertising, voting record information, and public statements of candidates
- How to pay a ticket and find a government auction in one place online

The VoxCap Network

The VoxCap Network consists of four sites: VoxCap.com, IntellectualCapital.com, Policy.com, and CongressVote.com. The home page for VoxCap.com is at *www.voxcap.com*.

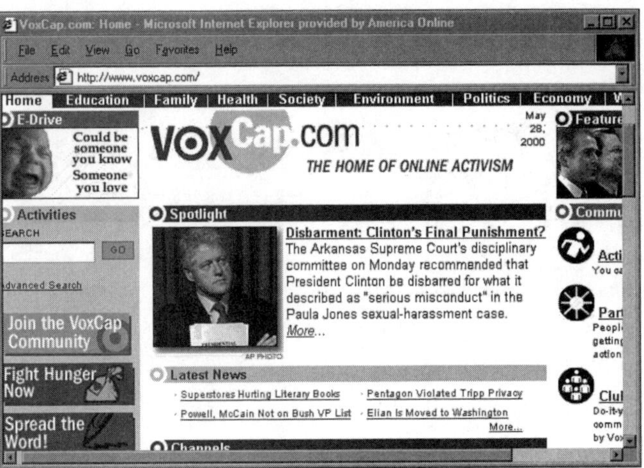

The home page for VoxCap.com, one of four VoxCap sites, focuses on online activism.

VoxCap.com

VoxCap.com is the group's activism site. It features nine channels that provide information on different broad topics, such as education and the environment. Each channel is divided into subchannels, and also lists a featured issue and a topic in the news. There are also ReadingRoom reviews of recent books on the topic.

Another VoxCap feature is the VoxCap community where, after you register, you can file your profile, sponsor VoxCap clubs, participate in discussion forums, and take advantage of other VoxCap services. VoxCap also has buttons that link you to forms for writing your congressman and a letter to the editor. The VoxCap Reader service is a weekly email in which VoxCap provides summaries of the week's articles and news items for an issue area of your choice. The summaries also contain links to the complete articles.

IntellectualCapital.com

IntellectualCapital.com is a weekly e-zine that provides articles about current news and issues. It also features articles from leading "think" magazines such as the *New Republic* and *National Review*.

Policy.com

Policy.com is focused on in-depth public policy analysis. It features studies, articles, and links from think tanks, advocacy groups, universities, media, and similar organizations. It also offers interviews with newsmakers on public policy topics.

CongressVote.com

CongressVote.com looks at issues before Congress. It posts articles and offers discussion groups and other interactive features about current federal legislation. Its home page contains a United States map from which you can obtain a list of members from a specific state. The site provides biographical and voting record information on these members of Congress, and an email form you can use to write their offices.

Grassroots.com, Democracy Network, and Related Sites

Grassroots.com is another "take action" site on the Web. It, too, can be most useful when used as part of a broader group of sites that includes Democracy Network (DNet) and Public Agenda.com, sponsored in part by DNet.

The Grassroots.com site provides action pages on almost thirty separate issues.

Grassroots.com

Grassroots.com offers information and action links on numerous issues. If you register with Grassroots.com, you can also customize your home page with news about the issues that interest you.

Try It Yourself

This takes you step-by-step through the registration procedure used by Grassroots.com. Other sites also provide custom information for registered users. The site deposits a cookie on you computer that tells the site what your interests are when you visit. The site loads the pages that reflect your choices.

1. From the URL *Grassroots.com*, choose the Sign In link at the left. This pulls up the sign-in form for registered users, and a link for you to register.
2. Click the Sign Up link, and you retrieve a simple form. It requires you to provide a username (which can be an alias) that other visitors will see, and a password. It also asks for optional address information.
3. Now that you are registered, you can customize the page based on your interests. When you click the Customize Now link, you are provided three lists: one of issues, one of cities, and one of states. Pick the issues and locale you want to follow.
4. The next time you visit the Grassroots.com home page, you can sign in and see the latest news and information about your custom choices.

Grassroots.com provides several action options for each issue. It has links to groups to which you can make donations, contact links for writing your congress member, chat and discussion forum links, and options to form or join a Grassroots.com group related to the issue.

Grassroots.com also provides links of general interest on its home page. For instance, as of this writing, a copy of a film the White House produced as a spoof on the President's waning days in office could be played from this site by using RealPlayer.

DNet

The Democracy Network, or DNet, is at *www.dnet.org*. This site provides one stop for information on candidates for national, state, and local offices. By entering your ZIP Code, you can retrieve a page with the listed offices on your ballot covered by the site. Some state and local offices might be blank, either because they are not contested in the next election or because the DNet site doesn't have information about them. If DNet is missing information on a race you think should be covered, you can write and request coverage by using the link next to that office.

When you see the race that interests you, click that link. DNet will load a page containing a grid that lists the names of the candidates for the office, and how they responded to a series of questions on issues. Some candidates respond to every question, others leave no comment for some or all questions. This chart on the issues can help you choose which candidate to support, or provide you with a basis for doing more penetrating research on one or more candidates.

From the DNet home page, you can also retrieve the national voter registration form. We discussed online voter registration in Chapter 11, "Surfing for the Cause: Interest Groups on the World Wide Web."

Public Agenda

Public Agenda, at *publicagenda.com*, provides policy analysis and public opinion results. From this site, you can link to briefings on numerous issues, and from there link to candidates' stands on these issues.

The page for each issue provides an overview of the subject, digest of recent stories, charts, opinions, sources to go to for additional information, and recent books on the topic. Each issue page also provides public opinion information about the topic so that you can see what concerns and views were found in polling. Then you can link from this site to DNet and other sites to obtain candidates' positions. You can also obtain contribution information from this links menu from the Center for Responsive Politics Open Secrets site. We will review contribution research in depth in Chapter 17, "The Future of the Internet in Politics."

Lobbyforme.com and Related Sites

Lobbyforme.com offers an interesting service: Voice your views and have 12 former members of Congress lobby for action on those issues. Lobbyforme.com is part of a group of sites that includes Politics1.com and Politicalwag.com.

Who Sees My Information?

You might be reluctant to register for custom features from a Web site if you thought that information could be traced back to you or used for advertising. As has been reported in the press, some commercial sites gather registration information to use commercially. Sometimes commercial use is limited to simply compiling demographics to show advertisers that the site has wide appeal, but your registration information might also be used to tailor the banner ads you see while on the site or, conceivably, to build email lists for direct advertising. If the use of your information concerns you, read the fine print. Sites usually tell registrants how information will be used, and might allow you to opt out of having your information used. Depending on what you find in the fine print, you might decide that the convenience of a custom site or registration for chats and forums is not worth the trouble.

Lobbyforme.com will dispatch one of 12 former Congress members to lobby for you.

Lobbyforme.com

When you first visit Lobbyforme.com, you will see a Hot Topics questionnaire. After you register with Lobbyforme.com, you can express your views on these questions, and see in realtime how other registered visitors voted on the questions. (Only one vote allowed per visitor!) You can also express your opinion to Lobbyforme.com by clicking the Make a Difference link. From there, you can register your views on a list of topics, and your views will be advocated by one of Lobbyforme.com's former congressional members. For a list and biographies of the members providing services for Lobbyforme.com, visit the information page at *lobbyforme.com/about*.

Another interesting link on Lobbyforme is Face Off. Here, two opinion leaders provide opinion editorials on two sides of an issue. Also, at the lower-right side of the page is a link to live voting from the capitol, where you can watch votes in Congress as they are taking place. It's best to use this feature if you already know that a vote is being taken; if you instead visit at random from time to time, you will find that most days nothing is happening. Congress is frequently meeting in committee or debating, and not voting.

Lobbyforme.com also has an Election 2000 link, which takes you to the Politics1.com presidential election page. We'll look at Politics1.com next.

Politics1.com

Politics1.com provides numerous links to specific political sites. Under the Presidency 2000 link are links to candidate campaigns, polls, and other sites. Under The States: Races & Links is a map of the nation and a list of state links. You can click a state on the map, or the state link below the map, to retrieve that state's Politics1.com page. For each state, Politics1.com provides a list of the candidates on the ballot with links to their Web pages, if available. Politics1.com also uses photos of old campaign buttons from state races to liven up these pages—see how many you can identify!

The Political Parties link takes you to links for the two major parties. Both the Democrats and Republicans have several national committees and other official groups with sites—we will look at these closely in Chapters 13, "Democrats Online," and 14, "Republicans Online." This page also contains links to minor parties, which we will review in Chapter 15, "Other Parties Online." There are also many unofficial party sites not covered here, which we will talk about in those chapters.

Under the Issues & Debates link, the links are presented first by ideology, and then by specific issues. You'll find activists, groups, and plenty of attitude in these directories. You can sign up for the Politics1.com newsletter under the Newsletter link. The Campaign Buttons link provides links to some interesting resources for buying and valuing old campaign mementos, such as buttons. There is a link to a Politics1.com archive of candidates in past federal and gubernatorial races for use in identifying campaign materials.

Politicalwag.com

Politicalwag.com at *http://politicalwag.com/servlet/home* is a political discussion site. It provides moderated forums for registered visitors to post messages about a wide variety of political topics. On the home page, you will see a list of featured discussions, and you can pull down a menu listing of all discussions. You can review the posts in these forums without registering. To participate in the discussion requires that you register with the site.

Politicalwag.com also has separate state pages for political issues related to specific states. A pull-down menu of states that links you to these pages is also on the home page. Politicalwag.com also hosts live chats with politicians from time to time.

Political News Sites

You can find political news at a number of specialty sites. Here is a sample for you to investigate:

- CNN/Allpolitics, at *cnn.com/allpolitics*
- ABC News's Political Nation, at *abcnews.go.com/sections/politics*
- *Roll Call*, at *www.rollcall.com*, and *The Hill*, at *www.hillnews.com*, both newspapers specializing in coverage of Congress
- Headlines from the Hotline, a daily electronic political news sheet, at *hotlinescoop.com*
- The *Washington Post*'s On Politics page, at *washingtonpost.com/wp-dyn/politics*
- The *Nando Times*'s politics page, at *www.nandotimes.com/politics*

Freedom Channel

Freedom Channel is a nonprofit site that supplies political news, campaign information, video, in-depth features on specific issues and races, and customizable features. It is at *www.freedomchannel.com*.

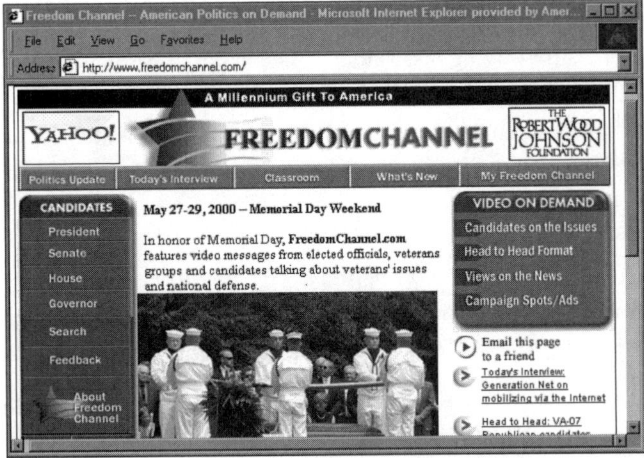

The Freedom Channel home page with links to news and campaign video.

The Video On Demand feature of this site is useful for researching public statements of candidates. By clicking the Candidates on the Issues link, you retrieve a page with pull-down menus of candidates (by office) and a list of issues. Select a candidate office and issue, and the next page provides a list of video of candidates talking about that issue. You can choose to watch the video using RealPlayer, listen to the sound without the video, or read the transcription. You can also connect to the candidate's Web page or email by selecting those links adjacent to the link to the video. The Head to Head Format link provides you with video of the candidates in one particular race discussing an issue—you select the issue from a menu. The Views on the News button provides links to video of groups and candidates expressing views on a specific issue of the day. The Campaign Spots/Ads button leads to links for party and issue ads, and campaign ads. You can see what a candidate or group is saying to voters in other parts of the country. Depending upon the campaign, this information can be quite illuminating.

Freedom Channel also provides additional services, such as email updates, to registered users. You also need to register to participate in Freedom Channel's polls. The registration form is under the My Freedom Channel link. It requires you to give your name and email address, and party registration for polling purposes. (If you object to disclosing your party affiliation, the form instructs you to enter "other.") You also pick a username and a password. If you want to participate in the polls, the form asks for additional demographic information. This information is used to calculate cross-tabulations from the polling information. That is, not only will the poll reveal how registered users generally feel about an issue, but how opinion is split by age and gender, for example.

More One-Stop Political Sites

Sites offering one-stop shopping for the news and politics junkie seem to appear every day. By necessity, I can show you only a sampling of what these various sites can do. New sites will come online, and existing ones will change focus, so you should review the field from time to time to see what might have turned up. For now, some other sites you might want to look at are

continues

continued

- *www.speakout.com*
- *govote.com*
- *onedemocracy. com*
- *votenet.com*
- *politicalinsider. com*
- *www.voter.com*
- *epolitics.org*
- *evote.com*

The proliferation of political portal sites has attracted attention. The Annenberg Public Policy Center's site, Netelection.org, has developed a grid comparing the features of many political sites. The grid is at the URL *netelection .org/features/portals*.

A Site That Makes Working with Government Less Work

At govWorks.com, you can chat about issues, participate in message boards with other visitors, check out campaign videos, and scan links to other government Web sites like these other sites we've visited. But, adding an interesting twist, govWorks.com can also help you pay your taxes, fees, and bills to government agencies online.

On the home page at *govworks.com*, you will see a column headed by the word Pay. Each of these headings links you to the govWorks.com payment system. For instance, if you want to pay a parking ticket online, you would click Parking tickets. You then retrieve a form that asks for the city and state issuing the ticket. After you provide that and click the Continue button, a form appears with the address of the ticket payment agency. If this doesn't match the agency on your ticket, you are given a form to type the proper information. You can then pay the ticket using a credit card over the govWorks.com secure server. Similar forms are provided for paying property taxes and utility bills. The Income taxes button links you to forms from the federal and state governments, additional articles and information on taxes, and information on how to file electronically.

As an incentive, govWorks.com offers govRewards to visitors who pre-register and then make payments using govWorks.com. Registered users can earn credits toward future governmental payments over govWorks.com by accepting offers advertised when they make online payments.

govWorks.com also provides a govHotline via email or telephone, where visitors can ask legal or governmental questions that are then answered by govWorks.com staff. govWorks.com posts the most interesting answers on the site.

You can also subscribe (for a fee) to govWorks.com's government auction listings. These listings provide information about government auctions around the country, where you can pick up seized or surplus goods at (one hopes) cut-rate prices.

Vote Smart

A slightly more specialized site for nonpartisan political research is sponsored by Project Vote Smart. This home page is at *www.vote-smart.org*.

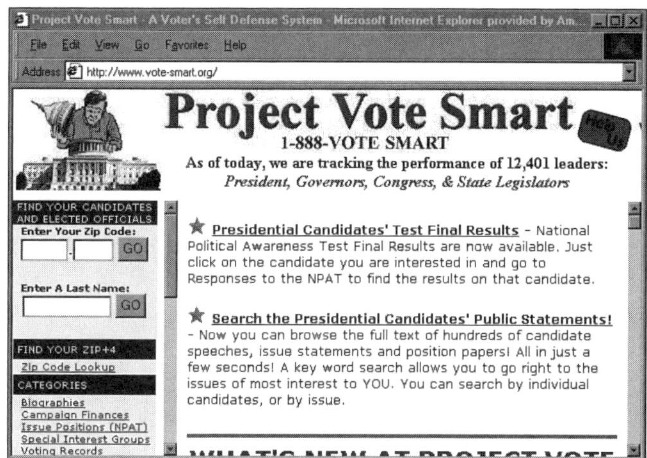

Track candidate statements and votes on Project Vote Smart's site.

This site specializes in providing issue and vote information about specific candidates. Project Vote Smart circulates its National Political Awareness Test (NPAT), which asks for candidates' positions on a variety of issues, each election cycle. Candidates' responses are then published and posted on this site. Additionally, Project Vote Smart has collected key votes from incumbents' terms in office, so you can learn how they cast their votes in issues of interest to you.

On the home page, you will see links on the left side of the page. Under Categories, you can retrieve candidates' biographies, campaign finance information, issue positions according to their answers to the NPAT, ratings and endorsements by interest groups, and voting records. When you click one of these links, you are taken to a map of the U.S., and can choose which state's candidate's information to retrieve. The site provides information on the candidates for president, Senate, House of Representatives, governor, and state legislature. If you are pulling up information on a presidential candidate, look for the Public Statements link. This link is to a page that enables you to read and search the candidate's public statements.

If you are researching state legislative candidates, you might find that Project Vote Smart has not posted voting record information, and might not have the most current information on ballot measures or other state-specific items. (It's a big country, after all.) A good alternative is to seek out a similar group in your state. For instance, in California, you could check out the California Voter Foundation at *www.calvoter.org*, which has a California-specific guide to the legislature and similar election information. The Proposition Song, which you can hear on this site at the URL *http://www.calvoter.org/2000/primary/propositions/song/index.html*, winks a deadpan eye at California's notoriously long initiative ballot. Or try your state's page on DNet, a site we looked at earlier in this chapter.

Wrapping It Up

The abundance of do-it-all political sites might seem daunting, but it also gives you numerous options. You should try a few. One site will fit your personal interests, tastes, and passions better than another. After reading this chapter, you should be able to

- Find political news, campaign information, discussions, registration, and polls on any one of a number of sites
- Voice your views to a lobbyist online
- Review candidate advertising, voting records, and public statements online, in text, audio, or video
- Research not just federal, but also state candidates
- Take care of inconvenient but important government payments online

PART IV

Come to the Party Online

CHAPTER 13

Democrats Online

Of the two major American political parties, the Democratic Party is the older. Thomas Jefferson won the presidency as a member of the Democratic-Republican Party (the predecessor of today's Democratic Party) in 1800. Under Andrew Jackson's leadership (elected president in 1828), the party developed into a national organization with a national convention and party platform. Jackson also adopted the donkey as a campaign symbol. The party acquired its current name in 1844. Its national committee, the Democratic National Committee, was established in 1848.

What You'll Learn in This Chapter:

- What the Democratic Party has to offer online
- What information is publicly disclosed from your campaign contributions
- Why committees ask so many questions of contributors
- How to find Democratic candidates on the Internet, and how to volunteer online
- What some unofficial Democratic groups do to support particular Democratic candidates

Official Democratic Party Organizations

The Democratic Party is made up of a national committee (the Democratic National Committee or DNC), congressional campaign committees, state party committees, county party committees, and other official Democratic organizations. In addition to looking at these, we also review Democratic candidate campaign sites. Also, we will visit some Democratic groups that are not official party organizations. These groups usually favor a particular vision of Democratic politics, and raise money for candidates and activities to move the party in their direction.

The Democratic National Committee

The Democratic National Committee is the national Democratic Party organization. Its home page is at *www.democrats.org*.

The home page provides links to the DNC's latest news stories and anti-Republican stories and links (it is a political committee, after all), and has a number of useful links along the left side of the page.

The Newsroom link connects you with the DNC's selected news items. As you would expect, these news items usually involve flattering portrayals of Democratic elected officials, and unflattering stories about Republicans. Some of the news is campaign related, and other news involves votes in Congress and more policy-oriented fare. The Action Center button takes you to a page where you can link to your state party's information via a pull-down menu, link to state voter registration information for your state through another menu, and sign up for campaign training.

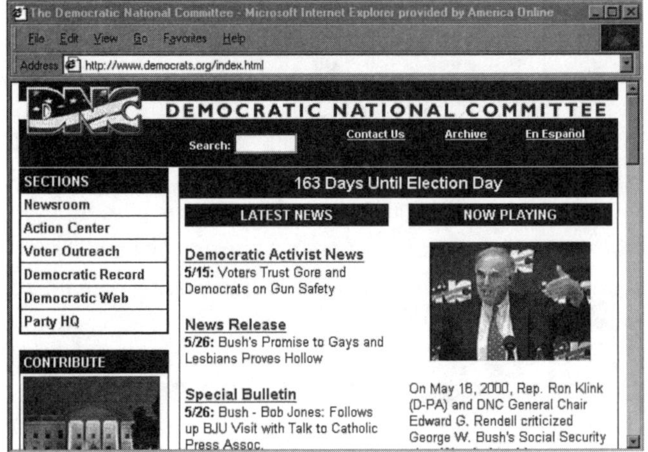

The home page for the Democratic National Committee with links to campaign information, political news, and other Democratic groups.

Under Voter Outreach are links to the party's official outreach offices for ethnic groups, gays and lesbians, older voters, women, and youth. The Democratic Record button leads to links for the party's platform and position papers. The Democratic Web button retrieves a page from which you can link to national Democratic organizations, state parties, and county committees. Not all state or county parties have active Web pages, so you might not find a state Democratic Party page for your state.

The Party HQ button takes you to materials about the Democratic Party, and about its history, platform, bylaws, and other administrative information. The party also has links to job and internship listings from this page.

Beneath these buttons on the home page is a link you can use to contribute to the DNC. From it, you are provided a form to complete, which asks for your name, address, occupation, and employer. Under federal law, committees must ask for this information, and include it when they itemize contributions on periodic reports. If you don't provide it, the committee will ask you for it again, and might choose to return your contribution if you still don't provide the information.

By using the DNC's contribution form, you can contribute via credit card or use the form to mail in a contribution by check. Contributions through this form are sent to the DNC's federal account.

Confidentiality and Political Contributions

When you contribute $200 or more to a federal political committee, your name, address, occupation, and employer are reported to the Federal Election Commission. These forms are publicly available online, and are reviewed by opponents, reporters, and researchers. If you do not want your information reported, there isn't much you can do about it after you make the $200 threshold. These disclosure laws were enacted after the Watergate scandal to shed light on what interests supported which candidates or committees. However, it might be some consolation to know that it is illegal to use these reports for commercial purposes or for fundraising.

Federal and Nonfederal Contributions

The DNC's online contribution form specifically solicits federal contributions. Why does it specify *federal* contributions? Political parties are concerned with both federal and nonfederal elections; in some states, everything from governor to dogcatcher involves a partisan political contest. Parties, therefore, raise funds for federal use under the strict federal rules, and raise funds for nonfederal use free from those rules. Parties can use a certain percentage of the nonfederal (or *soft*) money on party administration, voter education, and issue ads. They can also use it to contribute to state and local candidates, provided that the money is legal under the laws of those recipients' states. As you can imagine, this crazy quilt of state laws, combined with federal restrictions, makes for an accounting challenge. As a result, national political parties employ staffs of accountants and lawyers to keep it all straight.

Why All the Caveats on the Federal Contribution Forms?

If you've looked at the online contribution forms for a federal candidate or party committee, you've noticed that many forms require you to attest that you are not making the contribution out of corporate funds, are not contributing on behalf of another person, and are not a foreign national or a government contractor. These campaigns aren't being nosy or irrationally punctilious. In fact, federal laws prohibit these sources from making contributions in federal elections. The recipient candidates and committees need to make sure that you know the rules, both for their own protection and to prevent inadvertent violations of the law by uninformed donors.

Other National Democratic Committees

Under the umbrella of the DNC are numerous other official Democratic committees. The Democratic members of the U.S. Senate have a party committee, the Democratic Senatorial Campaign Committee or DSCC, at *www.dscc.org*. The Democratic members of the House of Representatives likewise have the Democratic Congressional Campaign Committee, or DCCC, at *www.dccc.org*.

At the national level, Democrats have a number of committees focused on the political interests of communities. The College Democrats at *www.collegedems.com*, and Young Democrats at *www.yda.org*, provide leadership opportunities and activities for younger Democrats. The Women's Leadership Forum at *www.wlf-online.org/wlf/*, and the National Federation of Democratic Women at *www.nfdw.org*, focus on Democratic women.

State Democratic Organizations and Committees

State-level Democratic officials also have Democratic campaign committees. One example is the Democratic Governors' Association, or DGA. Its URL is *www.democraticgovernors.org*.

The DGA is an independent, national committee that helps elected Democratic governors. On the home page, you can click the Governors button for a list of links to the Democratic governors now in office. You can find these governors' State of the State addresses, other accomplishments, and contact information. The home page also has a pull-down menu with links to governors' official Web sites and governors' campaign committee sites. If you can't find your governor's official site here, try your state's site. We covered online research of state officials in Chapter 5, "State Sites on the Web."

Under the Elections button is information on each Democratic race from 1998 to 2002, including filing deadlines, statistics from past campaigns, and which elections include Democratic incumbents. Under the Calendar button are upcoming events related to the DGA, and under the Policy and Press buttons are DGA submissions and public statements.

State party committees are an important part of the Democratic Party. State committees focus on in-state races, fundraising, volunteer recruitment, and activism. A link to state Democratic Party Web pages is at *www.democrats.org/dweb/states.html*. You might want to check out your own state's page or the following state party pages. These pages combine state news, events, volunteer recruitment and activities, and contribution solicitations, and give you a good idea of a state party committee's activities and purpose:

- The California Democratic Party, at *www.ca-dem.org*
- The New York State Democratic Party, at *www.nydems.org*
- The Democratic Party of Wisconsin Online, at *www.wisdems.org*
- The Massachusetts Democratic Party, at *www.massdems.org*

The Democratic Governors' Association, with links to Democratic governors' campaigns.

County Democratic Committees

Although not featured as prominently on the Web, county party committees are an important part of the state and national organizations. Party leaders might start as local party officials, and these groups produce volunteers, recruit candidates, and encourage small-donor support for the party. A list of links to county parties is posted at *www.democrats.org/dweb/counties.html.*

A good example of a county party page is the page for the Montgomery County, Maryland Democratic Party, at *www.mcdcc .org*.

From the Montgomery county Democratic Party home page, you can read the latest committee updates. Along the left, buttons link you to the committee's newsletter, with articles about local elections and events; a calendar of events; information about other Democratic clubs and groups in Montgomery County; a contribution form for online contributions to the committee; and a campaign 2000 link to candidate sites.

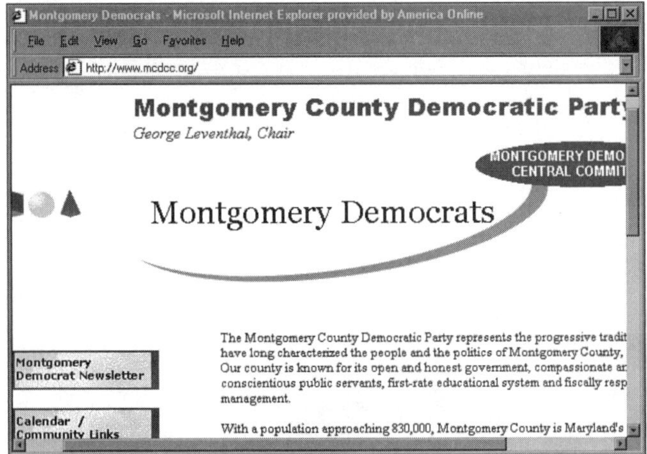

The Montgomery county Democratic Party Web page.

Democratic Candidate Sites

The primary function of any political party, including the Democratic Party, is to elect candidates for office. So, we next look at some Democratic candidate sites.

Gore 2000

The first is the home page for Vice President Al Gore's campaign for president. It is at *algore2000.com*.

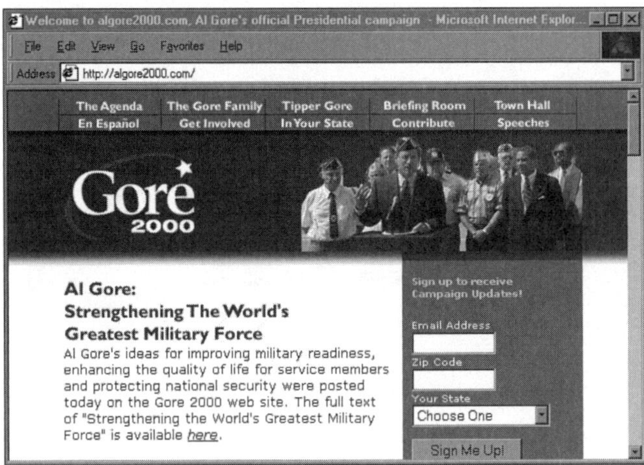

The Gore 2000 campaign site, with campaign news and links.

From the Gore home page, you can scan the campaign news from the last several days. Along the right side of the home page are several notable features. You can sign up for regular email campaign updates. You can also sign up as a volunteer and for voter outreach. The site also has a search engine, which you should use if you are looking for something specific. The site offers streaming video of advertisements, issue statements, and special Internet-only campaign video that you can watch using RealPlayer.

The home page also has two rows of buttons on the top that link to additional information. Under The Agenda are Gore's statements and press releases organized by topic. They cover such topics as the economy, education, health care, the environment, and foreign policy. Under The Gore Family and Tipper Gore buttons, you can learn more about Gore's family. The Briefing Room links you to press releases and other campaign statements sorted by date. Under Town Hall, you can correspond via email with the campaign and ask questions about Gore's positions. The site says that interactive town hall meetings will also be featured on this page. The En Español button provides Gore information in Spanish.

Under Get Involved, you can sign up to volunteer for Gore. The In Your State button links you to a map of the nation, from which you can link to Gore events and news specific to your state. There is a state pull-down menu, as well as a pull-down menu that links you to special Gore groups, such as Environmental Voters For Gore, Gay and Lesbian Americans For Gore, Students For Gore, and Women For Gore.

▼ Try It Yourself

In this exercise, we will review the steps to volunteering for the Gore campaign. Of course, you don't need to complete the steps if you do not support Gore, and you should not view this as a recruitment or solicitation on Gore's behalf.

1. From *algore2000.com*, click the Get Involved link and the Volunteer Form link or go directly to *www.algore2000.com/getinvolved/volform.php*.

2. You will retrieve a form that asks you to provide your name, address, phone number, and email information. A box is

checked to receive email updates from the campaign. You should uncheck the box if you do not want to receive these updates. If you later decide that you want to be removed from Gore email and update lists, you can unsubscribe by using the form at *www.algore2000.com/unsubscribe*.

3. Superimposed over this page you might also get a small box asking you to contribute to the campaign. If you do not want to contribute, click to close the box.
4. The form also asks you to indicate how you want to help. You should check whether you want to work in headquarters, write letters to the editor, organize in your neighborhood, register voters, or one of the other options.
5. You are also asked to provide some information about yourself, such as your party registration, whether you are retired or a union member, and similar details. You do not have to provide this information if you don't want to.
6. If you want to know more about Gore events in your state, check the In Your State button, under which the campaign has listed activities and events.

The Contribute button links you to the Gore 2000 contribution form. You can make a contribution to the Gore primary campaign from personal funds by using your credit card. If you prefer to contribute by check, you can print the form and mail it in with your check.

The final button, Speeches, links you to major speeches by Gore, organized by topic.

Contributions to Gore's Presidential Primary Only

The Gore site solicits contributions for only his primary election. Why not the general election, too? The Gore campaign has chosen not to take private contributions for the general election, in return for public funding. The public funding element of the presidential election is another Watergate-era reform, designed to reduce the influence of private contributors on candidates for the presidency, and to reduce campaign expenditures by placing a ceiling on general election funds. Gore will receive funding for his general election campaign from the government, in addition to having received matching funds in the primary. In contrast, George W. Bush decided to forgo public funding for his race. His is the first presidential campaign to do so since the reforms were enacted.

Hillary Clinton for Senate

Another interesting candidate campaign site is for Hillary Clinton's campaign for Senator of New York. It is at *www.hillary2000.org*. From the home page, you can read campaign news, or choose from one of the links to volunteer, watch campaign videos, contribute, read Hillary's policy proposals, review endorsements, or take the Hillary quiz.

To find your Democratic candidate's Senate campaign Web site, try looking through the links on the Democratic Senatorial Campaign Committee site, at *www.dscc.org/2000revised/campaignlinks.htm*. For links to Democratic candidates for the House of Representatives, look through the state-by-state database on the Democratic Congressional Campaign Committee site, at *www.takebackthehouse.com/campaignhq/dbaseindex.chtml*.

State Candidates

Candidates for state offices also use the Web to attract supporters and get out their campaign's information and materials. Look, for example, at the site for the Democratic candidates for governor and lieutenant governor in Indiana, Frank O'Bannon and Joe Kernan, at *www.obannon-kernan.com*.

The Democratic slate for governor and lieutenant governor in Indiana.

On this page you find many of the now-familiar features common to campaign sites. You can use the page's button to link to contribution and volunteer forms. You also find campaign news stories, candidate position papers, and advertisements to watch online. And you can sign up for regular email updates as the campaign progresses.

You can find your own state Democratic candidates for governor in 2000 on the DGA link page, at *www.democraticgovernors.org/dga/election/election2000/index.html*. Where can you find information about the Democratic candidates for your state legislature? The Democratic caucus of your state legislature or your state's central Democratic committee might have a campaign site with information about and links to those candidates. And, as we saw in Chapter 12, "The Cyber-Swiss Army Knife: Sites That Put It All Together," you can retrieve links to state races of both parties for your state through DNet, at *www.dnet.org*.

Unofficial Democratic Party Organizations

Unofficial Democratic groups can take several forms. They might be policy groups that seek to steer the ideological focus of the Democratic Party to the right or the left. They might have specific issues that they seek to further by recruiting and supporting candidates. I've selected a few for you to review, but there are many others with a wide variety of agendas.

The New Democrat Network

The New Democrat Network embraces centerist economic and social policies. Its Web page is at *www.newdem.org*.

The New Democrat Network raises funds for Democratic candidates that agree with these views. The group also makes contributions to like-minded state and local officials. If you are interested in this group's views, you might also be interested in the lobbying and policy research organizations for "new Democrats," the Democratic Leadership Council and the Progressive Policy Institute. They share a Web page at *www.dlcppi.org*.

The New Democrat Network home page.

EMILY's List

EMILY's List is committed to raising money for and electing pro-choice Democratic women to office. It is at *www.emilyslist.org*.

The EMILY's List home page.

EMILY's list raises money for its own projects, but also recommends pro-choice women Democratic candidates for member donors to support directly. Candidates soon learn that if they attract the support of EMILY's List, the group will then encourage its members to give. This activity is sometimes called *bundling*.

You can review EMILY's List recommendations only after you become a member because under federal rules, EMILY's List can only solicit from its members, not the general public. If you join EMILY's List, you pay a membership fee and also commit to contributions to at least two of the group's recommended candidates.

Bundling

As the term suggests, *bundling* contributions amounts simply to taking many separate contributions and delivering them together. Groups seek to bundle contributions because the group gets credit and status from gathering the funds. Providing it is properly reported, there is nothing illegal about bundling. Why wouldn't a group such as EMILY's List just contribute directly to a candidate? In fact, many such groups do just that. But direct contributions from political committees to federal candidates are limited to $5,000 per year. True, individual donors may contribute up to only $1,000 per federal candidate per election. But EMILY's List can bundle ten or fifteen such individual contributions—in fact, there's no limit on how many individual contributions can be bundled.

Democrats 2000

Democrats 2000 was founded by Jim Hightower and Senator Tom Harkin and was formed to recruit, support, and elect progressive populist Democrats to office. Its home page is at *www.dems2000.org*.

For this election, Democrats 2000 seeks to train and place 2,000 field workers in progressive Democratic campaigns. Interested? You can retrieve the training application from the site at *www.dems2000.org/2kapp.htm.*

Democrats 2000 recruits and supports progressive populist Democrats.

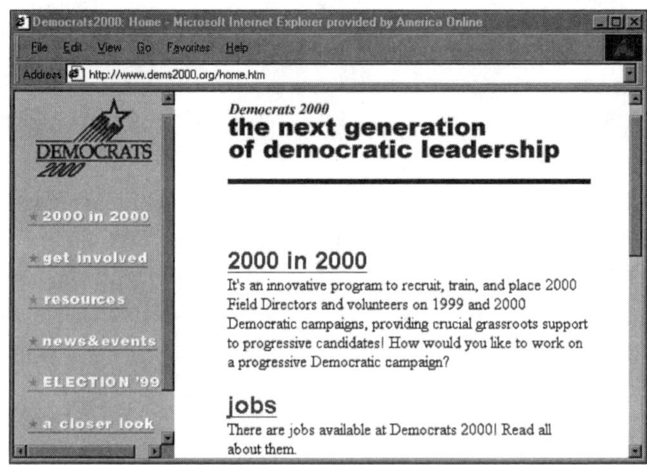

Wrapping It Up

The Internet provides a quick and convenient way for you to learn more about the Democratic Party and its candidates. It is also a great way for the party and its candidates to let potential supporters know about its positions, activities, and recruit volunteers and donors to the cause.

Now you should be able to

- Find national, state, and local Democratic committees online
- Find Democratic candidates online
- Better understand some technical campaign contribution rules, and recognize why campaign committees set limits and conditions on contributors
- Volunteer for a campaign
- Identify and, maybe, get involved with an independent Democratic Party group

CHAPTER 14

Republicans Online

The second major party in American politics is the Republican Party. Its roots are in the 1850s, with antislavery and proWestern expansion interests joined together. Its first candidate for president was John C. Fremont, who ran in 1856. In 1860, Abraham Lincoln won the presidency as the Republican nominee. The Republican mascot, the elephant, was popularized through the political cartoons of Thomas Nast in the 1870s.

First, we will look at what official Republican organizations have to offer on the Web. We will also review some Republican candidate campaign sites. Finally, we will visit some Republican groups that are not official party organizations. These groups usually raise money for Republican candidates and activities to move the party in a particular direction.

What You'll Learn in This Chapter:

- How to find official Republican Committees in the Web, and how to volunteer or contribute through these Web pages
- How to find national, state, and local candidates on the Web, and how to volunteer or contribute
- What special donor research tools are available on the Bush for President site
- Where to find independent Republican groups that seek to move the party to the right or left by supporting specific candidates in agreement with their views

Official Republican Party Organizations

The Republican Party is lead by a national organization called the *Republican National Committee,* or *RNC*. The party also includes congressional campaign committees, state party committees, county party committees, and other official Republican organizations.

The Republican National Committee

The Republican National Committee is the general party committee for the Republican Party. Its home page is at *www.rnc.org*.

From this page, you can access a great deal of information about the Republican Party and its candidates. Under Today's Features you will see a row of buttons. The Vote button takes you to voter registration information like that offered by pages we've already reviewed. Under Get Involved, you can sign up to receive one or many different news and information services offered by the RNC. Under Donate, you can make a contribution to the RNC. This form reflects the legal restrictions and limits we discussed in connection with the Democratic Party in Chapter 13, "Democrats Online." You can buy Republican merchandise under the Store button, and learn more about the national convention under the Convention button.

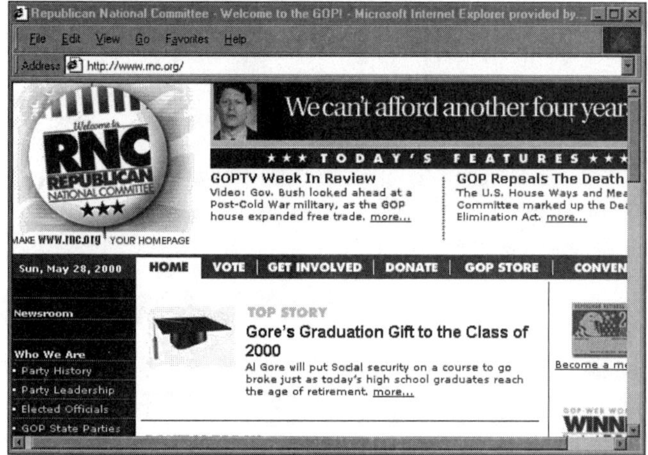

The home page of the Republican National Committee.

Along the right side of the page are buttons that connect you to special features, events, the Bush campaign page, anti-Gore campaign material, and other topical items.

Along the left side of the page are links to information about Republican history and issues. The Elected Officials and GOP State Parties links both take you to an interactive index for finding Republican elected officials, candidates, and party committees. The URL for this index is *www.rnc.org/rncweb/index.htm*. From the index, you can enter your ZIP Code, and the site will retrieve the names and (if available) Web links for your Republican elected officials. A pull-down menu allows you to select your state to retrieve information and Web links to your state Republican Party.

Other National Republican Committees

There are several national Republican Committees. The Republican members of the Senate have the *National Republican Senatorial Committee,* or *NRSC,* at *www.nrsc.org*. The Republican

House Members have the National Republican Congressional Committee at *www.nrcc.org*.

The Republican Party also has several official committees for Republicans in particular communities. Younger Republicans can check out the College Republican at *content.colleges.com/republicans* or the Young Republicans at *www.yrock.com*. The Insider feature on the Young Republican page contains lively and interesting commentary you might want to check out. The Republican National Hispanic Assembly is found at *www.rnha.org*. The National Federation of Republican Women is at *www.nfrw.org*.

State Republican Organizations and Committees

At the state level, information on the Republican Party is available from several national Republican organizations with a state-level focus, as well as Republican Central Committees in the states.

The Republican Governor's Association page is a good source for state-level Republican information and contacts. Its URL is *www.rga.org*.

The Republican Governor's Association home page.

Here, you can link to Republican Governor's own Web sites using the pull-down menu on the left. You can also check out the Republican Governor's headlines and news stories. Using the buttons at the top of the page, you can link to the RGA's Headquarters for information about their mission and activities.

The RGA News button provides links to radio addresses, newsletters, and campaign updates, and the Membership button links you to a membership and contribution form if you want to support the RGA. Under the Rising Stars button are links to biographical profiles of each Republican governor.

Under the State-by-State button, you will find a directory organized by state of links to state political statistics, historic election returns, government offices, state party offices, and state elections regulators. Only information for states with Republican governors are included, but if you live in one of those states, this directory provides a handy list of links to many useful state-level sites. The direct URL for this directory page is *www.rga.org/state_by_state/state_by_state.html.*

As mentioned previously, links to all Republican state parties are found through the RNC's page, at *www.rnc.org/rncweb/index.htm.* Here are the URLs for some Republican state party committee pages you might want to visit:

- The California Republican Party, at *www.cagop.org*
- The New York Republican Party, at *www.nygop.org*
- The Florida Republican Party, at *www.rpof.org*
- The Texas Republican Party, at *www.texasgop.org*

County Republican Committees

The Republican county central committees are an important part of party organization. Many Republican leaders get their start as local party leaders, and county parties recruit volunteers, donors, and new members to the party. You can probably find contact information for your county's party through your state party—and a Web link, if one is available.

You can also try the Republican Party county locator on the Web page of GOPAC, an independent Republican group. That county locator URL is *www.gopac.com/*. Links at the top left of that page will take you to information about state and local Republican contacts and Web links, if available.

A good example of a county party page is for the Cook County, Illinois Republican Central Committee, at *www.cookgop.org*.

The home page for the Cook County, Illinois Republican Central Committee.

This home page provides a good overview of the activities and projects pursued by county party committees. The home page features a list of buttons that follow along the right side of the figure of Illinois. Under Welcome is a message from the chairman of the County Central Committee. Under Our County is a map with the townships in Cook County. You can click on a township to get the name, address, and phone number of the township's committee representative. For the city of Chicago, by clicking on the area of the city, you retrieve another map of the wards of Chicago that link to the names and contact information of the representatives for each ward. Under Our Candidates are the pictures, names, and biographies of local Republican candidates.

Under GOP Events is a calendar with contact information for Committee events, other Republican events, and nonpartisan events that would be of interest to local Republicans. The Join the Party button links you to forms to contribute to the central committee via credit card, volunteer, or contact the party for an internship. The Other GOP Sites link provides a directory of other Illinois Republican sites as well as Illinois government sites.

Republican Candidate Sites

Now we will examine some Web pages for Republican candidates for public office. More and more candidates are using the Web to raise funds, attract volunteers, and get the word out to the press and the public.

George W. Bush for President

The Bush campaign Web page is at www.georgewbush.com

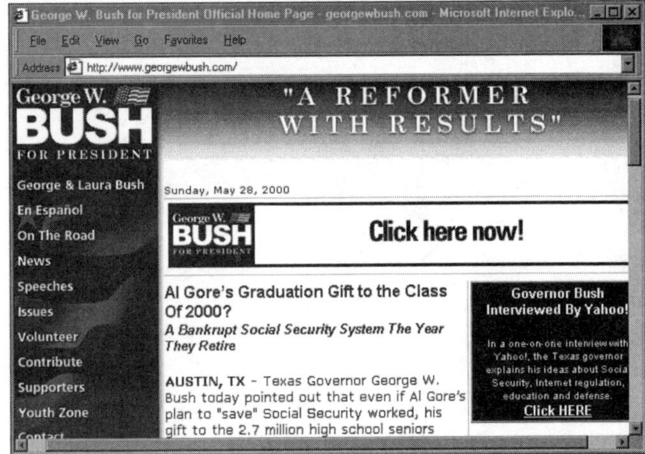

Campaign news and updates are featured on the home page, and buttons down the left side link you to the kinds of features found on campaign sites, such as biographies of Bush and his wife, a Spanish language option, event information, news, video and audio files of Bush speaking, and texts of major speeches and issues statements. Under the Volunteer button, you will find a pull-down menu from which you can select your state. You will then be provided an online volunteer form to fill out and submit.

Under the Contribute button are links for a credit card contribution and contributions by check. If you select the check option, you receive a PDF version of the contribution form to print, complete, and mail in with your contribution check. The credit card option links you to the online contribution form. A box at the bottom of the form is prechecked, and states your consent for your profile to be shared with third parties. If you do not want the campaign to share profile information, uncheck the box.

A distinctive feature of this site is on the left—a link to the campaign's own contributor database. The contributor search form allows you to search for contributors to the Bush campaign. It provides more complete information than FEC records because it has information on contributors who have given under $200, and it is updated more quickly. The federal contribution disclosure laws only require reporting of contributors of $200 or more. You can also link to this search feature from the home page (the link is on the lower right), or you can access it directly at *207.54.174.86/donorsearch/donorsearch.asp*.

Try It Yourself

Now we will walk through the steps for researching Bush's campaign donor database. You will see how the sites with official FEC contributor information work in Chapter 16, "The Money Game Online."

1. From the George W. Bush Home Page, click on the Search the Donor Database on the lower right side of the page, or point your browser to *207.54.174.86/donorsearch/donorsearch.asp*.
2. You will retrieve a search form. You can specify one or several names to search in the Name space, but separate names by commas.
3. Under Using, select either All Words if you want the entries you find to have all the names specified in them, or Any Words if you want to retrieve entries with any one of the names you entered. In other words, if you are searching for John Doe, you entered *John, Doe* and you would specify All Words. If you mistakenly specified Any Words, you would pull up a large list with every John and every Doe.
4. In the next space on the form, you can specify whether the search is for an individual, a PAC, or a political committee. You can also choose a state or a ZIP Code. If you wanted to see who had contributed to Bush from your area, you might consider searching your ZIP Code.
5. You can specify the size contribution you want to retrieve in the next spaces on the form, the date of contribution, and the order with which the list you retrieve is sorted.

6. When you retrieve donor entries, you will see the name, the type of donor (individual, PAC, or committee), the occupation and employer information, and the amount of the contribution. If you click the donor's name for more details, you will also see the city and state of the donor and the date of the contribution. The full address is not provided, both out of respect for the donor's privacy and to discourage the illegal use of that information for commercial purposes or for fundraising.

At the bottom-left side of the page is a pull-down menu, from which you can select your state and get state-level contact information from the campaign.

Unprecedented Internet Campaign by McCain

Bush's challenger in the 2000 Republican Primary was Senator John McCain. McCain won the New Hampshire Republican Primary on February 1, 2000. This prompted great national interest in his campaign, including unprecedented levels of contributions and volunteers into the campaign through the campaign Web site. McCain was the first political candidate to raise $1,000,000 online in only 48 hours, and raised roughly 25% of his total campaign contributions online. More than 60,000 new volunteers signed up in February to help the McCain campaign. The campaign said that nearly half of the campaign's online donors were first-time givers to a presidential campaign, and that sixty percent of the online donors were under 45 years old.

For more information on the McCain 2000 campaign's performance, you can review a special report and links to news articles on Politics Online at *www.politicsonline.com/specialreports/000202*.

Tom Campbell for Senate

Another Republican candidate site you might want to review is the Tom Campbell campaign for Senator from California. That site is at *www.campbell.org*.

Tom Campbell's site has a series of straightforward buttons from which you can get the now familiar mix of candidate and campaign information. The library of material under Issues is extensive and includes video clips in some cases.

A distinctive feature of this site is the Town Hall: from this button you can send Campbell questions, which he will answer and post on the page. His site states that he answers five questions a day, and will continue this practice once elected. His site also has the option to contribute or sign up as a volunteer with the campaign.

Specific Republican Senate campaigns can be found via the NRSC's page, at *www.nrsc.org/contents/gopcampaignhq2000*. This page also offers an overview of each race and links to media and Republican sites in that state. To find the contact information for Republican candidates for Congress, try the NRCC's list, organized by state, at *http://www.nrcc.org/distmap/index.htm*.

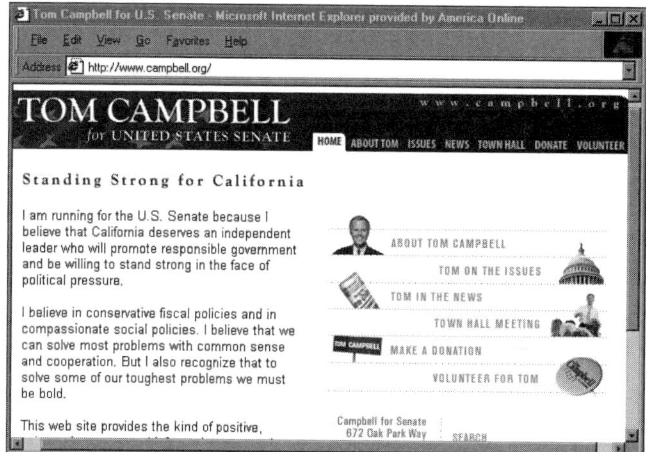

The Campbell Senate campaign Web page.

State Candidates

Republicans running for state office are using the Internet to attract support and inform voters. For an example, because we looked at the Democrat slate for governor and lieutenant governor in Indiana in Chapter 13, let's look at the Web page for the Indiana Republican slate of David McIntosh and Murray Clark, at *www.davidmcintosh.org*.

On the top of the page are buttons you can use to get information on the candidates' biographies, families, news items, and speeches. On the left, links provide ways for you to volunteer and contribute online, review campaign ads, and place buttons and banners on your site that link it to this campaign site. You can also sign up for campaign updates. Registered supporters can get insider briefings and advance review of campaign ads, and are credited for recruiting new supporters.

The home page for the McIntosh-Clark slate for governor and lieutenant governor of Indiana.

To find the state Republican candidates in your area, try the state Republican Party's page, the Republican legislative caucuses, or your state's page on Dnet, at *www.Dnet.org*.

Unofficial Republican Party Organizations

These Republican groups, like their Democratic counterparts, often work within the party to steer it toward their preferred philosophical views. We've selected a few for your review, but there are many others with a wide variety of missions.

GOPAC

GOPAC focuses on training and organizing Republicans to run for state and local office. Its Web page is at *www.gopac.com*.

GOPAC's mission is to support conservative Republican leaders early, and encourage strong candidates to move up to higher offices. From the home page, you can link to Local GOP Contacts which is GOPAC's Republican Directory (You can also register for training materials from The Training Center). Under State News and Info, you can review GOPAC's news items on races in a specific state. And, you can also make contributions to GOPAC online via credit card.

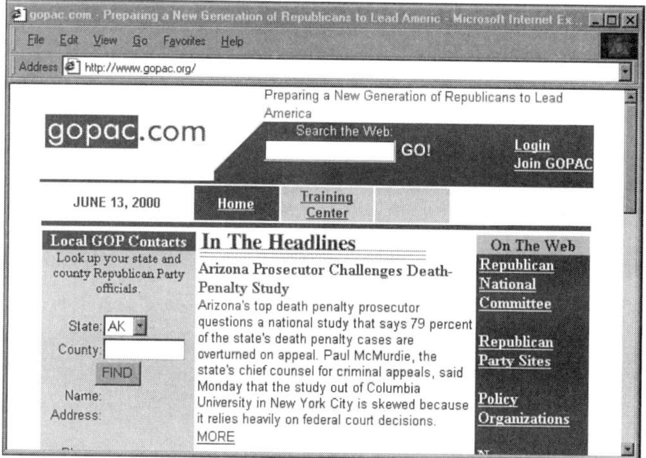

GOPAC provides training and information for Republican state and local candidates.

Republican Mainstream Committee

This independent Republican group supports moderate Republican candidates for office. It is at *www.mainstream.org*.

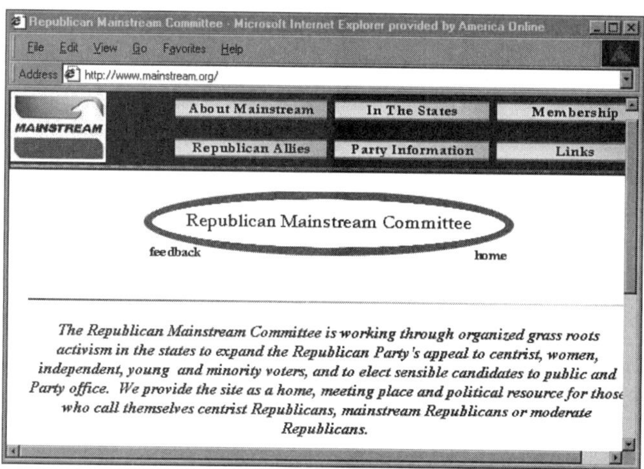

The moderate Republican Mainstream Committee.

The Republican Mainstream Committee has affiliated groups in most states. You can view a state contact list at *www.mainstream.org/states.htm*. You can contribute to the group online via credit card by clicking the Membership button. You can also peruse the Mainstream Committee's directory of likeminded groups under Republican Allies or at the URL *www.mainstream.org/likeminded.htm*.

The Club for Growth

The Club for Growth supports Republican candidates for Congress who are committed to lower taxes and less government. Its Web page is at *www.clubforgrowth.com.*

The Club for Growth home page.

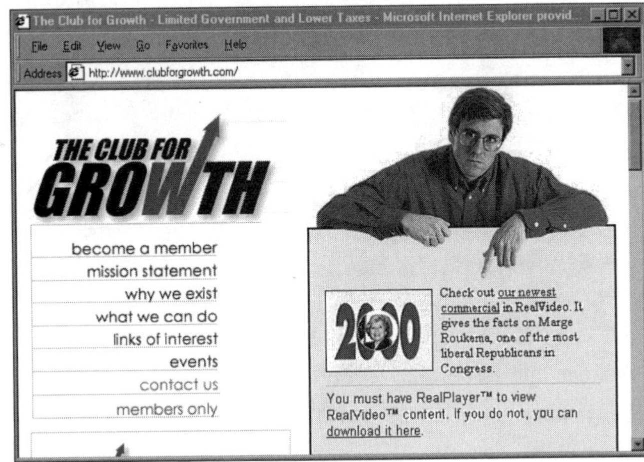

The Club for Growth endorses candidates, and recommends those endorsements to its members. They in turn make their own contributions to those endorsed campaigns. Hence, the Club for Growth, like EMILY's List that we discussed in Chapter 13, "bundles" the contributions of many individuals to specific candidates. To learn which candidates the Club endorses, you first need to become a member. Again, as with EMILY's List, the Club for Growth can only solicit members for contributions—not the general public. A membership form is available by clicking the Become a Member button on the home page. Members receive the Club's endorsement list, email updates, information on upcoming votes, and other information reflecting the Club's interest in reduced government spending and lower taxes.

Wrapping It Up

The Republican Party uses the Internet to inform supporters, recruit new members, encourage volunteers and donors to support the party and its candidates, and rouse the troops with anti-Democrat Party information. Republican candidates also surf the Web for these and similar functions.

Now you should be able to

- Find the Republican Party at the national, state, and local levels on the Web
- Find national, state, and local campaign sites
- Use the Bush donor database to research Bush's contributors
- Check out groups and their activities on the right side and the left side of the party

CHAPTER 15

Other Parties Online

In addition to the Republican and the Democratic Parties, a number of other political parties are active in American politics. Some have elected candidates to offices at the state and local level. Although none of these parties is likely to take the place of a major party in the near future, they are important to our system. They provide a place for new ideas to develop. They are also organizations where voters who reject the two major parties can look for candidates, issue positions, and camaraderie.

First, we visit a few of the other political parties on the Web. Then, we take a look at the presidential candidates online to see what their sites offer.

What You'll Learn in This Chapter:

- How to find other political parties online
- What the Green Party, Libertarian Party, Natural Law Party, Reform Party, and Constitution Party offer via the Internet
- What it takes to get on your ballot as a candidate
- Where to find presidential candidates from these parties online
- Why these candidates don't always make the presidential debates

Official Party Sites

This section reviews the party sites of some third parties with a national presence, namely the Green Party, Libertarian Party, Natural Law Party, Reform Party, and Constitution Party. Each party pursues a distinctive doctrine, and several have successfully elected candidates to office.

Green Party USA

The American branch of the international Green Party can be found at *www.greens.org/gpusa*.

From the Green Party home page, you can learn more about the positions of the party and its candidates. The Green Party supports a variety of environmental positions, as well as some left-leaning views on social justice and diversity. It also advocates direct nonviolent action as a means of achieving social change.

According to the party, it is organized in 46 of 50 states. You can find out who in your area is a Green Party contact by clicking the National Structure link. You can also find Web sites for state Green Parties under the Links button.

The home page for the Green Party USA.

International Green Parties

The Green Party is an international party with its roots (as it were) in the Green Movement in Germany. It now has national parties in many countries. Here are some English-language links that can tell you more about international Green Parties:

- The European Federation of Green Parties at *www.europeangreens .org*.
- The Green Party of England and Wales, at *www.greenparty.org.uk*.
- The Global Greens Conference, to be held in Australia in 2001, has an information site about the gathering at *www.global.greens.org.au*.

Libertarian Party

The Libertarian Party's home on the Web is *www.lp.org*.

Briefly put, the Libertarian Party stands for freedom from government. In particular, libertarians would abolish the drug war, the income tax, military involvement overseas, and most, if not all, regulation on human activity. If you are interested in state candidates or contacts, you should look up the links at *www.lp.org/organization/state.html*. You will find lists of Libertarians elected to office (more than 150 nationwide, mostly to local offices) as well as candidates and links to Libertarian state party Web sites.

The Libertarian Party home page.

Libertarian Political Philosophy

The Libertarian movement is more than a political party. Numerous writers and publications in the Libertarian fold are available online. Here are just a few resources you might want to try:

- Free-Market.Net, at *www.free-market.net*
- The Center for Libertarian Studies, at *www.libertarianstudies.org*
- A home page for Libertarianism, at *www.libertarian.org*
- The Cato Institute, at *www.cato.org*
- The Reason Foundation, at *www.reason.org*

Natural Law Party

The Natural Law Party's home page is at *http://www.natural-law.org*.

The Natural Law Party's mission is to "bring the light of science into politics." It advocates public policies based upon "prevention." The party's philosophy is shaped by the Transcendental Meditation teachings of Maharishi Mahesh Yogi. For more information about the Natural Law Party from the TM perspective, click on *www.alltm.org/nlp.html*. State-by-state contacts and candidate information are at *www.natural-law.org/states/index.html*. An e-zine, the Natural Law Party Monthly, is at *nlpmonthly.0pi.com*.

The Natural Law Party's home page.

Ballot Access

Can just anyone be a candidate on the ballot? No. Each state regulates the conduct of its elections. This includes how candidates make the ballot. For the established major parties, the nomination process is set in place and readily followed. For minor parties and new parties, fielding a candidate often entails massive volunteer petition efforts, fees, and sometimes a visit to the local courthouse. Ballot access rules vary by state. Therefore, administering a national campaign for a third-party candidate involves mastering complex ballot access requirements.

A publication that keeps abreast of ballot access news and views is the *Ballot Access News*. You can find its index, as well as a link to the latest issue, at *www.ballot-access.org/*.

Reform Party

The Reform Party has been subject to dissent within its ranks. As of this writing, the national party could be found at *www.reformparty.org*.

The Reform Party was born out of the 1992 presidential campaign of H. Ross Perot, who spent roughly $60,000,000 of personal money on an independent campaign for president. Perot ran again in 1996 as the Reform Party nominee. The Reform Party seeks to reform campaign finances, lobbying practices, and the ethics of government. It is also in favor of fiscal responsibility, and trade policies that protect domestic producers. A state-by-state directory of Reform Party contacts is at *http://www.reformparty.org/states/index.html*. You'll find links to the state Reform Party committees if available, and the names and email addresses of its officers. For links to Reform Party candidates in the 2000 election, point your browser to *www.reformparty.org/candidates2000*.

The National College Reform Party hosts a lively Web site that is worth a look if you are interested in Reform Party activities. Its URL is *www.college.reformparty.org/ncrp_index.html*.

Jesse Ventura, governor of the state of Minnesota, is the highest-ranking Reform Party candidate elected to office, although he has broken from the national Reform Party in favor of the new

Independence Party. Governor Ventura's campaign Web site is at *www.jesseventura.org*. His official site as the governor of Minnesota is at *www.mainserver.state.mn.us/governor*. An alternative Reform Party group is online at *www.americanreform.org*.

The Reform Party home page.

Presidential Debates

Minor political parties complain that the rules for presidential debates prevent their candidates from participating and their views from being heard. They have a point. Since the 1987 establishment of the Commission on Presidential Debates, Americans have been able to view regular debates between the top contenders in presidential elections. With only rare exceptions, these debates have excluded all but the candidates from the two major parties. The commission's criteria for inclusion in the debate include having support from at least 15% of the voters as determined by polling, and being on the ballot in enough states to win a majority of the electoral college.

Although excluding minor candidates might not seem entirely fair, the system has delivered regular and manageable presidential debates. Presidential debate scheduling was erratic at best before 1987. Debates were held only in 1948, 1956, 1960, 1976, 1980, and 1984. You can learn more about the Commission on Presidential Debates at *www.debates.org*. The candidate selection criteria are described at *http://www.debates.org/pages/candsel.html*. Links to summaries of each historic debate are at *www.debates.org/pages/debhis.html*.

Constitution Party

The Constitution Party, formerly known as the U.S. Taxpayers Party, is at *www.constitutionparty.com*.

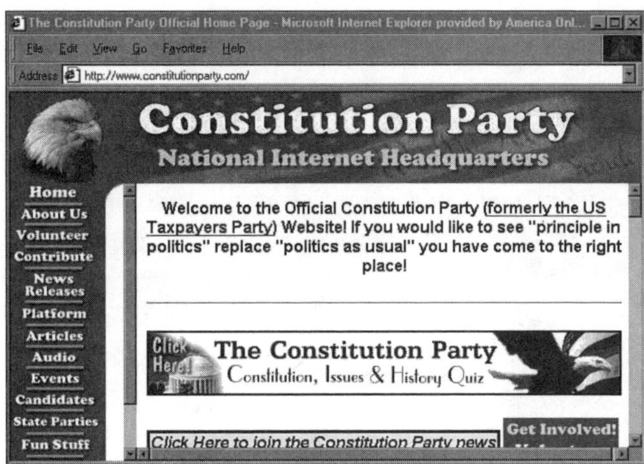

The National Internet Headquarters of the Constitution Party.

Finding Other Political Parties

There are numerous political parties in American politics. We are looking at only a few. If you don't find the party that you are looking for here, try the Political Parties links page on Politics1 .com at *www. lobbyforme.com/p1 /parties.htm*. Or try the Yahoo list of American political parties at *dir.yahoo .com/Government/ U_S__Government/ Politics/Parties/*. Another good directory is offered by 3rd Party Central, at *www.3pc.net/parties. html*. If you can't find a party's site through these directories, you might want to search for the party's name by using your Web browser's Search function.

The party expects to be on the ballot in all 50 states in November, 2000. The Constitution Party seeks to reduce the size and scope of government, in keeping with its view of the proper function of the Constitution. It seeks to abolish the present tax system, abolish the Federal Reserve, return to redeemable currency, declare a moratorium on immigration, and establish anti-abortion policies. Under the State Parties button on the party's home page, you can find links to state party representatives of the Constitution Party.

Presidential Candidate Sites

The following is a review of the candidate sites for a number of third-party presidential campaigns. Although chances are great that none of these contenders will be residing at the White House in 2001, these campaigns nevertheless serve to attract public attention to the issues of the parties.

Ralph Nader for President—Green Party

Consumer activist Ralph Nader (as of this writing) will be the Green Party candidate for president. His campaign site is at *www.votenader.com*.

The Nader site is like many other candidate sites we've seen. It contains issue information, a candidate biography, and donation and volunteer recruitment. You should note the emphasis on ballot access activities—in fact, the campaign specifically recruits volunteers to get Nader on the ballot in certain states. You can use the directory at *www.votenader.com/state/index.html* to see whether Nader is on the ballot in your state.

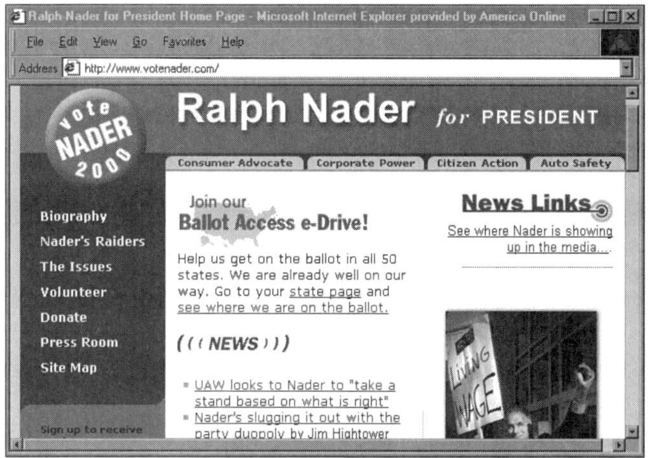

The Nader for President Web site.

Harry Browne for President—Libertarian Party

Harry Browne is the candidate for president from the Libertarian Party. This campaign site is at *www.HarryBrowne2000.org*.

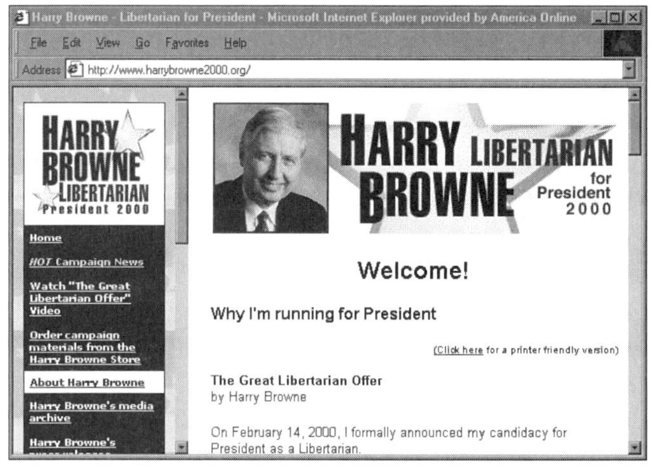

The Browne Web site is www.HarryBrowne2000.org.

Browne is an investment advisor and speaker. He was the Libertarian Party candidate in 1996 and again in 2000. This page provides numerous links to issues information, videos, and other materials about the Libertarian party and Harry Browne. For an insightful look into the life of a minor-party candidate for office, check out the link to Harry Browne's *Campaign Journal*.

John Hagelin for President—Natural Law Party

John Hagelin is a physicist and the candidate for president from the Natural Law Party. His campaign site is at *www.hagelin.org*.

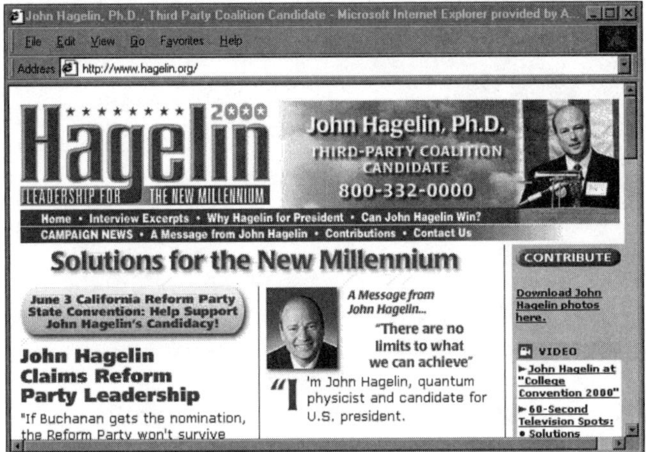

The Hagelin for President site.

Hagelin is also campaigning for the nomination from the Reform Party, as you can see from his site. From this site, you can learn about his views on issues, campaign events, and contribute to his primary campaign.

Hagelin is also Director of the Institute of Science, Technology and Public Policy, in Fairfield, Iowa, which you can reach at the URL *istpp.org*. The Maharishi University Institute of Management, which houses the ISTPP, is at the URL *mum.edu*.

Pat Buchanan for President—Reform Party

Pat Buchanan is a conservative commentator and candidate for the nomination from the Reform Party. His campaign site is at *www.buchananreform.com/index.asp*.

Buchanan's page provides information about his views on issues such as trade, abortion, immigration, corruption, and job protection. As of this writing, the campaign was seeking support for Buchanan's inclusion in the presidential debates, and debate petitions were available for supporters to sign. The site also has links to Buchanan's calendar, and forms for you to use to make a contribution or volunteer online.

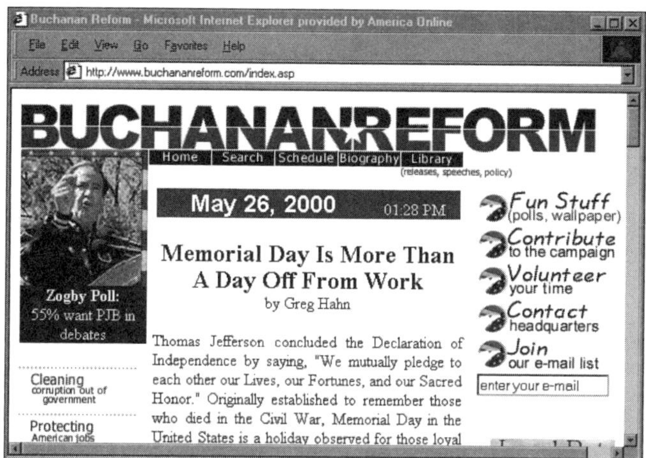

Buchanan recently departed from the Republican Party to campaign as a Reform Party candidate.

Wrapping It Up

Although it is unlikely that a candidate from one of these political parties will be moving into the White House in the near future, these parties do provide different perspectives and a home for people who are seeking something different.

Now you should be able to

- Find several different political parties on the Internet, and link to your local representatives
- Look up candidates for office from these parties
- Find out why some parties are on the ballot when others aren't
- Find out why some candidates make the presidential debates when others don't

CHAPTER 16

The Money Game Online

In our political system, campaigns are financed almost entirely through private donations. The impact that private financing has on political decisions is a controversial issue that persists despite continuing efforts to fix perceived problems with the campaign finance system.

There is no doubt that money is important in campaigns. It pays for staff, research, polling, literature, advertisements, and other necessary campaign expenses. Even candidates in relatively easy races raise money to help support their political parties and to help bolster the campaigns of colleagues in rougher contests.

Political parties continually seek funds to support candidates, recruit members, register voters, and encourage the vote on election day. Corporations and labor unions raise funds for political committees, give directly in states that allow such contributions, and pay for voter education, registration, and internal campaign materials. Independent groups with views on issues raise political money to support the candidates who agree with them on the issues, and sponsor issue advertising to the general public.

One of the enduring reforms in campaign finance has been disclosure. We know much more about who gives to whom than we used to know. In this chapter, we consolidate and expand on the political contribution and disclosure information you've seen in previous chapters. We visit the sites that will help you understand the federal rules and limits. At the end, you should have a pretty good idea how the major rules work, how to find information you want, and how to evaluate what you find.

What You'll Learn in This Chapter:

- How the basic federal campaign contributions rules work
- How to find reports and contributions using the FEC's site
- How to research donors from specific occupations or from your neighborhood
- Where to go for state campaign finance information
- How to find out more about big donors and soft money

The Federal Election Commission

The Federal Election Commission is the agency that regulates political fundraising and reporting at the federal level. States have their own agencies that govern these activities at the state level. The URL for the FEC home page is *www.fec.gov*.

The Federal Election Commission page provides federal campaign finance information.

From the FEC home page, you can link directly to the national voter registration form under the Register to Vote button. There are also links on the home page to the most recent releases and announcements from the FEC.

You can also connect to directories of campaign finance information under the Citizen Guide, Candidate & Committee Guide and Media Guide links. These links are designated in the center of the page with drawings of citizens, a candidate, and a reporter, respectively.

- The Citizen Guide link takes you to campaign finance brochures, explanatory materials, and links to use to research campaign finance reports.
- The Candidate & Committee Guide link takes you to reporting forms, brochures, and guides that you would need to comply with the law, and also links you to research reports.
- The Media Guide focuses on resources to help reporters research contributions and other campaign finance issues.

Links along the left side of the page provide additional information. Under About the FEC link is information about the commission's mission, personnel, and job opportunities. Under FEC

Services, you will find information about information services from the FEC, including the 24-hour fax line for obtaining documents (such as copies of forms, instructions, and advice letters), the fee-based direct access program for researching contributors, and research guides. Under Campaign Finance Reports and Data, you'll find the search function for federal campaign reports, the image viewer for the actual reports (in PDF), and statistical summaries of campaign finance information. Under Reporting Forms and Filing Information are summaries, copies of forms, and instructions for committees and others who are required to file reports.

Campaign Finance Law Resources links to FEC regulations, advice letters (called *advisory opinions*) in which the FEC explains how the laws apply in specific situations, and guides for candidates, corporations (for-profit and non-profit), nonconnected committees (usually ideological PACs), and political parties. Case abstracts, summaries of state campaign finance laws, brochures on specific issues, and agenda information for FEC meetings are also available. Elections and Voting links to information about federal requirements for elections and statistics. Check the News Releases link for the latest from the commission. There is also a Spanish-language alternative for this site at the bottom of the list.

Rules for Making Contributions Online (or Offline)

Press coverage might have given you the impression that contributions in federal elections are not regulated. Vivid media stories often refer to the "swamp" quality of campaign finances, and of cash "flooding" American elections. But do not be misled. Numerous rules regulate your personal political activity, and forbid contributions by corporations, labor unions, and foreign nationals. When the news of the day emphasizes the exceptions to these rules, do not assume the rules have vanished. They haven't.

You should also have a basic understanding of federal finance rules if you are researching a candidate and want to examine the reports filed by that candidate.

Here's a brief summary of some of these rules, taken from the more extensive FEC online guide Supporting Federal Candidates: A Guide For Citizens, which is at the URL *www.fec.gov/pages/citn0001.htm.*

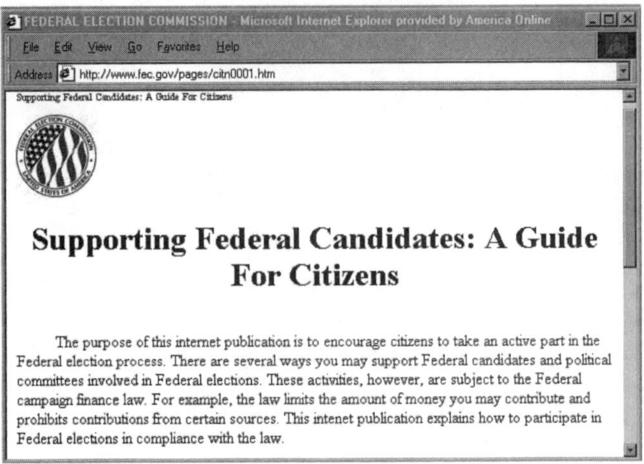

The FEC's Internet publication Supporting Federal Candidates: A Guide For Citizens.

Briefly, an individual may give

- $1,000 per election to a federal candidate committee—Primaries, runoffs and general elections are considered separate elections.
- $5,000 per calendar year to a PAC or state party committee—This limit applies to a PAC (political action committee) or a state (or local) party committee that supports federal candidates. (PACs are neither party committees nor candidate committees. For instance, some PACs are sponsored by a corporation, membership group, or a union. Other PACs, often ideological, do not have a corporate or labor sponsor and are, therefore, called *nonconnected PACs*. Groups such as the NRA and NOW have PACs they use to contribute to federal campaigns.) Party committees and PACs use your contributions to make their own contributions to federal candidates to fund other election-related activities.
- $20,000 per calendar year to a national party committee—This limit applies separately to a party's national committee, House campaign committee, and Senate campaign committee.
- $25,000 per year total—This annual limit places a ceiling on your total contributions to all federal candidates and committees.

- $100 in currency (cash) to any political committee—(Anonymous cash contributions may not exceed $50.) Contributions exceeding $100 must be made by check, money order, or other written instrument.

Contributions include donations of money or anything of value. You can volunteer your time without limit, but if you buy pizzas for a campaign, pay for flyers, or pay long-distance phone tolls for a federal candidate, you have made a contribution that is subject to limits and reporting requirements. You don't need to report it yourself, but you should let the campaign know what you spent so that it can report your donation.

If you are a not a U.S. citizen, you may not contribute unless you hold a green card. You may not make contributions from a corporate account, nor should you be reimbursed for your contribution by another donor or by a corporation.

Employees of members of Congress are prohibited from contributing to their employers. Elected officials are also prohibited from using official resources, such as their office phones, staff, and stationery, for raising political contributions. As I mentioned in Chapter 2, "Going Online with the U.S. Senate and the House of Representatives," congressmen are not permitted to link their campaign Web site to their official site.

If you have a specific question not covered in the guide, check the links to FEC brochures at *www.fec.gov/brochures.html*.

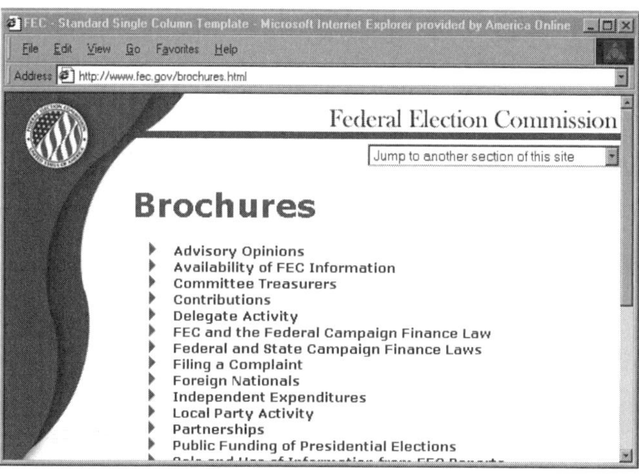

Brochures about several FEC topics are available online.

Chances are good that the FEC has written a brochure that answers your question. The FEC also has a toll-free information line to call with questions, at 1-800-424-9530.

What Is Reported?

If you are researching a candidate, or are active in a campaign and want to know more about how campaign reporting works, this section is a brief summary of the reporting basics.

A filer's FEC report consists of a cover page, a summary page, and schedules that contain information to back up the numbers on the summary page. Filers must itemize contributions of $200 or more per year from a donor. Although $200 might seem like a big contribution, if you are active in a person's campaign it can add up quickly. After you contribute $200, your name, address, occupation, and employer will be listed on the report's Schedule A along with other individual contributors. If the filer is paying you as staff, you will be listed on the Schedule B, where disbursements are itemized. As I mentioned earlier, it is against the law for others to use these reports for commercial purposes or fundraising.

You can retrieve images of filed FEC reports online from the FEC at *herndon1.sdrdc.com/info.html*. Use the Search the Report Image System link to retrieve the search form. Enter a word or words from the name of the candidate or committee whose reports you want to see. There might be more than one filer that matches your request, so if you get a list, click the name of the specific filer you want. You'll retrieve a chart with the reports filed by that candidate or committee. Click the report you want, and page through the scanned image of the report. The reports are in an image form that you can print or can be loaded in PDF form and read using Adobe Acrobat Reader.

If you are looking for a specific contributor or recipient, the FEC site has a query form at *herndon1.sdrdc.com/fecimg/query.html*. From this page, choose an individual, committee, or query search. You want the Individual search option if you are trying to find contributions made to federal candidates or committees by a particular donor. (For fun, enter your own name and see what comes up.)

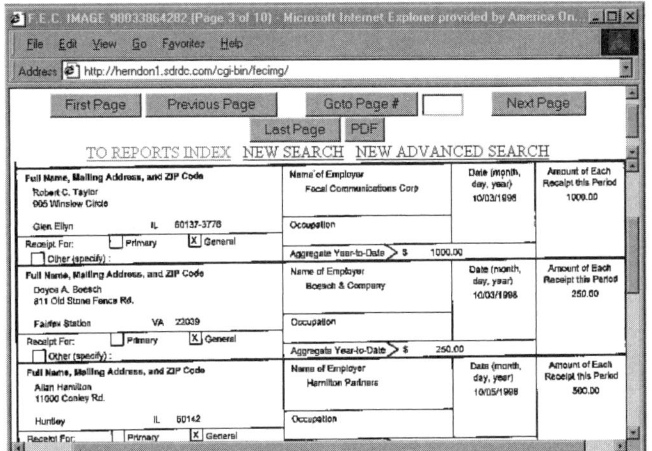

An image of a candidate's Schedule A of contributions.

The search result will link to the image system so that you can also view how the contributions were reported. The result will list federal contributions to federal candidates and committees, as well as nonfederal contribution to political parties (also known as *soft money*).

Researching Contributions: Other Useful Sites

Several private campaign finance sites are available online. They offer the same information as the FEC, as well as additional information of interest to political researchers, such as lobbying reports. These sites are easy to use and can provide you with quick answers.

Public Disclosure with FECInfo

Public Disclosure's FECInfo site provides a wide variety of campaign finance information. It is at *www.publicdisclosure.org*.

The top of the FECInfo page is devoted to statistics and links to the presidential candidates. Below on the left are links to database queries you can run, such as summary information on congressional campaigns and politician PACs (also known as *Leadership PACs*), presidential queries from 2000 back to 1991, and PAC and party committee databases. Of particular interest are database searches of contributors by name, occupation or employer, donors who contribute to out-of-state candidates, donors by ZIP Code, and highest contributing ZIP Codes in the country.

FECInfo has data on FEC filings and invitees to presidential coffees.

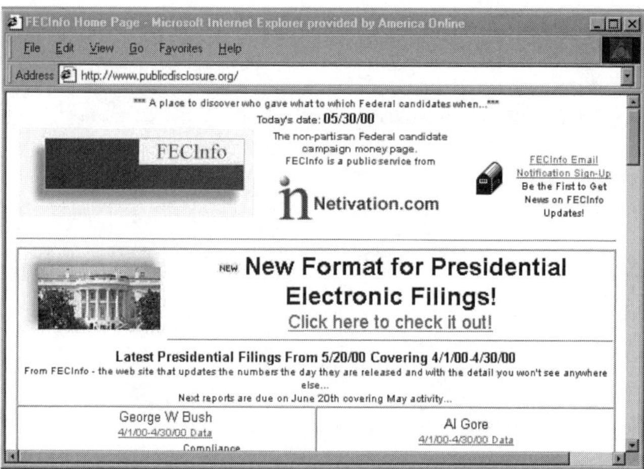

Try It Yourself ▼

To see how the database queries on FECInfo work, we will search for donors from a particular occupation.

1. From the FECInfo home page at *www.publicdisclosure.org*, click the link to Contributor Occupation/Employer Look-up or point your browser to *www.publicdisclosure.org/fecinfo/_employ.htm.*

2. Choose which election cycle—from 1980 to 2000—you want to search. You can search one two-year reporting cycle at a time.

3. Then enter the occupation or employer information you want to search. You might want to see whether employees from a specific company made contributions, or search for a job description such as *actor* or *scientist.* If you pick a common job description, you might retrieve a lengthy list that is hard to work with. I used *actor* and searched the 2000 election cycle, and retrieved 126 contributions. Your entry must be at least five letters long for the search to run.

4. If the list you get is too long—or too short—or after scanning it you want to change the parameters of your search, just click your browser's Back button to return to the search page, and enter a new search.

▲

The middle column on the FECInfo page provides links to donor information for the president's "off the books" committees, such as the Clinton Legal Defense Trust, Clinton Library, and Clinton Birthplace Foundation. It also has specific results on which invitees to Clinton White House coffees and Lincoln Bedroom sleepovers made contributions, and when. The right-side column on FECInfo provides links to the subscription-only version of FECInfo. These subscription databases provide more information on soft money donors, and lobbying registrations and expenses.

Open Secrets with the Center for Responsive Politics

Another private site that provides campaign finance information is opensecrets.org, sponsored by the Center for Responsive Politics. Its home page is at *www.opensecrets.org/home/index.asp*.

The opensecrets.org home page.

This home page starts with a set of links for data on presidential campaign finances. As of this writing, the candidates included were George W. Bush, Al Gore, and Pat Buchanan. It breaks out the total raised, contributions by geography, top contributors (this site combines corporate PAC contributions with contributions by individual employees to get these numbers), and a database.

The site provides a pull-down menu that links you to maps showing contribution levels to the presidential candidates from the top

ZIP Codes in each state. The site has another pull-down menu that provides state-by-state information on congressional races. Finally, it has a search engine from which you can find contributions to presidential candidates from a specific ZIP Code.

Try It Yourself

In this exercise, we will use the opensecrets.org search-by-ZIP-Code option to learn who gave to which presidential campaigns in some areas.

1. From the opensecrets.org home page, *www.opensecrets.org*, locate the Get Local feature and the search box titled Your Zip.
2. For a start, enter the ZIP Code for Manhattan: 10012. You'll retrieve a page with links to several search results. Under Presidential Race by Zip, you can see what candidates the donors in this ZIP Code prefer. As of this writing, Bill Bradley was the favorite.
3. Scan down this page to the Top Contributions link and you can retrieve a list of the top contributors from this ZIP Code. The top several contributions are usually to political party soft money accounts because these contributions are not subject to the strict federal limits.
4. For a contrast, try a new ZIP Code search with the ZIP Code for downtown Louisville, Kentucky: 40202. Again, you can see which presidential candidates Louisville donors prefer. (As of this writing, it was George W. Bush.) You can also see who made the top contributions from this ZIP Code.
5. Now try your home ZIP Code. If you don't retrieve many contributions, it might be because donors sometimes prefer to use their business addresses for privacy reasons. Look under the Presidential Race by Metro Area link, or try another search using the ZIP Code for the nearest downtown area, and see what you get.
6. You can also search for donors to all federal campaigns from a ZIP Code. Click the Donor Lookup button at the bottom of the opensecrets.org home page, and then fill in the donor search form with the ZIP Code only. You might want to limit the date or the amount parameter as well, or you might retrieve a lengthy list.

The opensecrets.org page has several interesting searches you can perform using the buttons at the bottom of the page. Under PACs, you can search PAC contributor and financial information. The Donor Lookup button pulls up a form you can use to find a donor by name, state, ZIP Code, occupation, or recipient. You can search more than one election cycle at a time, back to 1989–90. You can search specifically for soft money contributions under the Soft Money button, as well as link to several reports about soft money.

Under the States button are profiles of the federal contributions in specific states, and links to several state campaign finance databases assembled by the Center for Responsive Politics. Under Politicians, you can pull the campaign finance profile of specific federal elected officials.

The Lobbyists button links to a report on lobbying expenditures with a searchable database of 1997 and 1998 lobbyist filings. This information is taken from reports that lobbyists and their clients file with Congress. It is not campaign contribution information, but rather reports of what these entities spend on lobbying.

State Campaign Finance Disclosure

States have their own contribution and disclosure laws. Some states require more disclosure than the federal law, and some require less. Moreover, some states provide easy access to this data, but others provide little, if any online search capability.

To research state level contributions, try the database assembled by the National Institute on Money in State Politics, at *www.followthemoney.org*. The Institute compiled information from many different sources, and the lag time involved might mean that the information here is not as current as the information you could get directly from the state.

Here are links to several state campaign disclosure sites that you might want to try:

California: *cal-access.ss.ca.gov*

Florida: *election.dos.state.fl.us/campfin/cfindb.shtml*

Hawaii: *www.hawaii.gov/campaign/index.html*

Illinois: *www.elections.state.il.us*

Michigan: *www.sos.state.mi.us/election/elect.html*

New York: *www.elections.state.ny.us/finance/finance.htm*

Ohio: *www2.state.oh.us/sos*

continues

continued

Pennsylvania: *www.dos.state.pa.us/bcel/camp_fin/campaign.html*

Texas: *www.ethics.state.tx.us*

Vermont: *vermont-elections.org/soshome.htm*

If your state isn't listed here, try your state home page and search for *elections* or *campaigns*. Often the Secretary of State is in charge of contribution paperwork, so try that site for your state. A directory of state offices, with some Web links, is at *www.fec.gov/pubrec/cfsdd.htm*.

How can you find your state law on campaign contributions? Some of the sites listed here might also have links to their state laws. The National Institute on Money in State Politics also has a summary of state contribution restrictions, at *www.followthemoney.org/database/statedir.html*. Remember, these laws change constantly. So, you might want to call the state disclosure office directly to get the latest information. Again, that directory is at *www.fec.gov/pubrec/cfsdd.htm*.

Be Your Own Gumshoe with the Investigative Reporters and Editors' Campaign Finance Information Center

Another useful site for campaign money research is the Campaign Finance Information Center (CFIC) at *www.campaignfinance.org*, hosted by Investigative Reporters and Editors, Inc. (IRE).

The IRE Campaign Finance Information Center home page.

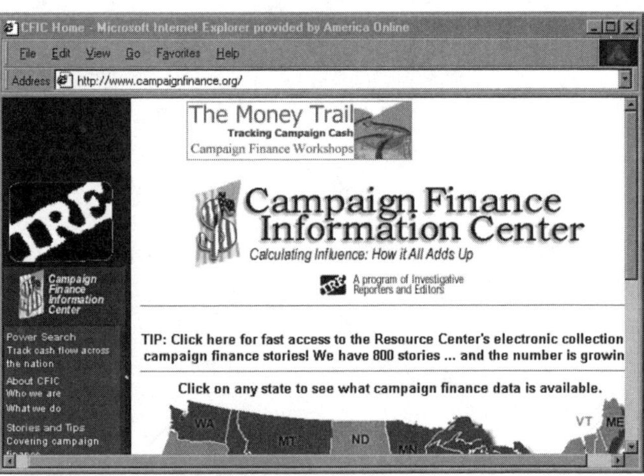

The CFIC page can help you perform national campaign finance searches. It has more than 20 state databases (colored red on the map) that you can search using the Power Search link at the top of the column of buttons on the left side. If the CFIC doesn't have the database, when you click on the state under the Source link, you are told where to obtain contributor information. The results page frequently has a Web link to the source, too.

When you use Power Search for a name, you will find contributions both from and to that person, so choose carefully. If you enter John Doe in the search field, you will retrieve contributions from John Doe to candidates from these state databases, as well as the FEC's database, and contributions to any candidates, vendors, or other reported recipients named John Doe.

Maintaining such a database is an enormous task, and the CFIC page contains a disclaimer about the quality of the data. This is a good stop for casual research or to begin a project, but you should double-check your results from this site with an official site, such as the FEC or official state site.

The Campaign Finance Information Center also has many articles and resources on money in politics. If you are doing serious research in this area, these materials are worth a look. You'll find them under the Stories and Tips link. Links to past issues of the CFIC newsletter are available under the Tracker button.

Sites Focused on Specific Campaign Finance issues

Some campaign finance sites limit their focus to a particular area of the issue. Here are two sites that might be worth checking out. Both sites reflect animosity toward the current system and toward money in politics in general. Whether you agree with that sentiment or not, the data on these sites makes interesting reading.

Common Cause's Soft Money Laundromat

Common Cause, a government reform advocacy group, sponsors the Soft Money Laundromat, at *www.commoncause.org/laundromat*.

Here, you can find soft money contribution information by donor name, city and state, or industry group. The site also offers a link to profiles of the top soft money donors at *www.commoncause.org/laundromat/profiles.html*. The site has data from the current election cycle as well as the previous two cycles.

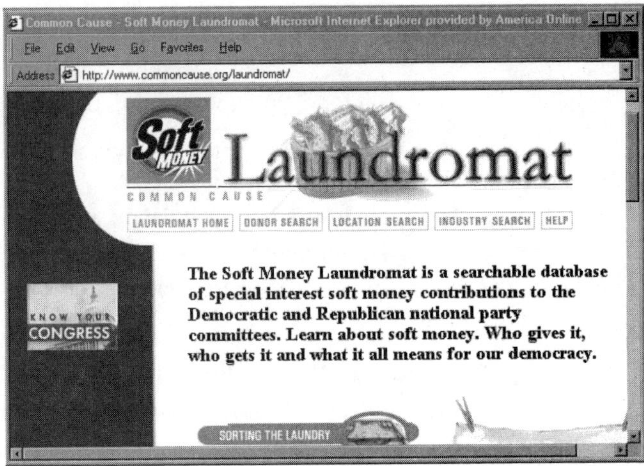

Common Cause's Soft Money Laundromat.

Mother Jones: The Coin-Operated Congress

This site is brought to you by the liberal magazine *Mother Jones*. It is at the URL *www.motherjones.com/coinop_congress*.

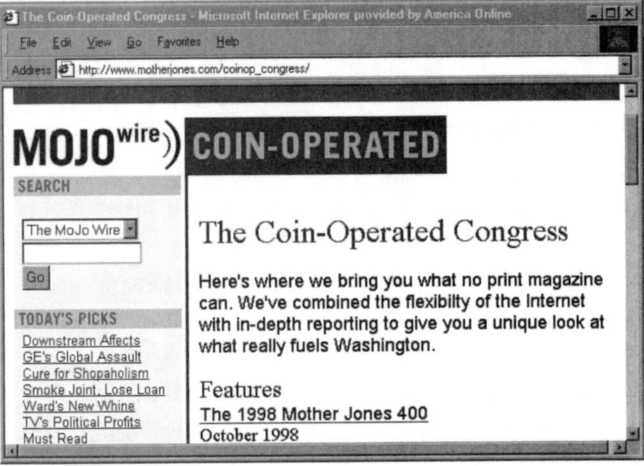

The Coin-Operated Congress site, by Mother Jones.

The Coin-Operated Congress site features the *Mother Jones* 400, which provides contribution information for the top 400 federal contributors. It includes profiles for the top 10 donors. The site also provides reports and *Mother Jones* articles about campaign finance. The most recent version, as of this writing, is the 1998 report.

Wrapping It Up

Campaign finance research can seem like a tangled web. But now, as never before, most of this information is readily accessible to anyone with a computer and a modem. You can read commentary on money in politics, and then see what the evidence is yourself.

Now you should be able to

- Find the rules governing campaign contributions, expenditures, and disclosure
- Retrieve an FEC report
- Research contributions made by a particular person or group
- Find out whether someone in the neighborhood or at the office has donated to a federal campaign
- Know where to look for state campaign finance information
- Get more information about big donors and soft money

PART V

The Future

CHAPTER 17

The Future of the Internet in Politics

What You'll Learn in This Chapter:

- How Internet elections might become a reality
- What trends are occurring in e-politics
- Whether you might someday vote for a Web page for office

Only a few years ago, email was the province of technical computer specialists and academics. Internet use was generally confined to moving files via FTP and discussing specialized topics on a few bulletin boards. Now, people surf the Web using the family television, load news and stock quotes into handheld computers, and work from home or the airplane by using email.

We can expect the integration of everyday life and technology to continue. So, it's only natural that the melding of politics and the Internet will continue. This chapter looks into the future by examining the cutting edge of cyberpolitics.

Your Precinct Moves Online: Voting on the Internet

Voting in elections on the Internet might quickly become a reality for citizens. One company that has administered elections online is *election.com* at *www.election.com*.

The home page for *election.com* provides links for election information and for voters participating in online elections. If you were voting in an online election, you would use the Vote Now button to link to your election, and would follow the instructions you were given by your election officials. No election site would be complete without voter registration, and you can register to vote using the national form by clicking the Register to Vote button. (There's also a link to the voter registration form at the lower left.)

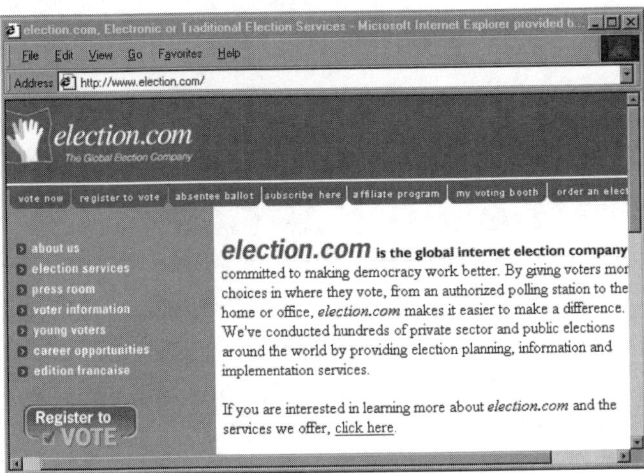

Your future e-precinct workers might be with election.com.

A Browser in Every Rec Room and a Chicken in Every Pot

According to *www.messagingonline.com*, at the end of 1999, there were 569 million email accounts, and by 2002, there will be 1 billion email accounts. According to NetValue, 48.7% of the U.S. population is on the Net at home. Besides sending email, checking stocks, and shopping, people are using their computers for politics. According to a survey by E-thepeople.com, 12% of American households used the Internet in the previous year to communicate with a government official.

If you live overseas or are in the military, you can apply for an absentee ballot online using the Absentee Ballot button. Under the Subscribe Here button is a form you can use to sign up for election updates from *election.com*. If you want *election.com* to administer an election for you, contact the company using the Order an Election button.

election.com has some other links on the left side of the page that you might find interesting. Under Voter Info is a list of the elections in the United States, with registration deadlines. Under Young Voters is information about Youth-e-Vote, a student exercise in which students will be able to vote for president, senator, representative, and governor one week before the general election on November 7, 2000.

Online Elections: The Beginning

election.com administered the first online binding public election for the Arizona Democratic Party. In March of 2000, the party held its presidential primary online. Voters could vote online as well as in their local precinct. A total of 45,000 votes were cast, and 30,000 were cast online.

Just as with a regular election, it is vital in an online election that ballots remain secure and confidential, and that polling is available for voters. Reports from the Arizona primary were generally good.

Elections are a substantial expense for local governments in particular, given the printing, staffing, and tabulation costs. If online election services can promise fair elections, address voter fraud concerns, increase voter participation, and lower costs, we can expect that more jurisdictions will be investigating online voting. Of course, polling places or voting by mail would still be provided for voters who lack access to the Internet.

election.com also administers elections for large private groups. According to its site, it conducted elections for the Sierra Club and the Florida State Bar Association.

The Cybercampaign: Online Fundraising, Organization, and Activities

A good source for information about the Internet and politics is PoliticsOnline. It is at the URL *www.politicsonline.com.*

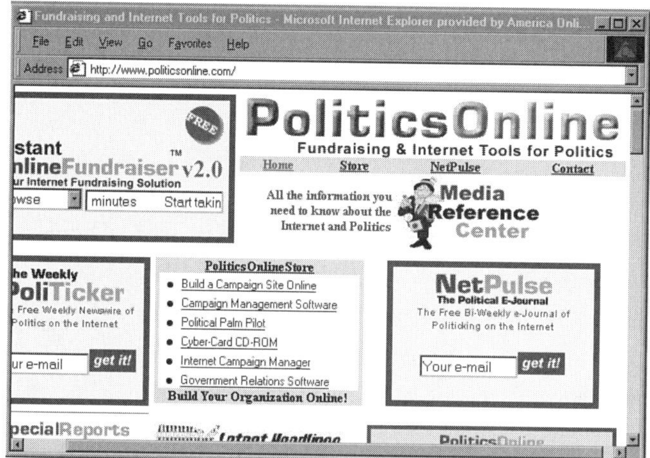

The PoliticsOnline home page.

Check the Latest Headlines link to read the latest stories about trends and uses for the Internet in politics. Also click the link to the Media Reference Center, a page designed for informing media about e-politics, but also a good source for the latest news about research you might be doing.

PoliticsOnline publishes two regular email newsletters covering this topic: the Weekly Politicker and the biweekly NetPulse journal. You can sign up for both of these publications by using the sign-in forms on the PoliticsOnline home page.

Another good source for news about cutting-edge technology and politics is Wired News's Politics page, at *www.wired.com/news/politics.*

Here is a rundown of some of the latest developments in using the Internet in politics.

Fundraising Online

More and more campaigns are opting to use the Internet, Web pages, and email for fundraising. In 1988, less than 2% of all political donations were made through the Internet. In 2000, the figure is expected to be 20%. Raising funds online is easier and more convenient for the donor and cheaper for the candidate than direct mail and telemarketing techniques.

Most security concerns are addressed by using secure servers and other protection measures. If you are comfortable shopping online with a credit card, you should be at ease using the Internet to make a political contribution.

e-Volunteers

More and more campaigns are using the Internet to recruit and keep in touch with volunteers and supporters. Web sites and email lists can get out the word on a candidate's views or schedule, without disrupting supporters with dinnertime phone calls, and without hefty postage or advertising bills.

More volunteers are being asked to work for the campaign online, rather than stuff envelopes at headquarters. Online volunteers distribute campaign news and information to their email contacts and write letters to the editor of the local paper online, for example.

Candidates are making great efforts to get email addresses for supporters, and communicate with them online. Candidates have also used live online chats, although at present the interface can be frustratingly slow and unpredictable. What happens when the email traffic gets so thick that "delete" is the only response that a candidate gets? What happens, too, to the person-to-person contact between candidate and voters that takes place at headquarters and on precinct walks? What about less-privileged voters who don't have access to the Internet? Chances are that person-to-person campaign techniques will still be important to campaigns, especially at the state and local levels. The Internet provides a new tool for voter communications, but will never be a complete substitute for getting out and meeting the public.

The Growth of e-Politics

To appreciate how fast politics on the Internet is changing, take a look at these Internet political milestones from a list compiled by PoliticsOnline .com. Web features that seem commonplace today were novel just a few short years ago.

- First email campaign: Jerry Brown (CA, 1992)
- First U.S. Senator with Web site: Ted Kennedy (MA, 1993)
- First candidate Web site: Dianne Feinstein (CA, 1994 Senate campaign)
- First candidate to buy an online banner ad: Ted Mondale (MN, 1998 Democratic gubernatorial primary)
- First candidate to list contributor information online: Ed Garvey (WI, 1998 gubernatorial campaign)
- First candidate to sell merchandise online: Barbara Boxer (CA, 1998 Senate campaign)
- First candidate who would not have won without the Internet: Jesse Ventura (MN, 1998 gubernatorial campaign)
- First negative banner ad: Peter Vallone (NY, 1998 gubernatorial campaign)
- First candidate to raise $1,000,000 online in a campaign: Bill Bradley (NJ, 2000 presidential campaign)
- First governor to deliver a state budget online: Jeb Bush (FL, 1/2000)
- First candidate to collect $500,000 online in one day and $2,000,000 in one week: John McCain (AZ, 2/2/2000–2/7/00 presidential campaign)

The complete list of firsts is at *www.politicsonline.com/specialreports/firsts/politicalfirsts.shtml*.

"Independent" Candidate Sites

Another campaign technique used on the Internet is "independent" candidate sites. A campaign sets up separate Web sites either to promote specific issues of interest to the candidate or to criticize the candidate's opponent. These are explicitly campaign sites—with a clear message in favor of one candidate over another.

Because these sites have separate domain names, they might have more credibility than if the same information were posted on the candidate's site. And, if you are looking for information on an issue through a Web search engine or directory, these sites will come up in a search that might not find the campaign's general sites.

An example of an independent candidate site is titled BushInsecurity.com, at *www.bushinsecurity.com.*

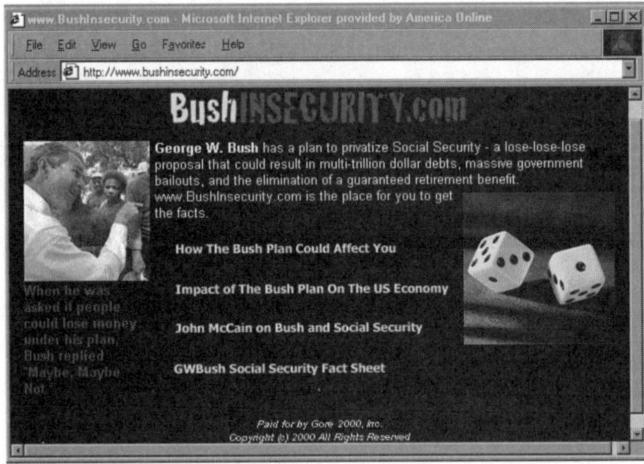

BushInsecurity.com is a Gore campaign site with a separate domain name.

BushInsecurity.com is a Gore campaign site that criticizes George W. Bush's Social Security reform plans. Check the fine print at the bottom of the page. The Gore campaign is required to disclose that it paid for the site. That's how you know it is a Gore site and not an independent site.

Another example of an independent candidate site is HillaryNo.com at *www.hillaryno.com.*

The HillaryNo.com site is sponsored by Friends of Giuliani.

This site is hosted by the campaign of her onetime opponent for a Senate seat from New York, N.Y., Mayor Rudy Giuliani. The site criticizes Hillary Clinton's lack of experience in government. The campaign ad disclaimer appears at the bottom of the page.

Attack and Response in e-Politics

A big technological change in politics is the way the Internet has changed how political stories develop. Candidates can blast their opponents via email. With another quick click, the attack is in the opponent's Inbox, and before much time has passed, the response or counterattack is on the way to reporters. Claims can be verified, research reviewed, and errors exposed faster than ever before.

News reporters and commentators can quickly obtain background on candidates and groups from a wide variety of sources with the click of a mouse. With another click, the candidates' contributors can be reviewed, and comparisons made between their support and campaign promises.

The advantage is obvious. Voters get more complete information more rapidly than before. False and misleading information is countered quickly and effectively. The downside is that the ease with which information is retrieved and shared also means more material flying over the Internet. Some of the information is accurate, and some of it isn't. Few of us have the ability to sort through it all, and reporters, campaigns, groups, and ordinary citizens might face factoid overload.

Can a Web Page Run for Office?

We've seen candidates begin to run Web campaigns. What's the next step? How about a Web site as a candidate for office?

Leave it to the British to lead the trend with London Virtual Mayor, a Web site that is running (only half-facetiously) as a candidate for Mayor of London. It is at *http://www.virtualmayor.com/index2.html*.

The sponsors of Virtual Mayor seek to use technology to make government more responsive to citizens. The London Virtual Mayor site provides bulletin boards and petitions as a way for Londoners to express their views. The Virtual Mayor would govern based on citizen input, and provide governmental services and information through its site.

Despite its campaign, which attracted attention in England and in the U.S., after the ballots were counted, the Virtual Mayor was not elected as Mayor of London in May, 2000. Nevertheless, the site remains active, and is a creative political example for others to follow. It also provides useful links to London city government information.

Virtual Mayor campaigned in London.

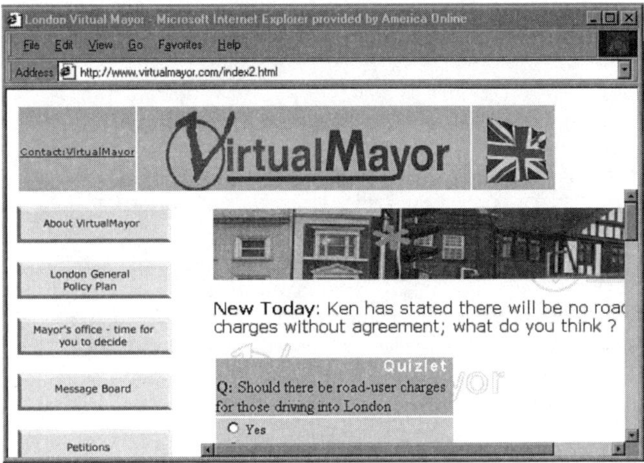

Wrapping It Up

If the last few years are indicative of the future, the Internet will continue to grow as a tool for campaigns and voters. Now you should be able to

- Understand the new role of the Internet in politics
- Appreciate the limitations of e-politics
- Review the latest trends on campaigning on the Internet

CHAPTER 18

Campaigns in the Future: Campaign Finance Reform

In this final chapter, we use the tools we've acquired in this book to take a look at the issue of federal campaign finance reform. As discussed briefly in Chapter 16, "The Money Game Online," our system of privately funded political campaigns is criticized for the potential for donors to "buy" influence with politicians, and for the opportunity politicians might have to use legislation to "shake down" donors for contributions. Our present system of regulation—which includes contribution limits, prohibitions at the federal level on corporate and labor contributions, and disclosure—has critics because it restricts political activity.

This chapter takes a whirlwind tour through some of the sites we've used before. We'll pass by those sites that don't relate to federal laws, such as those discussed in the chapter on state and local government, and international sites. After you've seen how these sites can be used to find out more about campaign finance reform, you might have some ideas of your own on how to gather information about other topics.

What You'll Learn in This Chapter:

- How to research a topic using the skills acquired in this book—in this case, the topic is campaign finance reform
- Learn about current campaign finance laws and review reform proposals
- Find court cases on campaign finance reform
- Learn what independent groups and politicians say about campaign finance reform

Campaign Finance Law and Reform Information

To understand the reform debate, you should first have an idea of the scope of our present laws. First, you'll review the relevant parts of the Constitution, and then take a look at the portion of the federal code that regulates campaigns. Finally, you'll visit the federal election regulations that are drafted, interpreted, and enforced by the Federal Election Commission.

The Constitution

The first stop in our tour is the Constitution. Campaign finance reform restrictions must be compatible with the protections of freedom of speech and association in the First Amendment.

A transcription of the Bill of Rights as originally adopted is available from the National Archives at *www.nara.gov/exhall/charters/billrights/billrights.html.*

The First Amendment to the U.S. Constitution is the first of ten amendments that make up the Bill of Rights.

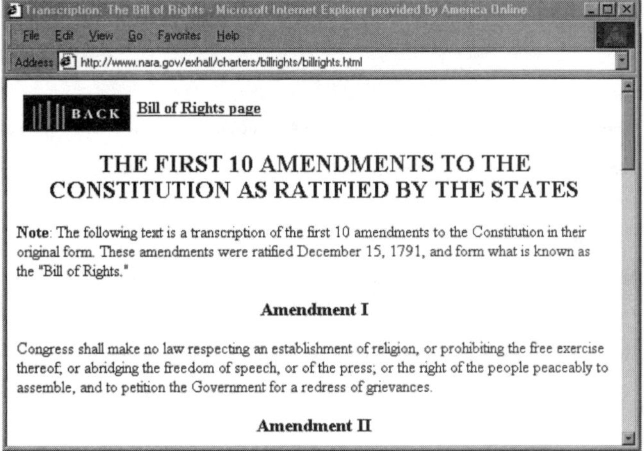

When you look at cases that interpret the Constitution, the actual language is often enhanced by decades of court decisions. For instance, the First Amendment does not use the word *association,* but numerous court cases have found that the First Amendment protects the right to associate with others to express opinions and discuss politics.

You can also learn more about what the authors of the constitution thought about the First Amendment by using the research links on the National Archives page, as we discussed in Chapter 1, “Where It All Started: The Declaration of Independence and the Constitution.” The home page for the National Archives and Records Administration is *www.nara.gov*.

The Congress

Congress enacted the present campaign finance laws, and would have to draft and enact any reform of those laws.

The bulk of current federal campaign finance laws are found in the U.S. Code, Title 2, Chapter 14. Most of the Federal Election Campaign Act, or FECA, is codified in that reference. You can review the contents of Title 2 on the House Web site, at *http://uscode.house.gov/title_02.htm*.

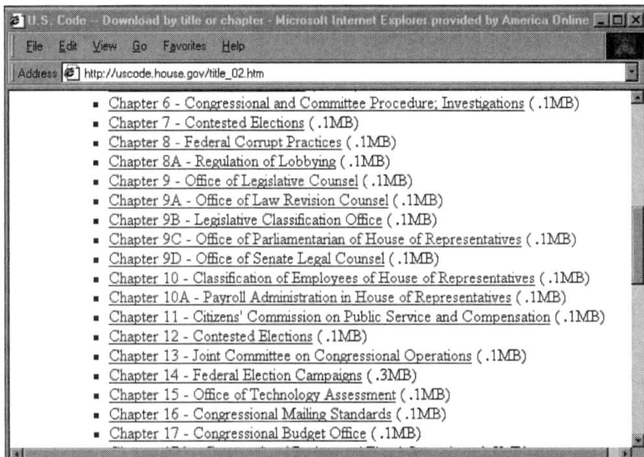

FECA is in Title 2, Chapter 14 of the U.S. Code.

From here, you can download Chapter 14 and read as much—or as little—of the present law as you choose.

Reforms of these laws have been introduced in Congress in a number of bills. To review this legislation, we will return to THOMAS, the Library of Congress's legislative information site, at *thomas.loc.gov*.

▼ Try It Yourself

This exercise will retrieve campaign finance reform legislation from the Senate and the House.

1. Go to THOMAS, at *thomas.loc.gov*. Click the Bills in the News link at the top-left side of the page. Either scroll through the list of topics or click the letter C and find the topic Campaign Financing.

2. You will find several House and Senate bills about campaign finance reform under the Campaign Financing heading. Click the bill numbers to retrieve the summary and text of each bill, as we did in Chapter 2, "Going Online with the U.S. Senate and the House of Representatives."

3. After you review these bills, you might want to see whether anything else has been introduced. To find other relevant bills, go back to the THOMAS home page, and enter the phrase **`campaign finance`** in the search By Word/Phrase box at the top of the home page.

4. You will retrieve a longer list of legislation. The list begins with bills that contain the phrase *campaign finance*. Below that is legislation that contains both words, but not as a phrase.

The Executive Branch

The executive branch contains two important decision-makers in the campaign finance reform arena. The first, the president, can use his stature to encourage and cajole Congress into enacting particular reforms. The president also can veto reform legislation with which he disagrees. The second decision-maker is the Federal Election Commission, the agency responsible for enforcing the laws.

To find the president's views and documents on campaign finance reform, go to the White House Web site at *www.whitehouse.gov*. From there, click the link to The Virtual Library. You can search the archive of all documents by selecting the link Archive of All White House Documents, or you can selectively search press briefings, radio addresses, or executive orders. Here, we'll search the archive of all documents by clicking the Archive of All White House Documents link.

You retrieve a page with a search form. You can put the phrase *campaign finance reform* in the Words box, and leave the rest of the parameters as they are. If you wanted to narrow your search to a specific week or month, you could enter those date parameters in the fields under the Words box.

The figure shows the list of documents retrieved with this search. If you want to review a document in the list, click its title, which downloads the document to your computer. Then, open the document in a word-processing program such as Microsoft Word and read it.

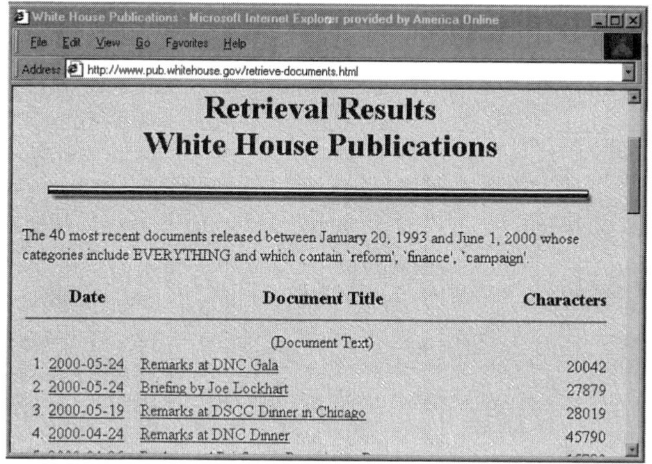

The White House site's documents on campaign finance reform.

The Federal Election Commission is the executive branch agency authorized to enforce campaign finance laws. It has adopted numerous regulations that interpret the law in this area. Those regulations are located in Title 11 of the *Code of Federal Regulations*. The FEC has a link to those regulations under the Campaign Finance Law Resources link on the home page at *www.fec.gov*. On the Campaign Finance Law Resources page, select the Annual Compilation January 1, 2000 link. Or, alternatively, you can go directly to the URL at *www.access.gpo.gov/nara/cfr/waisidx_99/11cfrv1_99.html*.

11 CFR Ch. I (1-1-00 Edition) - Microsoft Internet Explorer provided by America Online
File Edit View Go Favorites Help
Address http://www.access.gpo.gov/nara/cfr/waisidx_00/11cfrv1_00.html

Title 11--Federal Elections

CHAPTER I--FEDERAL ELECTION COMMISSION

Part	
1	Privacy Act
2	Sunshine regulations; meetings
4	Public records and the Freedom of Information Act
5	Access to Public Disclosure Division documents
6	Enforcement of nondiscrimination on the basis of handicap in programs or activities conducted by the Federal Election Commission
7	Standards of conduct
8	National Voter Registration Act (42 U.S.C. 1973gg-1 et seq.)
100	Scope and definitions (2 U.S.C. 431)
101	Candidate status and designations (2 U.S.C. 432(e))

The contents of Title 11 of the Code of Federal Regulations.

We looked at the FEC page's contribution research capabilities in Chapter 16. The FEC also has numerous documents that relate to campaign law and reform. For instance, you might want to see what the FEC has to say in its legislative recommendations to Congress. That document is at *www.fec.gov/legrec2000.html.*

The Courts

The Supreme Court and federal courts have considered many cases raising constitutional questions about campaign finance laws. One of the first such cases to consider FECA's constitutionality was *Buckley v. Valeo.*

You can retrieve the *Buckley* decision from a number of sources. From the Cornell Legal Information Institute site (*supct.law.cornell.edu/supct*) discussed in Chapter 3, "The Wired White House and Bitmap Bureaucracy," click the link to Historic Decisions on the right side of the page. Then select the By Topic link, and click the Elections topic. *Buckley v. Valeo* is one of several cases listed within that topic.

The *Buckley* decision is quite long. If you want an abstract of the case, try the FEC's Selected Court Case Abstracts, at *www.fec.gov/info/cca98.htm.* You can search for *Buckley* by name or scroll through the list of cases. After you select it, the abstract of *Buckley* is retrieved in a frame for you to review.

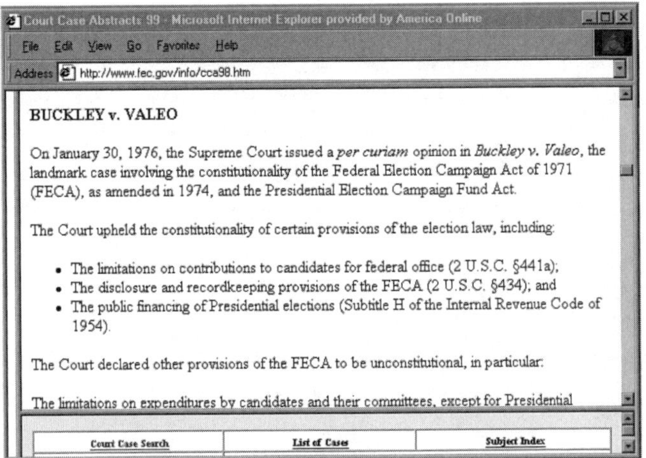

The Buckley v. Valeo case abstract at www.fec.gov /info/cca98.htm.

The Supreme Court also hears constitutional challenges to state campaign finance laws. Its interpretation of these laws is relevant to federal campaign finance reform because these cases indicate what kinds of reforms are unconstitutional. The body of cases in this area is too massive to cover using the court sites, so you can cheat a little by reading about these cases in the FEC's Selected Court Case Abstracts site.

Another good place to find information about campaign finance reform cases and other recent legal developments is the Brookings Institute's Campaign Finance Reform page, at *www.brookings.org/gs/cf/cf_hp.htm.*

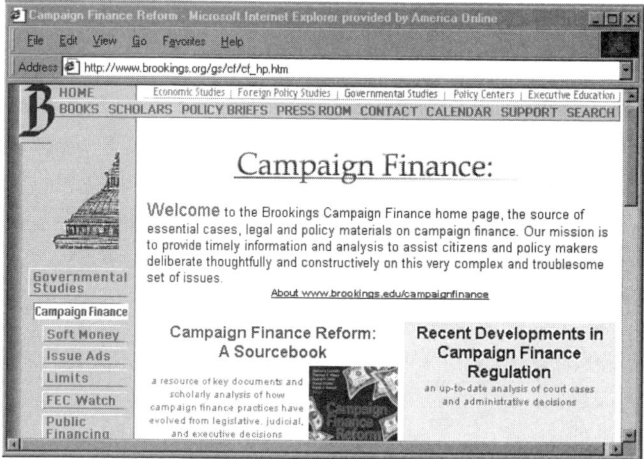

The Brookings Institute's Campaign Finance Reform page.

This page has summaries of campaign finance cases at the Key Court Cases link toward the bottom of the page or at the URL *www.brookings.org/gs/cf/courts.htm.* From the Brookings Campaign Finance page, you can also link to articles, texts of decisions, summaries of the law, and recent developments in campaign finance.

Organizations, Groups, and Campaign Finance Reform

Campaign finance reform is a hot topic, and many groups have views about how reform should be pursued. To give you a sense of the debate, here are descriptions and URLs to sites from some of these groups.

As you review these materials, you might want to keep some questions in your mind: Should campaigns be funded entirely with public money—that is, tax dollars? If not, how should private funding be limited under the Constitution? Is disclosure alone adequate, or are other restrictions necessary? Does it make sense to ban corporate and union contributions in federal elections, yet permit their soft money contributions to political parties? Should the individual contribution limit be $1,000 per election? Should it be higher? Should it be lower?

Reform Groups

A number of groups tout campaign finance reform as a policy goal, and seek to achieve it through public education, activities, lobbying, and litigation. Although each reform group seeks reduced influence of private money on government, each group advocates a different means.

Common Cause, at *www.commoncause.org*, is a membership-funded lobbying organization that was founded in 1970. Its main goal is to reform government. Common Cause has advocated reforms in government operations, sunshine laws, reforms of gift restrictions, and campaign finance reform. It has long been a critic of soft money.

Public Campaign, at *www.publiccampaign.org*, provides news and research about money in politics. It advocates "clean money" reforms. In brief, "clean money" provides public funding to candidates in return for forgoing private contributions and agreeing to spending limits.

The Center for Public Integrity, at *www.publicintegrity.org*, investigates and analyzes public officials and their conduct. The Center publishes books and studies on the role that money plays in politics.

The State Public Interest Research Groups' Democracy campaign, at *www.pirg.org/demos*, provides news and information on state campaign finance as well as reports on money in politics at the federal level.

Groups Critical of Conventional Reform

Other groups are critical of reform proposals that seek to reduce money in politics. These groups often argue that such reforms are futile, would make the system worse, or that the reforms are unconstitutional.

The Claremont Institute's Campaign Finance project, at *www.claremont.org/1_campfin.cfm*, offers articles, commentaries, documents, and editorials critical of the campaign finance reform agenda. It also has related materials about "paycheck protection," which addresses the use of compulsory union dues in elections.

The Cato Institute, *www.cato.org*, is dedicated to reducing the size and scope of government. Its Center for Constitutional Studies has produced papers and commentaries criticizing campaign finance reform measures.

Partisan Politics and Campaign Finance Reform

Everyone is in favor of good government, but the parties do not see eye-to-eye on how to achieve that goal. In general, the Democratic Party and its candidates seek to protect the role of labor organizations in politics because those groups are traditional Democrat supporters. Republicans generally seek to protect corporate activities because corporations tend toward supporting Republicans (although not to the same degree as labor supports Democrats). Democrats rail against soft money because (at least for now) Republicans have a relative advantage there. Republicans rail against using union funds in politics because Democrats benefit from that activity. Of course, there are exceptions to these generalities, but as you read about reform proposals, remember to consider whose ox is being gored.

Political Parties and Candidates on Campaign Finance Reform

Campaign finance reform is an election issue, and many parties and candidates have something to say about it. Be sure to read between the lines. Unlike other policy issues, campaign finance reform has a direct effect on how campaigns operate, and whether candidates can vigorously challenge incumbents.

The DNC and RNC

The Democratic National Committee (DNC), at *www.democrats.org*, has audio and text documents about campaign finance reform—many of which are critical of Republicans. You can retrieve the DNC's documents about campaign finance reform by entering the phrase *campaign finance reform* in the Search box at the top of the home page. You'll retrieve a list of links to documents on the site.

The Republican National Committee (RNC), at *www.rnc.org*, also has materials related to campaign finance reform under its Newsroom link. The site does not offer a search function, but if you look through the releases and articles posted in the Newsroom, you will find materials about the campaign finance issue, mostly criticizing Gore's fundraising activities in 1996.

Al Gore for President

At *www.AlGore2000.com*, the campaign Web site, you will find speeches and campaign material touting Gore'e campaign reform credentials.

Using the search box at the lower right, enter the phrase `campaign finance reform`. You'll retrieve a number of statements that Gore has made, as well as other campaign literature.

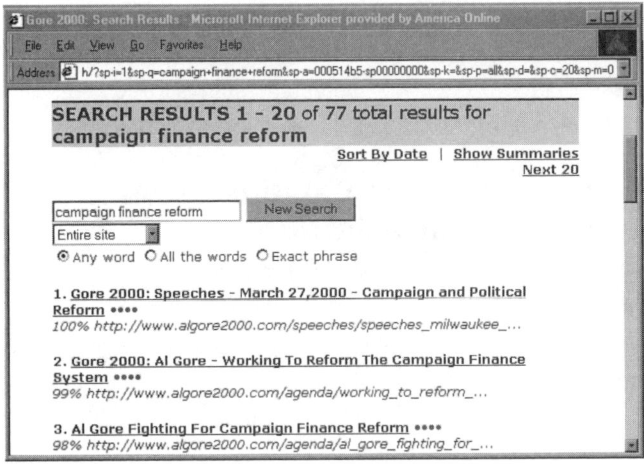

Documents from a search of the Gore Web site for campaign finance reform.

George W. Bush for President

At *www.GeorgeWBush.com*, his campaign's Web site, you can also find campaign materials and speeches on campaign finance reform.

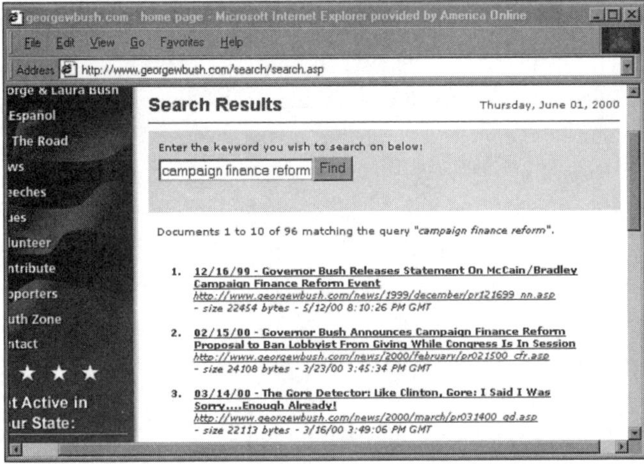

Documents from a search of the George W. Bush Web site for campaign finance reform.

You can search the site by using the Search feature, found at the bottom of the home page. Simply enter the phrase **`campaign finance reform`** to retrieve a list of campaign documents about the issue.

Nader, Buchanan, and Browne Campaign Sites

Ralph Nader, the candidate from the Green Party, has made governmental reform a focus of his campaign. On Nader's campaign site, at *www.votenader.com*, you can find his statements and relevant material under the Issues & Agenda link, and more information under the Citizen Action link. The site does not offer a search engine.

Pat Buchanan, the Reform Party candidate, also emphasizes reform of politics in his campaign. At *www.buchananreform.com/index.asp*, check out the materials under the Cleaning Corruption Out of Government link.

Harry Browne, the Libertarian Party candidate, advocates vastly less government regulation in all areas. Reading through his campaign site, at *www.HarryBrowne2000.com*, you can conclude that Browne's reform measures would scrap the current regulations. See specifically his commentary on the Bill of Rights under the Discover Harry Browne's Stand on the Issues link.

Wrapping It Up

You have now revisited many of the information sources I discussed earlier in the book, to gather a wealth of information on one topic: campaign finance reform. Now, when researching campaign finance reform or another topic of your choice, you should be able to

- Find the federal law—Constitutional and code—about that area
- Retrieve legislation about that topic
- Learn what the president has said about the issue
- Find relevant regulations on that issue
- Review what nongovernmental groups and activists think of the issue
- Find out what the parties and candidates advocate about that topic

APPENDIX A

Web Site Directory

The following is a directory of the Web sites discussed in each chapter. The sites are listed in order of their appearance in the indicated chapter. At the end of each list are additional sites you might want to take a look at.

You should not treat this as a comprehensive list of all relevant directories. Instead, view it as a sample of the kind of sites you'll find in each area, and as a starting point for your own exploration. Nor should you assume that this is a rating system including only the best sites. This book has tried to provide a good cross section for your review, and makes no claim that the sites included are superior to other sites.

Chapter 1, "Where It All Started: The Declaration of Independence and the Constitution"

The National Archives (*www.nara.gov*) contains numerous historic documents of interest. Some include

- The Declaration of Independence: *www.nara.gov/exhall/charters/declaration/decmain.html*
- The U.S. Constitution: *www.nara.gov/exhall/charters/constitution/conmain.html*
- Questions and Answers Pertaining to the Constitution: *www.nara.gov/exhall/charters/constitution/conqa.html*
- The Bill of Rights: *www.nara.gov/exhall/charters/billrights/billmain.html*

U.S. Constitution Net (*www.usconstitution.net/const.html*): More links to the Constitution, Declaration, and related documents

Avalon Project at Yale Law School (*elsinore.cis.yale.edu/lawweb/avalon/avalon.htm*): Research information about the Constitution

The *Federalist Papers* at Emory School of Law (*www.law.emory.edu/FEDERAL/federalist*)

Library of Congress (*memory.loc.gov/ammem/amhome.html*): Link to documents on the founding, including

- Journals of the Continental Congress at the Library of Congress (*memory.loc.gov/ammem/amlaw/lwjc.html*)
- Farrand's *Records of the Federal Convention of 1787* (*memory.loc.gov/ammem/amlaw/lwfr.html*)

Founding.com—A User's Guide to the Declaration of Independence (*www.founding.com*): Information about the Declaration, hosted by the Claremont Institute

Chapter 2, "Going Online with the U.S. Senate and the House of Representatives"

U.S. Senate (*www.senate.gov*): Home page for the Senate with links to members, committees, and legislative information

Index of senators: (*www.senate.gov/senators/index.cfm*)

Index of Senate committees: (*www.senate.gov/committees/index.cfm*)

U.S. House of Representatives (*www.house.gov*): Home page for the House, with links to members, committees, and legislative information

Index of House members: (*www.house.gov/house/MemberWWW.html*)

Index of House committees: (*www.house.gov/house/CommitteeWWW.html*)

Specific congressional committees of interest:

- Senate Foreign Relations Committee (*www.senate.gov/~foreign*)
- Senate Appropriations Committee (*www.senate.gov/~appropriations*)

- Senate Judiciary Committee (*www.senate.gov/~judiciary*)
- House Ways and Means Committee (*waysandmeans.house.gov*)
- House Committee on Standards of Official Conduct (*www.house.gov/ethics*)
- House Commerce Committee (*www.house.gov/commerce*)
- House Judiciary Committee (*www.house.gov/judiciary*)

THOMAS (*thomas.loc.gov*): The Library of Congress's legislative information site

Adobe Acrobat Reader (*www.adobe.com/products/acrobat/readstep.html*): Free download of reader software needed to view PDF documents

The Congressional Budget Office (*www.cbo.gov*): Congress's budget and economic research office

The General Accounting Office (*www.gao.gov/main.html*): Congress's fiscal oversight office

Government Printing Office (*www.access.gpo.gov/*): Source of government documents and information

Architect of the Capitol (*www.aoc.gov*): Source of history and information on the U.S. Capitol

Center for Legislative Archives at the National Archives (*www.nara.gov/nara/legislative/*): Historic congressional documents and records

Chapter 3, "The Wired White House and Bitmap Bureaucracy"

The White House, or Executive Office of the President (*www.whitehouse.gov*): Site with links to presidential documents, statements, and biographical and other information

The White House Virtual Library: (*www.whitehouse.gov/library*)

The White House Briefing Room: (*www.whitehouse.gov/WH/html/briefroom.html*)

Executive orders (*www.pub.whitehouse.gov/search/executive-orders.html*)

Social Security Online (*www.ssa.gov*): The Social Security Administration's Web site with information about benefits and eligibility

The IRS Digital Daily (*www.irs.gov*): The Internal Revenue Service's site with federal tax information and forms

The Census Bureau (*www.census.gov*): Information about the census, statistics, and maps

The Federal Bureau of Investigation (*www.fbi.gov*): Federal crime and law enforcement information

The Department of State (*www.state.gov*): Diplomatic information, passport applications, and travel advisories for foreign travel

The Immigration and Naturalization Service (*www.ins.usdoj.gov*): Immigration news, policies, and information

The Food and Drug Administration (*www.fda.gov*): Information about safe food, drugs, and cosmetics

Department of Education (*www.ed.gov*): Information about education, statistics, and student loan services

Federal Information Center (*fic.info.gov*): One stop for links and information to federal government agencies

The *Federal Register* (*www.access.gpo.gov/su_docs/aces/aces140.html*): Where regulations are published

Federal Consumer Information Center (*www.pueblo.gsa.gov*): Consumer product information and advice

Patent and Trademark Office (*www.uspto.gov*): Information about patents, inventions, and intellectual property rights

Selective Service System (*www.sss.gov*): Registration form required for men on reaching their 18th birthday

Office of Personnel Management (*www.usajobs.opm.gov*): Job vacancies with the federal government

Post Office ZIP Code Locator (*www.usps.gov/ncsc/*): Find a ZIP Code or other address information

Equal Employment Opportunity Commission (*www.eeoc.gov*): Investigates discrimination and harassment complaints

Executive Branch Television (*www.exbtv.com*): Streaming video from federal agencies and departments

U.S. government "blue pages" online (*bp.fed.gov*): Online government phone directory

Chapter 4, "A Web Court Appearance"

U.S. Supreme Court (*www.supremecourtus.gov*): Official Web site for the Supreme Court

Legal Information Institute (LII) (*supct.law.cornell.edu/supct*): Supreme Court site hosted by Cornell Law School

FindLaw's Supreme Court site (*supreme.findlaw.com/supreme_court/resources.html*): Web portal with a vast and growing law library

Findlaw's legal dictionary (*dictionary.findlaw.com*): Quick reference for legal definitions

The Oyez Project (*oyez.nwu.edu*): Multimedia Supreme Court information site

The Supreme Court Historical Society (*www.supremecourthistory.org*): Historic information on the Court

The New York Times Guide to the Supreme Court (*www.nytimes.com/library/politics/scotus/index-scotus.html*)

Court TV's "A Journey Through Time," (*www.courttv.com/multimedia/supremecourt/index.html*): A multimedia presentation of the Court through history

The USAToday Supreme Court page (*www.usatoday.com/news/court/nscot000.htm*)

Washingtonpost.com's Supreme Court page (*www.washingtonpost.com/wp-srv/national/longterm/supcourt/supcourt.htm*)

The Law News Network's Supreme Court Report (*www.lawnewsnetwork.com/supremecourt/*)

Federal Judiciary home page (*www.uscourts.gov*): Maintained by the Administrative Office of the Courts

PACER (*pacer.psc.uscourts.gov/pubaccess.html*): Docket information for federal cases; registration and fee payment required

The United States Court of Federal Claims (*www.law.gwu.edu/fedcl*)

The United States Court of International Trade (*www.uscit.gov*)

The United States Tax Court (*www.ustaxcourt.gov/ustcweb.htm*)

The U.S. Federal Courts Finder (*www.law.emory.edu/FEDCTS/*): Sponsored by Emory Law School; provides links to federal courts

Federal Courts of Appeal Web sites:

- First Circuit (*www.law.emory.edu/1circuit*)
- Second Circuit (*www.tourolaw.edu/2ndCircuit*)
- Third Circuit (*www.law.vill.edu/Fed-Ct/ca03.html*)
- Fourth Circuit (*www.law.emory.edu/4circuit*)
- Fifth Circuit (*www.ca5.uscourts.gov*)
- Sixth Circuit (*www.ca6.uscourts.gov*)
- Seventh Circuit (*www.ca7.uscourts.gov*)
- Eighth Circuit (*ls.wustl.edu/8th.cir*)
- Ninth Circuit (*www.ce9.uscourts.gov*)
- Tenth Circuit (*www.ck10.uscourts.gov*)
- Eleventh Circuit (*www.ca11.uscourts.gov/opinions.htm*)
- D.C. Circuit (*www.cadc.uscourts.gov*)
- Federal Circuit (*www.fedcir.gov*)

USSC+ (*www.usscplus.com/current/index.htm*): An alternative fee-based source for Supreme Court opinions and information

The Federal Court Locator (*vls.law.vill.edu/Locator/fedcourt.html*): Find federal courts here; sponsored by the Villanova School of Law

Jurist Supreme Court Guide (*jurist.law.pitt.edu/supremecourt.htm*): News and analyses from law professors and Court watchers

Chapter 5, "State Sites on the Web"

Commonwealth of Massachusetts (*www.state.ma.us*): State home page with links to state agencies, tourism information, business development, and similar materials

GovSpot (*www.govspot.com/categories/stategovernment.htm*): Provides directory of links to state government sites

California Department of Motor Vehicles (*www.dmv.ca.gov*): Regulates cars and drivers in California

Virginia Department of Taxation (*www.tax.state.va.us*): Tax information for Virginians

Louisiana State University Library (*www.lib.lsu.edu/govdocs/taxes.html*): Directory to all state tax agency Web sites

New Jersey Division of Taxation (*www.state.nj.us/treasury/taxation/updiscl.htm*): Page for searching for unclaimed property in New Jersey

Similar unclaimed property sites:

- Texas (*www.cpa.state.tx.us/comptrol/unclprop/upsearch.html*)
- California (*www.sco.ca.gov/col/ucp*)
- Florida (*up.dbf.state.fl.us*)

Missing Money (*www.missingmoney.com/main/index.cfm*): National database of unclaimed property; registration required

Texas House of Representatives (*www.house.state.tx.us*): The lower house of the Texas legislature

National Conference of State Legislatures (*www.ncsl.org*): Links and information about state legislatures

Council of State Governments (*www.states.org*): Information targeted at officials in state government

Colorado courts Web site (*www.courts.state.co.us/ct-index.htm*): Links and information about state courts in Colorado

New York courts Web site (*www.courts.state.ny.us*)

Illinois links to judicial offices and courts (*www.state.il.us/judicial.htm*)

Georgia state courts (*www2.state.ga.us/courts/supreme*)

Arizona state courts (*www.supreme.state.az.us*)

National Center for State Courts (*www.ncsc.dni.us/COURT/SITES/Courts.htm*): Links to state courts across the country

Stateline.org (*www.stateline.org/*): Site for state news and information from across the nation

NewsDirectory.com state governments (*www.newsdirectory.com/cities/states/*): Directory to state and local government sites

Google's government page (*www.google.com/unclesam*): Search engine for .gov and .mil sites

Yahoo! Get Local (*local.yahoo.com/*): Listings of state-specific directories on Yahoo!

State Justice Institute (*www.statejustice.org/*): Administers grants to improve the quality of state courts

Chapter 6, "All Politics Is Local—And Online"

City of Tumwater, Washington (*www.tumwater.wa.us*): Provides links to city information and services

City of Las Vegas, Nevada (*www.ci.las-vegas.nv.us*): Provides links to city services, information, and travel and tourism materials

Official City Sites (*officialcitysites.org/usa.htm*): Index of official city sites for easy reference

Piper Resources' guide to government sites (*www.piperinfo.com/state/states.html*): Lists the states in alphabetical order, with links to cities, counties, and regions

National Association of Counties site (*www.naco.org/counties/index.cfm*): County-level information and links

California small claims courts (*www.courtinfo.ca.gov/courts/trial/smallclaims/*): Information about county-level courts in California

Yahoo K–12 school directory (*dir.yahoo.com/Education/K_12/Schools/*)

Home Education Magazine (*www.home-ed-magazine.com*): Homeschooling information from *Home Education* magazine

Crosswalk.com's HomeSchool channel (*Homeschool.crosswalk.com/learnathome*): Information about homeschooling

Ann Zeise's Homeschooling site (*www.gomilpitas.com/homeschooling*): Maintained by a homeschooling parent in Milpitas, California; contains links to articles, directories, guides, and other helpful information

South Coast Air Quality Management District (*www.aqmd.gov*): Smog control agency for the southern California air basin

Twin Cities Metropolitan Council of the Minneapolis–St. Paul region (*www.metrocouncil.org*): Regional government for the seven counties in the Twin Cities, MN region

ERIC Clearinghouse on Urban Education (*eric-web.tc.columbia.edu*): Provides news and information about education in cities and urban districts

EducatorsNet (*www.educatorsnet.com*): Portal for teachers and educators, with news, information, and resources

EduHound (*www.eduhound.com/*): Directory with K–12 links, information, and resources

Neighborhoods Online (*www.libertynet.org/nol/natl.html*): Site covering neighborhood revitalization and civic renewal

Municipal World (*www.municipalworld.com/*): Monthly magazine about municipal government

Chapter 7, "The Web IS Worldwide: International Political Research on the WWW"

Worldwide Governments on the WWW (*www.gksoft.com/govt/en/world.html*): English-language directory to government sites across the globe

WWW Virtual Library—international affairs resources page (*www.etown.edu/vl/*): Provides another index for finding international governmental sites

The *CIA World Factbook* online (*www.odci.gov/cia/publications/factbook/*): The CIA's public summaries of other nations

Library of Congress Country Studies (*lcweb2.loc.gov/frd/cs/cshome.html*): The Library of Congress's summaries and analyses of other nations

Political Resources on the Net (*www.politicalresources.net*): Good resource for international political information

Trinidad and Tobago (*www.gov.tt/home.html*): Example of a nation's home page

U.S. State Department's Travel Warnings and Consular Information Sheets (*travel.state.gov/travel_warnings.html*): Provides travel warnings of problem areas in other nations

State department's list of embassies and consular offices overseas (*www.state.gov/www/regions_missions.html*)

Foreign embassies in Washington, D.C. site (*www.embassy.org*)

EmbassyWeb.com (*www.embpage.org*): Directory of domestic and foreign embassy information

The Internet edition of the *Times* of London (*www.sunday-times.co.uk/news/pages/Times/frontpage.html*)

The International News page of the *New York Times* (*www.nytimes.com/yr/mo/day/world*)

The *International Herald Tribune* (*www.iht.com*)

The BBC (*news.bbc.co.uk*)

The Nation & World page of LATimes.com (*www.latimes.com/news/nation*)

News and Newspapers Online (*library.uncg.edu/news*): By the Walter Clinton Jackson Library at The University of North Carolina at Greensboro; links you to descriptions of a country's online media

The E&P Online Media Links (*emedia1.mediainfo.com/emedia*)

United Nations (*www.un.org*): Web site for the international organization

The United States representative to the United Nations (*www.un.int/usa*): Web site for our representative to the United Nations

North Atlantic Treaty Organization (*www.nato.int*): Site for the European security alliance

GIANT (Global Information Access Net) (*www.ucis.pitt.edu/dbinfo*): Hosted by the University Center for International Studies at the University of Pittsburgh; a database of governmental, educational, political, and similar groups

FindLaw's international and foreign law search page (*www.findlaw.com/search/list.html*)

Washburn University School of Law foreign and international law page (*www.waslaw.edu/forint*)

International Constitutional Law (*www.uni-wuerzburg.de/law*): German university site; provides an index with links to the constitutional documents and laws of more than 100 nations

The Nuclear Files (*www.nuclearfiles.org/prolif/index.html*): Information about nuclear proliferation

Human Rights Watch (*www.hrw.org*): Group monitors human rights internationally

Amnesty International (*www.amnesty.org*): An international human rights group

Interpol (*www.interpol.int/Default.asp*): International law enforcement organization

U.S. site for Interpol (*www.usdoj.gov/usncb*)

National Council for Science and the Environment (*www.cnie.org*): Library provides information on international environmental protection

The World Bank (*www.worldbank.org*): International lending institution

World Trade Organization (*www.wto.org/*): International trade organization

WTO Watch (*www.wtowatch.org/*): World Trade Organization watchdog group

Transparency International (*www.transparency.org/*): Organization evaluates international political corruption

Organization of American States (*www.oas.org/*): International organization of Western Hemisphere nations

Organization of African Unity (*www.oau-oua.org/*): organization of African nations

Internationalaffairs.com (*www.internationalaffairs.com/*): One-stop portal for international news, policy, and analysis

Council on Foreign Relations (*www.cfr.org/p/*): Studies and discusses foreign affairs

The Trilateral Commission (*www.trilateral.org/*): Elite group focused on relations among America, Europe, and the Far East

Foreign Affairs magazine (*www.foreignaffairs.org/*): Published by the Council on Foreign Relations; in-depth scholarly articles on international issues

Chapter 8, "Left-Brain Activity: Progressives and Liberals on the Web"

Macrocosm USA (*www.macronet.org*): Site with information and directories of liberal information

ZNet (*www.lbbs.org/weluser.htm*): Describes itself as "a community of people concerned about social change"

Turn Left (*www.turnleft.com/liberal.html*): Bills itself as "the home for liberalism on the Web"

Jay's Leftist and 'Progressive' Internet Resources Directory (*www.neravt.com/left/frontpage.html*): Liberal and progressive information and news

IGC Internet Progressive Gateway (*www.igc.org/igc/gateway/index.html*): Provides news and information about its members, which are a collection of liberal and progressive groups

American Association of University Women (*www.aauw.org/home.html*): Advocates women's rights, especially in higher education

New Moon Publishing (*www.newmoon.org*): Feminist publishing company

Off Our Backs (*www.igc.org/oob*): Feminist news and information

Cafe Progressive (*www.cafeprogressive.com*): Online community coffeehouse for visitors interested in progressive political issues

Communications for a Sustainable Future (*csf.colorado.edu*): Group dedicated to progressive change

ProActivist.com (*www.proactivist.com*): Information for the liberal activist

Essential Information (*www.essential.org*): Founded by Ralph Nader in 1982; directory of consumer groups, social change groups, and similar organizations

The Direct Action Network, (*www.directactionnetwork.org*): Information about protests and similar activities

Yahoo! directory of Liberal Opinion (*dir.yahoo.com/Government/U_S__Government/Politics/Political_Opinion/Liberal/*)

AdBusters (*adbusters.org/home*): Progressive criticism of modern consumer society

Mother Jones's The MOJO Wire (*www.motherjones.com*): Articles from the progressive print magazine as well as original Web content

The Nation (*www.thenation.com*): Site for weekly magazine of liberal politics and current events

The Progressive (*www.progressive.org*): Site for monthly magazine focused on peace and social justice

The American Prospect (*www.prospect.org*): Site for magazine of liberal philosophy, politics, and public life

Dissent (*www.dissentmagazine.org*): Quarterly focused on progressive culture and politics

Utne Reader (*www.utne.com*): Selects articles from the alternative press for republication

Ms. Magazine (*www.msmagazine.com*): Offers news, commentary, and articles from a feminist perspective

Pacific News Service (*www.pacificnews.org*): Provides a liberal alternative to mainstream news wires

Bad Subjects (*eserver.org/bs*): Electronic version of a magazine dedicated to "political education for everyday life"

Alternative Press Center's Alternative Press Index (*www.altpress.org*): Provides listings of alternative and independent publications, including Web addresses

Protest.Net (*www.protest.net/*): Information about political protests

World Campaign (*www.worldcampaign.net/intro1.htm*): Information about global responsibility and citizenship

Steven Biko Page (*www.biko.com/*): Remembering Biko and fighting apartheid and discrimination

E-Activism (*www.eactivism.com/*): Information about political activism

Progressive Magazine search (*activistshop.8m.com/progressive-magazines.html*): Search engine for leftist and progressive magazines

Chapter 9, "Place Your Right Hand over Your Keyboard: Conservative Web Sites"

Town Hall (*www.townhall.com*): Directory, news, and information about conservative topics sponsored by the Heritage Foundation, a conservative think tank

RightBot (*rightbot.com*): Conservative Web directory

RightGuide.com (*www.rightguide.com/conservative.htm*): Conservative Web directory

Free Republic (*www.freerepublic.com*): Provides news and information for conservatives, and a forum area with a number of topics to choose from

Rightgrrl (*www.rightgrrl.com*): Refers to its site as "a Meeting Ground for Conservative and Prolife Women"

Enter Stage Right (*www.enterstageright.com*): Describes itself as a "Journal of Modern Conservatism"

The Heartland Institute (*www.heartland.org*): Links to conservative policy studies and other information

The American Enterprise Institute (*www.aei.org*): Moderately conservative public policy foundation

Claremont.org (*www.claremont.org*): The Web site for the Claremont Institute, a conservative foundation in southern California

The Conservative Caucus (*www.conservativeusa.org*): News, links, and information of interest to conservatives

The Common Conservative (*www.commonconservative.com/index.html*): Information and commentary for conservatives

ConservativeHQ.com (*www.conservativehq.com/chq/home*): Conservative portal; registration required

The Drudge Report (*www.drudgereport.com*): Perhaps the best-known news service site on the Internet, with original reporting, and links to other news sites, columnists, and similar information

WorldNet Daily (*www.worldnetdaily.com*): Conservative news site

National Review Online (*www.nationalreview.com*): Articles from the conservative monthly magazine, as well as Web-only content

American Vibe (*www.americanvibe.com*): Conservative news and information

Conservative News Service (*www.cnsnews.com*): Conservative news site

America News Net (*www.americanewsnet.com/home.htm*): News, opinion, audio files, and links to *The American Freedom* magazine

ConEye (*www.coneye.com*): Conservative analysis and opinion

My Right Start (*www.myrightstart.com*): Conservative news, analysis, links, and general information

FrontPage Magazine (*www.frontpagemag.com*): Conservative news and opinion from the Center for the Study of Popular Culture

The American Spectator (*www.spectator.org/*): Monthly conservative magazine

Insight Magazine: (*www.insightmag.com*): Conservative news magazine from the *Washington Times*

The Weekly Standard (*www.weeklystandard.com/*): Weekly conservative news and opinion magazine edited by Bill Kristol

Policy Review (*www.policyreview.com*): Journal on conservative policy issues from the Heritage Foundation

Chapter 10, "Is There a Ministry of Silly Walks? Iconoclastic, Humorous, and Hard-to-Describe Political Sites"

The White House (parody site) (*www.whitehouse.net*): Note that the real White House doesn't fly the Jolly Roger

Dave Barry for President (*www.herald.com/content/archive/living/barry/dave2k/main.htm*): Humor site of columnist Dave Barry's campaign for president

Doonesbury (*www.doonesbury.com/ieindex.html*): Web site of the political comic

The Daily Feed (*www.dailyfeed.com/washingtonpost.html*): Satirical daily radio program

The Capitol Steps (*www.capsteps.com*): Singing troupe with barbed wit

The Onion (*www.theonion.com*): Satirical newspaper

News of the Weird (*www.newsoftheweird.com*): Weird and true news from everywhere

Slick Times (*www.slick.com*): Political humor magazine

The Warper (*www.msintergate.com/warped/warp.html*): Warp a photo of your favorite politician or celebrity

Ficus 2000 (*www.ficus2000.com*): Your office plant might be a candidate for public office

Dumb Laws (*www.dumblaws.com*): Dumb laws from international, federal, state, and local jurisdictions

Speechmaker (*www.europa.com/~bknotts/speechmaker.html*): This might be why all politicians sound the same

Paunch Magazine (*www.paunchmagazine.com*): A modern take on the classic magazine *Punch*

Humor is Dead (*www.humorisdead.com/news/index.html*): Humorous look at current events, with a more international focus

National Lawn Care Now (*www.jefflindsay.com/NLCN.shtml*): Activist group seeking nationalized lawn care

Campaign Central (*www.campaigncentral.com/*): Campaign and political humor

Jackie Strike for President (*www.jackiestrike.com/*): Virtual candidate for president

Politically Incorrect with Bill Maher (*abc.go.com/pi/pi_home.html*): Web page for the television show

Chapter 11, "Surfing for the Cause: Interest Groups on the World Wide Web"

Electronic Frontier Foundation (*www.eff.org*): Group that monitors developments in technology and cyberspace regulation

Center for Democracy and Technology (*www.cdt.org*): Organization that analyzes technological policy proposals

Common Cause (*www.commoncause.org*): Political reform group

Mothers Against Drunk Driving (MADD) (*www.madd.org*): Well-known for its campaign to stop drunk driving, lower DUI blood-alcohol levels, and prevent underage drinking

Public Citizen (*www.citizen.org*): Consumer watchdog group

The Sierra Club (*www.sierraclub.org*): Environmental advocacy group

Greenpeace (*www.greenpeaceusa.org*): Environmental activism group

American Association of Retired Persons (AARP) (*www.aarp.org*): Monitors issues related to aging, retirement, Social Security, and Medicare

Be a Voter (*BeAVoter.org*): Online assistance with voter registration

American for Tax Reform (*www.atr.org/main.htm*): Taxpayer advocacy group

About.com (tax reform) (*law.about.com/newsissues/law/msub30.htm*): Directory of groups and views about tax reform

The Leadership Conference on Civil Rights (*www.civilrights.org*): Civil rights advocacy group

Lawyers Committee for Civil Rights Under Law (*www.lawyerscommittee.org/index2.html*): Civil rights advocacy and litigation organization

Hatewatch (*hatewatch.org/frames.html*): Monitors Internet "hate" activities

National Association for the Advancement of Colored People (NAACP) (*www.naacp.org*): Civil rights organization

National Council of La Raza (*www.nclr.org*): Civil rights group focused on Hispanic interests

Japanese American Citizens League (*www.jacl.org*): Civil rights group focused on Japanese-American and Asian-American interests

Anti-Defamation League (*www.adl.org*): Civil rights group focused on members of the Jewish community

Native American Rights Fund (*www.narf.org*): Civil rights group focused on Native American interests

Adversity.Net (*www.adversity.net*): Group focused on effects of reverse discrimination

Center for Equal Opportunity (*www.ceousa.org*): Research and analyses critical of racial preferences

The Christian Coalition (*www.cc.org*): Advocates traditional values

The Human Right Campaign Fund (*hrcusa.org*): Political action group advocating rights for homosexuals

The National Organization for Women (NOW) (*www.now.org*): Women's rights group

National Right to Life (*www.nrlc.org*): Pro-life group

People for the American Way (*www.pfaw.org*): Group critical of conservative social policies and organizations

The Gay and Lesbian Victory Fund (*www.victoryfund.org/templates/victoryfund/index.html*): Political fund for gay and lesbian candidates and supporters of gay and lesbian rights

Eagle Forum (*www.eagleforum.org*): Traditional values organization

The National Abortion Rights Action League (*www.naral.org*): Political group favoring abortion rights

U.S. Chamber of Commerce's site (*www.uschamber.org*): Business advocacy organization

Service Employees International Union (SEIU) (*www.seiu.org*)

United Farm Workers (UFW) (*www.ufw.org*)

International Brotherhood of Teamsters (*www.teamsters.org*)

Laborers International Union of North America (*www.liuna.org*)

Chapter 12, "The Cyber-Swiss Army Knife: Sites That Put It All Together"

VoxCap (*www.VoxCap.com*): Site providing information about activism in several issue areas

Intellectual Capital (*www.IntellectualCapital.com*): Weekly e-zine with "think" pieces on political issues

Policy.com (*www.Policy.com*): In-depth policy analysis and interviews

CongressVote (*www.CongressVote.com*): Information about issues before Congress and votes on legislation

Grassroots.com (*Grassroots.com*): A "take action" site with information and action links about a number of issues

The Democracy Network (*www.dnet.org*): One stop for information on federal, state, and local campaigns

Public Agenda (*PublicAgenda.com*): Provides policy analysis and public opinion results

Lobbyforme (*Lobbyforme.com*): Voice your views and have 12 former members of Congress lobby for action on those issues

Politics1.com (*Politics1.com*): Provides numerous links to specific political sites

Politicalwag (*Politicalwag.com*): Political discussion site

Politics.com (*Politics.com*): One-stop political news and information

CNN/Allpolitics (*cnn.com/allpolitics*): CNN's political news site

ABC News's Political Nation (*abcnews.go.com/sections/politics*): ABC's political news site

Roll Call (*www.rollcall.com*): Site for paper focused on Congress

The Hill (*www.hillnews.com*): Paper specializing in coverage of Congress

Headlines from the Hotline (*hotlinescoop.com*): Headlines from the daily political news sheet

The *Washington Post*'s On Politics page (*washingtonpost.com/wp-dyn/politics*): Politics page from the *Washington Post*

Nando Times's politics page (*www.nandotimes.com/politics*): Internet news service politics page

Freedom Channel (*www.freedomchannel.com*): Political news, campaign information, video, in-depth features on specific issues and races, and customizable features

Speakout.com (*www.speakout.com*): Site with news and links to contact officials about your views

GoVote.com (*govote.com*): Personalizable political site with news, issues, ad search features, and more

Onedemocracy.com (*onedemocracy.com*): Political news and information tailored to registered visitor's preferences

Votenet.com (*votenet.com*): Political information with special features on campaign finance and minority politics

The Political Insider (*politicalinsider.com*): Political news, campaign tools, search features, and email news services

Voter.com (*www.voter.com*): Political news, candidate issue comparisons and contact, featured political and special interest Web pages

Epolitics.org (*epolitics.org*): News and polls, plus searchable political database

Evote.com (*evote.com*): Political news with an edge

GovWorks (*Govworks.com*): Can help you pay your taxes, fees, and bills to government agencies online

Project Vote Smart (*www.vote-smart.org*): Candidate stands on issues and voting records

California Voter Foundation (*www.calvoter.org*): California-specific guide to the legislature and election information

GovernmentWatch.com (*www.governmentwatch.com*): Enables you to submit Freedom of Information Act requests to the federal government through this service; fee required

This Nation (*www.thisnation.com*): News, political information, email updates, special features for students and teachers, and a glossary

Chapter 13, "Democrats Online"

Democratic National Committee (DNC) (*www.democrats.org*): The national Democratic Party organization

Democratic Senatorial Campaign Committee (DSCC) (*www.dscc.org*): Political committee of Senate Democrats

Democratic Congressional Campaign Committee (DCCC) (*www.dccc.org*): Political committee of Democratic members of the House of Representatives

College Democrats (*www.collegedems.com*): Party organization for college-age Democrats

Young Democrats (*www.yda.org*): Party organization for post-college young Democrats

Women's Leadership Forum (*www.wlf.online*): Party organization for Democratic women

National Federation of Democratic Women (*www.nfdw.org*): Party group for Democratic women

Democratic Governors' Association (DGA) (*www.democraticgovernors.org*): Democrat state governor's organization

California Democratic Party (*www.ca-dem.org*): California's state Democratic organization

New York Democratic Party (*www.nydem.org*): New York's state Democratic organization

Wisconsin Democratic Party (*www.wisdems.org*): Wisconsin's state Democratic organization

The Massachusetts Democratic Party (*www.massdems.org*): Massachusetts's state Democratic organization

Montgomery County, Maryland Democratic Party (*www.mcdcc.org*): The county party committee for Montgomery county, Maryland

Al Gore 2000 (*algore2000.com*): Vice President Al Gore's campaign for president

Hillary 2000 (*www.hillary2000.org*): Hillary Clinton's campaign for Senator of New York

O'Bannon-Kernan (*www.obannon-kernan.com*) Campaign slate of Frank O'Bannon and Joe Kernan, for governor and lieutenant governor of Indiana

New Democrats Network (*www.newdem.org*): Group embraces centrist economic and social policies

Democratic Leadership Council and the Progressive Policy Institute (*www.dlcppi.org*): Shared site of these two New Democrat policy groups

EMILY's List (*www.emilyslist.org*): Committed to raising money for and electing pro-choice Democratic women to office

Democrats 2000 (*www.dems2000.org*): Founded by Jim Hightower and Senator Tom Harkin, formed to recruit, support, and elect progressive populist Democrats to office

Chapter 14, "Republicans Online"

Republican National Committee (RNC) (*www.rnc.org*): The national party committee for Republicans

National Republican Senatorial Committee (*www.nrsc.org*): The political committee for Republican senators

National Republican Congressional Committee (NRCC) (*www.nrcc.org*): Political committee for Republican House members

College Republicans (*content.colleges.com/republicans*): Party group for college-age Republicans

Young Republicans (*www.yrock.com*): Party group for post-college young Republicans

Republican National Hispanic Assembly (*www.rnha.org*): Party group for Hispanic Republicans

National Federation of Republican Women (*www.nfrw.org*): Party group for Republican women

Republican Governors Association (*www.rga.org*): Organization for Republican state governors

The California Republican Party (*www.cagop.org*): California's Republican state party committee

The New York Republican Party (*www.nygop.org*): New York state's Republican state party committee

The Florida Republican Party (*www.rpof.org*): Florida's Republican state party committee

The Texas Republican Party (*www.texasgop.org*): Texas's Republican state party committee

Cook County, Illinois Republican Central Committee (*www.cookgop.org*): County Republican central committee for Cook County, Illinois

George W. Bush for President (*www.georgewbush.com*): The Bush campaign Web page

Tom Campbell for Senator (*www.campbell.org*): Campbell's campaign site for senator from California

David McIntosh and Murray Clark (*www.davidmcintosh.org*): Site for Republican slate for governor and lieutenant governor of Indiana

GOPAC (*www.gopac.org*): Focuses on training and organizing Republicans to run for state and local office

Republican Mainstream Committee (*www.mainstream.org*): Republican group supporting moderate Republican candidates for office

The Club for Growth (*www.clubforgrowth.com*): Supports Republican candidates for Congress who are committed to lower taxes and less government

Chapter 15, "Other Parties Online"

Green Party USA (*www.greens.org/gpusa*): American branch of the international Green Party

Libertarian Party (*www.lp.org*): Libertarian Party home page

Natural Law Party (*www.natural-law.org*): Natural Law Party home page

Reform Party (*www.reformparty.org*): Reform Party home page

Minnesota Governor Jesse Ventura (*www.jesseventura.org*): Ventura's campaign Web site

American Reform (*www.americanreform.org*): An alternative Reform Party group

The Constitution Party (*www.constitutionparty.com*): The home page of the Constitution Party, formerly known as the U.S. Taxpayers Party

Ralph Nader for President (*www.votenader.com*): Nader's Green Party campaign site

Harry Browne for President (*www.HarryBrowne2000.org*): Browne's Libertarian Party campaign site

John Hagelin for President (*www.hagelin.org*): Hagelin's Natural Law Party campaign as candidate for president

Pat Buchanan for President (*www.buchananreform.com/index.asp*): Reform Party candidate for president

Chapter 16, "The Money Game Online"

Federal Election Commission (FEC) (*www.fec.gov*): Federal agency responsible for regulating campaigns

FECInfo (*www.publicdisclosure.org*): Public Disclosure's FECInfo site provides a wide variety of campaign finance information

opensecrets.org (*www.opensecrets.org/home/index.asp*): Sponsored by the Center for Responsive Politics, contains federal and state campaign finance information

National Institute on Money in State Politics (*www.followthemoney.org*): Database for researching state-level contributions

California Secretary of State (*cal-access.ss.ca.gov*): Campaign finance reports filed in California races

Florida Department of State (*election.dos.state.fl.us/campfin/cfindb.shtml*): Campaign finance search page for Florida campaigns

State of Hawaii (*www.hawaii.gov/campaign/index.html*): Campaign finance information for Hawaii campaigns

State of Illinois (*www.elections.state.il.us*): Campaign finance information on Illinois campaigns

Michigan Secretary of State (*www.sos.state.mi.us/election/elect.html*): Campaign contribution searches for Michigan races

State of New York (*www.elections.state.ny.us/finance/finance.htm*): Campaign finance information for New York campaigns

State of Ohio (*www2.state.oh.us/sos*): Campaign finance information in Ohio

Pennsylvania Department of State (*www.dos.state.pa.us/bcel/camp_fin/campaign.html*): Campaign finance information in Pennsylvania

State of Texas (*www.ethics.state.tx.us*): Campaign contributions in Texas

State of Vermont (*vermont-elections.org/soshome.htm*): Contribution information in Vermont

Campaign Finance Information Center (*www.campaignfinance.org*): Federal and state contribution information and research guides, hosted by Investigative Reporters and Editors, Inc. (IRE)

Common Cause Soft Money Laundromat (*www.commoncause.org/laundromat*): Common Cause is a government reform advocacy group; the Soft Money Laundromat provides information about soft money donors and recipients

Mother Jones Coin-Operated Congress (*www.motherjones.com/coinop_congress*): Site with information about donors to Congress

Chapter 17, "The Future of the Internet in Politics"

Election.com (*election.com*): Company that administers online elections

PoliticsOnline (*www.politicsonline.com*): Source for information about the Internet and politics

Wired News's Politics page (*www.wired.com/news/politics*): Source for news about cutting-edge technology and politics

BushInsecurity.com (*www.bushinsecurity.com*): Gore campaign's site critical of Bush's Social Security proposals

HillaryNo.com (*www.hillaryno.com*): Giuliani site critical of Hillary Clinton's political inexperience

Virtual Mayor (*www.virtualmayor.com/index2.html*): A web site that ran as candidate for Mayor of London

Chapter 18, "Campaigns in the Future: Campaign Finance Reform"

Note: Because this chapter provides a review for the book, some sites listed in this section were also listed earlier.

National Archives Bill of Rights (*www.nara.gov/exhall/charters/billrights/billrights.html*)

U.S. Code Title 2 (*uscode.house.gov/title_02.htm*): Copy of the Code for the House Web site

THOMAS (*thomas.loc.gov*): The Library of Congress's legislative information page

The White House (*www.whitehouse.gov*)

FEC regulations (*www.access.gpo.gov/nara/cfr/waisidx_99/11cfrv1_99.html*)

Cornell Legal Information Institute (*supct.law.cornell.edu/supct*): Site for Supreme Court cases and information

FEC's Court Case Abstracts (*www.fec.gov/info/cca98.htm*)

Brookings Institute Campaign Finance Reform page (*www.brookings.org/GS/CF/CF_HP.HTM*): Campaign finance reform cases and other recent legal developments in this area

Common Cause (*www.commoncause.org*): Group focused on governmental reform

Public Campaign (*www.publiccampaign.org*): Provides news and research about money in politics

Center for Public Integrity (*www.publicintegrity.org*): Investigates and analyzes public officials and their conduct

State Public Interest Research Group Democracy campaigns (*www.pirg.org/demos*): Provides news and information about state campaign finance

Claremont Institute Campaign Finance Project (*www.claremont.org/1_campfin.cfm*): Articles, commentaries, documents, and editorials critical of the conventional campaign finance reform agenda

Cato Institute (*www.cato.org*): Dedicated to reducing the size and scope of government

The Democratic National Committee [DNC] (*www.democrats.org*)

The Republican National Committee [RNC] (*www.rnc.org*)

Al Gore 2000 (*www.AlGore2000.com*)

Bush for president (*www.GeorgeWBush.com*)

Ralph Nader (*www.votenader.com*): The presidential candidate from the Green Party

Pat Buchanan (*www.buchananreform.com*): The Reform Party presidential candidate

Harry Browne (*www.HarryBrowne2000.com*): The Libertarian Party presidential candidate

APPENDIX B

Glossary of e-Politics Terms

accountability The extent to which leaders are held responsible for their words and actions.

activism An involvement in political affairs, by actions such as taking part in demonstrations and getting support for issues.

advisory opinion (AO) A formal ruling from the Federal Election Commission regarding the legality of a specific activity proposed in an advisory opinion request.

agenda Things to be accomplished. Often used to describe political platforms, as in the Republican (or Democratic) agenda, meaning the policies that each party hopes to enact.

appellate Having power to review decisions of lower courts.

appropriation An allotment of specific dollar amounts for specific programs or purposes.

archives The place where public records and documents are kept, and also the documents themselves.

Articles of Confederation The document that established a "firm league of friendship" between the 13 states during the Revolutionary War. The Articles of Confederation was replaced by the Constitution.

ASCII American Standard Code for Information Interchange. A common format for text files in computers and on the Internet.

attorney general The highest legal officer in the United States, who heads the Justice department, and is the chief legal advisor to the president. Each state also has an attorney general.

authorization The creation and empowerment of a program to spend money for specified purposes.

ballot initiative A public policy question decided by a vote of the people. The placement of the question on the ballot is initiated by the people (usually by petition). Used only at the state level.

bicameral A term describing a legislative branch that is divided into two houses, such as the United States Congress, which consists of the House of Representatives and the Senate.

Bill of Rights The first ten amendments to the Constitution, which establish the fundamental rights enjoyed by the people of the United States.

bills The form used for most legislation. A bill originating in the House of Representatives is designated by the letters *H.R.*, signifying "*House Resolution*," followed by a number that it retains throughout all its parliamentary stages. Senate bills as designated with an *S.* Bills are presented to the president for action when approved in identical form by both the House of Representatives and the Senate.

bipartisanship Cooperation between members of the two major political parties (Republicans and Democrats).

Boolean logic Many search engines use this logic, in which documents containing two or more terms can be retrieved by using the AND connector, and documents containing either of several terms can be retrieved by using the OR connector.

bundling Gathering contributions from many separate donors and delivering them together to a candidate or committee.

bureaucracy The administration of a government; all government offices taken together; all the officials of a government. Also applied to the career civil service employed in the federal agencies.

campaign A candidate for a federal office, his or her authorized agents, principal campaign committee, and any other authorized committees.

candidate A person seeking public office via election. An individual seeking election to federal office becomes a candidate when he or she or agents acting on his or her behalf raise contributions or make expenditures that exceed $5,000.

caucus A private meeting of members of a political party to plan action or to select delegatesfor a nominating convention. It may also refer to groups, either official or unofficial, in Congress.

censorship The prevention of publication, transmission, or exhibition of material considered undesirable for the general public to possess or view.

census An official enumeration or count of the population of the United States conducted by the national government every ten years, as dictated by the Constitution.

chat room A place on the Internet where people go to "chat" with other people in the room. Chat rooms are usually organized by topic.

checks and balances Powers held by one branch of government that enable it to limit another branch's exercise of its own powers; for example, the president's ability to veto legislation.

citizen A person who is a member of a state or nation, either by birth or naturalization. Anyone born in the United States is a U.S. citizen and is entitled to full civil rights.

civil liberties The freedoms that people have in a society. The idea of civil liberties is deeply embedded in the United States; it is enshrined in the Bill of Rights.

civil rights The rights granted by a state to all its citizens. In the U.S., this refers to the rights enshrined in the constitution and Bill of Rights. Civil rights prevent the government from intruding on personal liberties.

civil servants All nonmilitary employees of the government.

common law The legal system of most English-speaking countries, including the United States, common law is based on precedent. Common law is supplemented by statutory law, which is established by legislation. The distinction between common law and statutory law has become blurred in modern times because much of common law has been enacted into statutes.

concurrent powers Powers that are shared and exercised jointly under the Constitution by both national and state governments. Examples include taxation and law enforcement.

conference committee A committee comprised of both House and Senate members charged with working out the differences between House and Senate versions of a bill.

conservative Tending to support the free market in economic affairs, and against big government—an excessive federal bureaucracy that intervenes in a wide range of social and economic areas. On social issues, conservatives are pro-family, anti-abortion, and in general, support traditional moral values and religion. Conservatives usually favor a strong military.

constitution A document that describes the fundamental legal and political structures of a state. A constitution may be written or unwritten.

constitutional amendment A formally proposed and ratified change to a constitution that becomes a fully binding provision of the constitution itself.

constitutional government A form of government in which a constitution details the powers available to each branch of government, and the rights of the individual in relation to the government. Any action by the government that is not in accord with the constitution is considered illegitimate.

contribution A payment, service, or anything of value given to influence an election.

cookie A small file built into a Web page you visit that identifies you to the site on your return. A cookie could make research easier by identifying you, tracking sites you visit and topics you search, and getting a general feel for your preferences. A cookie can also be used to collect your email address for marketing purposes. You can set your browser to warn you before you accept cookies or not accept them at all.

database A collection of data that is organized so that its contents can easily be accessed, managed, and updated.

democracy Government by the people; the rule of the majority. Participation by the mass of people in the decisions that shape their lives; government by majority rule, with recognition of the rights of minorities; freedom of speech, press, and assembly; freedom to form opposition political parties and to run for office.

Democratic Party One of the two major American political parties (the other being the Republican Party). The Democratic Party is the more liberal of the two.

download The transfer of information from the Internet to your computer. Use care when downloading files or programs from unfamiliar email addresses or Web sites.

earmarked (bundled) contribution A contribution that the contributor directs (either orally or in writing) to a clearly identified candidate or authorized committee through an intermediary or conduit.

election Any one of several processes by which an individual seeks nomination for election, or election, to public office.

election cycle In federal law, the period beginning the day after the previous general election (for federal office) and ending on the day of the next general election. (For House candidates, the election cycle is two years; for Senate candidates, six years.)

electoral college The mechanism by which the president of the United States is chosen. Each state has a number of electoral votes equal to the number of members it sends to the U.S. Senate and House of Representatives.

email Usually provided by your Internet Service Provider. Email enables you to send and receive mail (messages) over the Internet.

embassy The official residence and offices of an ambassador in a foreign country.

encryption The conversion of data into a form, called a *cipher*, that cannot be easily understood by unauthorized people. Decryption is the process of converting encrypted data into its original form.

executive branch The branch of government, headed by the president at the federal level, and charged with executing or implementing and enforcing the laws.

FAQ An acronym for Frequently Asked Questions. A FAQ can serve as a help and information file.

Federal Election Commission (FEC) The executive branch agency charged with enforcement and interpretation of federal election laws.

Federalist Papers A series of essays written in support of ratifying the Constitution. *The Federalist Papers* were written by Alexander Hamilton, John Jay, and James Madison.

flat tax A tax collected at the same rate or percentage regardless of income level.

foreign national An individual who is not a citizen of the United States and has not been lawfully admitted to the U.S. for permanent residence (that is, a green card holder).

FTP File Transfer Protocol. A technique used to transfer files through the Internet from one computer to another.

hard disk Part of a unit—often called a *hard drive* or *hard disk drive*—that stores and provides relatively quick access to large amounts of data. Today's computers typically come with a hard disk that contains several billion bytes (gigabytes) of storage space.

HTML Hypertext Markup Language. HTML is a way to format text by placing marks around the text. HTML is the foundation for most Web pages.

ideology The political doctrine of a party or group, as in Communist ideology.

impeachment The process by which members of the executive branch or the judiciary are formally charged with crimes that could be grounds for removing them from office. A trial follows impeachment to determine the fate of the impeached individual.

interest group A group that lobbies for the interests of its members. An interest group might also promote its interests by working to elect officials who are sympathetic to its cause, and might make donations to election campaign funds.

Internet This electronic network connects hosts together so that you can efficiently go from one site to another. The electronic connection began as a government experiment in 1969 with four computers connected together over phone lines.

ISP Internet Service Provider. A company that provides individuals and other companies access to the Internet and other related services such as Web site building and hosting.

issue advocacy Political communications that discuss an issue in the context of an election. They are controversial because issue speech is protected from regulation, but campaign messages are not.

judicial branch The branch of government, headed by the Supreme Court at the federal level, that hears and settles legal disputes.

legislative branch The branch of government with the authority to make and change the laws of the land. The federal legislative branch is comprised of the U.S. Senate and House of Representatives.

liberal A person who believes it is the duty of government to ameliorate social conditions and create a more equitable society. Liberals generally favor generous spending on the welfare state; they exhibit a concern for minorities, the poor, and the disadvantaged, and often see these conditions as a product of social injustices rather than individual failings. Liberals also tend to be concerned about environmental issues, the defense of civil liberties, and do not favor military spending.

Libertarian A political philosophy that seeks to reduce the size and scope of government, preserve individual liberties, and reduce regulation to a minimal level.

link A connection that transports you from one Internet site to another with a click of your mouse. Links can be text or graphic. Text links are usually underlined and often a different color than the rest of the text on your screen. A graphic link usually has a frame around it.

lobby Any individual or group that attempts to exert an influence over legislation or other government action.

moderate Not extreme. Moderate political policies are those that occupy the middle ground, between the right and the left, and that do not try to effect fundamental societal change.

MP3 A compressed storage format for sound files that permits easier moving and storing of sound files.

national party committee The political committee established and maintained by a national political party. A party's national committee (RNC, DNC), House campaign committee, and Senate campaign committee are defined as national party committees.

newsgroups Also called Usenet, these are ongoing discussion groups among people on the Internet who share a mutual interest.

nomination Naming a candidate as the political party representative in an upcoming election. An appointment of a person to fill a particular office by the executive branch of the U.S. government, subject to the confirmation of the Senate.

operating system (Sometimes abbreviated as OS.) The program that, after being initially loaded into the computer by a bootstrap program, manages all the other programs in a computer.

party platform An official statement and proclamation of the beliefs, values, and policy positions of a political party. Specific statements or positions in a platform are sometimes called *planks*.

PDF Portable Document Format, which allows documents to be posted on a Web site and read, downloaded, and printed by visitors equipped with Adobe Acrobat Reader software.

Political Action Committee (PAC) The popular term for a federal political committee that is neither a party committee nor an authorized committee of a candidate. PACs sponsored by a corporation or labor organization are called *separate segregated funds*; PACs without a corporate or labor sponsor are called *nonconnected* PACs.

portal A World Wide Web site that is a major starting site for users when they get connected to the Web or that users tend to visit as an anchor site. There are general portals and specialized or niche portals.

primary election A popular election that usually selects a nominee from each party to contest against each other in the general election.

radical A person favoring fundamental social change.

referendum A national or local vote on a single issue. Most states in the U.S. require referendums on amendments to the state constitution.

Reform Party One of the minor American political parties. It was founded in large measure because of the efforts of American billionaire H. Ross Perot and his independent campaign for president in 1992.

Republican Party One of the two major American political parties (the other being the Democratic Party). The Republican Party is the more conservative of the two.

runoff election An election held after a primary or a general election when no candidate wins the previous election.

scroll The action required to look at the parts of the page that fall below (or above) what you see on your screen.

site A place on the Internet. Every Web page has a location where it resides, which is called its site. And every site has an address, usually beginning with **http://**.

server A Web server is the computer program that serves HTML pages or files as requested by your browser.

soft money Contributions by corporations, unions, and others to the nonfederal accounts of national political party committees. Soft money is controversial because its donors are sources that are otherwise not permitted to make federal election contributions.

standing The legal right to bring a suit before a court. To have standing, an individual must show that he or she has been harmed in a real way, not merely that he or she *might* be harmed in the future.

state party committee A committee that, by virtue of the bylaws of a political party, is responsible for the day-to-day operation of the party at the state level.

statute A law enacted by legislation.

think tank Popular term used for public policy research foundations that analyze public policy issues.

third parties Term applied to minor national parties in American elections—that is, parties other than the Republican and Democratic parties. Some third parties include the Reform Party, the Libertarian Party, the Green Party, and the Constitution Party.

upload The process of transferring information from your computer to another computer through the Internet.

URL An acronym for Uniform Resource Locator. It's the address of each Web site.

Usenet A collection of ongoing discussion groups among people on the Internet who share a mutual interest.

user ID The unique identifier (like your logon name) that you use to identify yourself on a computer. You probably type your user ID (and password) when you log on to the Internet.

veto The Constitution authorizes the president to reject, or veto, any bill passed by both houses of Congress if he disapproves of it for any reason. The Congress may, however, override the veto by a two-thirds majority vote in both houses. The bill then becomes law the President's objections notwithstanding.

virus A virus is a program that, after it is on your computer, can wipe out information on your computer or damage files. You can unintentionally download a virus from a Web site or by opening an attachment to an email message.

Web browser The tool (program) that enables you to move around the Web. The most popular Web browsers now are Netscape's Navigator and Microsoft's Internet Explorer.

Web ring A series of Web pages with a common subject or interest, linked together in a ring.

World Wide Web A multimedia database of information on the Internet, consisting of independent individual sites.

WWW An acronym for the World Wide Web.

INDEX

SYMBOLS

3rd Party Central Web site, 190

A

AARP Web site, 133
abandoned property, 62
absentee ballots, 214
accountability, 261
activism, 132, 261
Adams, John, 8
AdBusters (The Culture Jammers Network) Web site, 103
addresses (URLs), 8
Adobe Acrobat Reader, 22
Adversity Net, 137
advisory opinion (AO), 261
advocacy groups, Common Cause, 207
AFL-CIO, 139
agencies
  federal government, 29, 35
  states, 61
agendas, 163, 261
Al Gore Web site, 162-164
Almanac of Politics and Government (Chile) Web site, 81
Alternative Press Center's Alternative Press Index Web site, 104
American Enterprise Institute Web site, 113
The American Prospect magazine, 104
Americans for Tax Reform (ATR), 135
Amnesty International Web site, 243
Annenberg Public Policy Center Web site, 152
Anti-Defamation League, 137
AO (advisory opinion), 261
Arizona courts Web site, 66
Articles of Confederation, 10, 261
ATR (Americans for Tax Reform), 135
Avalon Project at Yale Law School, 12

B

back taxes, 31
Bad Subjects magazine, 104
Ballot Access News, 188
Barry, Dave, 118
BBC Web site, 88
BeAVoter.org Web site, 134
bicameral, 262
Bill of Rights, 10
bills
  Congressional Record, 22
  looking up with THOMAS, 21
  numbers, 22
  searching older legislation, 24
  versions, 22

bookmarks, 11
Boolean logic, 40, 262
branches. *See* government
Browne, Harry, 191, 231
Buchanan, Pat, 192, 231
bulletin boards, 102
bundling contributions, 168
bureaucracy, 27
Bush, George W., 164, 176-177, 230
BushInsecurity.com Web site, 218
bylaws (DNC), 158

C

Cafe Progressive Web site, 102
California Democratic Party Web site, 161
California Department of Motor Vehicles, 61
Campaign Finance Information Center (CFIC), 206
campaigns, 195
  ballot access, 188
  Clinton, Hillary, 165
  contributions
    information, 202-205
    rules, 197-200, 203
    soft money, 207
  Federal Election Commission, 196
  finance law, 221-225
    political parties, 229
    reform, 258
    reform groups, 228
    related Web sites, 256-257
    Supreme Court, 227
  funding, 164, 216
  Gore, Al, 162
    agenda, 163
    contributing, 164
    updates, 163
    volunteering, 163-164
  House of Representatives, 165
  Kernan, Joe, 165
  O'Bannon, Frank, 165
  political humor, 248
  presidential debates, 189
  restrictions on Senate/House of Representatives members, 16
  Senate, 165
  state candidates, 165-166
  third-party presidential, 190, 192
  volunteers, 216
Campbell, Tom, 178
candidates
  campaigns, 195
  Democratic party, 162-166
  Independent Web sites, 217
  Republican, 176
  states, 165-166
Capitol Steps, 122
Cato Institute Web site, 187
caucuses, 263
CDT (Center for Democracy and Technology), 128
Census Bureau, 236
  Statistical Abstract of the United States, 34
  Web site, 33
Center for Democracy and Technology (CDT), 128
Center for Equal Opportunity, 137

Center for Responsive Politics, 203
CFIC (Campaign Finance Information Center), 206
CFR (*Code of Federal Regulations*), 36, 39-40
chat rooms
courtesy/respect, 102
Doonesbury, 119
govWorks.com, 152
politicians, 150
Chile, 80, 82
Christian Coalition of America, 138
CIA (Central Intelligence Agency), World Factbook Web site, 83
city government Web presence, 69-71
finding your city, 72
portals, 73
civil rights, 136
Claremont Institute Web site, 114
Clinton, Hillary, 165, 218
Club for Growth, 182
Code of Federal Regulations (*CFR*), 36, 39-40
Coin-Operated Congress Web site, 208
College Democrats Web site, 160
Colorado courts Web site, 64
Commission on Presidential Debates, 189
committees, 23, 160-161
Common Cause, 128, 207
common law, 263
Communications for a Sustainable Future Web site, 103
ConEye Web site, 247
confidentiality (political contributions), 159
Congress. *See* House of Representatives
Congressional Budget Office, 24, 235
Congressional Research Service, 25
CongressVote.com Web site, 145
conservatives, 107
defined, 97
Enter Stage Right, 112
Free Republic, 109-111
news, 114
online resources, 114
related Web sites, 246-247
think tanks, 113
Web directories, 109
women, 111
Constitution Party, 190, 255
Constitutional Convention, 10
constitutions, 222
Federalist Papers, 12
James Madison, 10
location of, 7
online resources, 10-11
transcription, 10
Texas, 64
U.S. Constitution, 10, 222
viewing online, 9
consumer protection organizations, 131
contributions
Al Gore for president, 164
bundling, 168
confidentiality, 159
DNC, 158

federal, 159
George W. Bush for president, 176
limitations, 159, 168
nonfederal, 159
Cook County, Illinois Republican Central Committee, 175
cookies, 111, 264
cosponsors (bills), 21
Council of State Governments Web site, 64
counties, online searches, 73. *See also* local government
Court TV, 51, 237
courts
Court International Trade, 237
Court of Federal Claims, 238
Court TV, 51, 237
federal, 226
Federal Courts of Appeals, 238
states, 64-66
Tax Court, 238
venues, 65
Web sites, 237
Crosswalk.com Web site, 75

D

The Daily Feed Web site, 120
databases (George W. Bush's campaign donor), 177
DCCC (Democratic Congressional Campaign Committee), 159, 165
debates, 189
Declaration of Independence
location of, 7
viewing online, 8
Democracy Network (DNet), 146
Democratic Congressional Campaign Committee (DCCC), 159, 165
Democratic Governors' Association Web site, 160
Democratic Governors Web site, 166
Democratic Leadership Council Web site, 166
Democratic National Committee. *See* DNC
Democratic Party, 157. *See also* DNC
candidates, 162-166
committees
county, 161
DNC 157-158
governors, 160
organizations, 157-161, 166-168
outreach programs, 158
races, 160
related Web sites, 252-253
state committees, 160-161
Web site (official), 160-161
Democratic Senatorial Campaign Committee (DSCC), 159, 165
Democratic women, 167
Democrats 2000 Web site, 168
Department of Education Web site, 35
Department of State Web site, 35
Digital Daily (IRS) Web site, 32-33
Direct Action Network Web site, 103
directories (left oriented)
groups/causes/issues, 95
Jay's Leftist and Progressive Internet Resources Directory, 99

Yahoo! Directory of Liberal Opinion, 101
Dissent magazine, 104
district courts (federal), 51
DNC (Democratic National Committee), 157-158
bylaws, 158
campaign finance reform, 229
contributions to, 158
history, 158
internship listings, 158
job listings, 158
news stories, 157
platform, 158
Web site, 157-159
DNet (Democracy Network), 146, 166
documents
agency notices, 38
PDF format, 22
searching online, 13
Supreme Court, 44
UN General Assembly and Security Council Resolutions, 89
Doonesbury, 119, 248
downloading
The Daily Feed audio clips, 121
IRS forms, 32
RealAudio's RealPlayer, 49
DSCC (Democratic Senatorial Campaign Committee), 159

E

Eagle Forum, 138
education
Department of Education Web site, 35
finding schools online, 74
home schooling, 75
elder issues, 133
election.com Web site, 213, 215
elections
cycles, 265
electoral college, 265
online, 213-215
runoff, 269
Elections Around the World (Chile) Web site, 81
electoral college, 265
Electronic Frontier Foundation (EFF) Web site, 127
email
congress members, 18
presidents, 27
senators, 17
statistics, 214
embassies, 86-87
EmbassyWeb.com Web site, 87
EMILY's List Web site, 167-168
Emory School of Law Web site, 12
encryptions, 265
Enter Stage Right Web site, 112
environment related organizations, 132
Environmental Voters For Gore, 163
EO, 29
Equal Employment Opportunity Commission, 236
Essential Information Web site, 103
ethnicity issues, 136
European Federation of Green Parties Web sites, 186

executive branch, 27
campaign finance law, 224
states, 60
executive orders, 29

F

FBI (Federal Bureau of Investigation) Web site, 34, 236
FDA (Food and Drug Administration), 35, 236
FEC (Federal Election Commission), 196, 225
FECA (Federal Election Campaign Act), 223
FECInfo Web site (Public Disclosure), 201
federal appeals courts, 54
Federal Consumer Information center, 236
federal contributions, 159
Federal Courts of Appeal, 238
federal district courts, 51
Federal Election Campaign Act (FECA), 223
Federal Election Commission (FEC), 196, 225
federal government
agencies, 29, 35
appeals courts, 54
bureaucracy, 27
district courts, 51
judicial branch, 43
trial courts, 53
Federal Judiciary Web site, 51
Federal Register, 36-37
federal trial courts, 53
federalism, 61
Federalist Papers, 12, 266
feminist Web sites, 100, 244
ficus2000.com Web site, 125
final rules (regulations), 38
finding Web rings, 99
FindLaw Web site, 49
flames, 102
Food and Drug Administration (FDA), 35, 236
Form 990, 132
forms, downloading (IRS), 32
Founding Fathers, 9
Founding.com Web site, 234
frames (Web pages), 81
Franklin, Benjamin, 8
Free Republic, 109, 246
free speech issues, 137
Freedom Channel Web site, 150
Freedom of Information Act (FOIA) site, 35
Fremont, John C., 171
funding campaigns, 164, 216

G

Gay and Lesbian Americans For Gore, 163
Gay and Lesbian Victory Fund, 138
General Accounting Office Web site, 25
General Assembly (UN), 89
Georgia courts Web site, 66
GIANT (Global Information Access Net), 91
Giuliani, Rudy, 219
Global Greens conference, 186
global positioning systems (GPS), 86
gomilpitas.com Web site, 75

GOPAC, 180
GOPAC Web site, 174
Gore, Al, 162-164
campaign
agenda, 163
contributing, 164
volunteering, 163-164
official Web site, 229
government
campaigns
ballot access, 188
contributions, 197-207
Federal Election Commission, 196
finance law, 221-229
finance reform, 258
finance related Web sites, 256-257
fundraising online, 216
presidential debates, 189
third-party presidential, 190-192
volunteers, 216
chat sites, 152
city, 69-73
federal courts, 226
history, 233
humor, 117-120, 124, 247-248
international, 79-80, 84
Chile, 80, 82
CIA accounts, 83
country Web sites, 85
diplomatic information, 86
embassies, 87
law resources, 91
Library of Congress Country Studies Web site, 84
local news, 87
NATO, 90
organizations, 88
source reliability, 87
Web sites, 82, 241
Internet functionality, 219
local, 147, 240-241
news and information Web sites, 250-252
PACs, 138
parties, 269
Constitution, 190
contributions, 198
Democratic, 157, 166-168, 252-253
Green Party USA, 185
Libertarian, 186, 267
Natural Law, 187
other, 185, 190
other parties, 255
Reform Party, 188
Republican, 171-180, 254-255
political news sites, 150
states, 59
agencies, 61
campaign finance disclosures, 205
executive branches, 60
judicial branches, 64-65
legislative branches, 63-64
Web sites, 60, 239-240
Government Printing Office, 36
governors, 160
GovSpot Web site, 60
govWorks.com Web site, 152
GPS (global positioning systems), 86

grass-roots groups, 128
Grassroots.com Web site, 145-146
Green Party of England and Wales Web site, 186
Green Party USA, 185
  Ralph Nader for President, 190
  Web site, 255
Greenpeace, 249

H

Hagelin, John, 192
Handbook of Latin American Studies, 82
Harkin, Tom, 168
HateWatch web site, 137
Heartland Institute's Web site, 113
Helms, Jesse, 23
Heritage Foundation's Town Hall Web site, 107
Hightower, Jim, 168
The Hill Web site, 150
Hillary2000 Web site, 165
HillaryNo.com Web site, 218
Hispanic Reading Room, 82
history (DNC), 158
Home Education magazine, 75
home schooling, 75
House Commerce Committee, 24
House Committee in Standards of Official conduct, 23
House Foreign Relations Committee, 23
House of Representatives, 17
  campaigns, 165
  committees, 23
  Congress sessions, 23
  emailing congress members, 18
  legislation from specific representatives, 23
  Texas, 63
  Web sites, 17
human rights, 89
Human Rights Campaign, 138
Human Rights Watch Web site, 92
human rights Web sites, 243
humor, 117-120, 124, 247-248

I

IGC Internet Progressive Gateway Web site, 99-101
Illinois courts Web site, 66
immigration, 86
Immigration and Naturalization Service (INS), 35, 236
impeachment, 266
IntellectualCapital.com Web site, 144
International Brotherhood of Teamsters, 140, 250
international government, 79-80, 84
  Chile, 80, 82
  CIA accounts, 83
  country Web sites, 85
  diplomatic information, 86
  embassies, 87
  law resources, 91
  Library of Congress Country Studies Web site, 84
  local news, 87
  organizations
    NATO, 90
    United Nations, 88
  source reliability, 87
  Web resources, 82, 241

International Herald Tribune Web site, 88
Internet
  EFF, 127
  hate and bigotry online, 137
  organizations, 128
  political ramifications, 219
  privacy and other issues, 127, 147
  voting online, 213, 215
internship listings, 158
Interpol Web site, 92, 243
IRS
  Form 990, 132
  Tax Trails, 33
  United States Tax Court, 53
  Web site, 32-33, 236
issue advocacy, 135, 267

J - K

Japanese American Citizens League, 137
Jay's Leftist and Progressive Internet Resources Directory Web site, 99
Jefferson, Thomas, 8
job listings, 158
Journals of the Continental Congress, 13
judicial branch, 43
  federal appeals courts, 54
  federal courts, 51
  federal trial courts, 53
  states, 64-65

Kernan, Joe, 165
keyword searches, 13

L

labor organizations, 140
Laborers' International Union of North America Web site, 140
Las Vegas, NV Web site, 70
law
  campaign finance law, 221-225
    disclosure, 206
    political parties, 229
    reform groups, 228
    Supreme Court, 227
  common, 263
  dumblaws.com, 125
  international, 88, 91
  regulations, 36
  states, 64
  Web sites, 237
Law News Network Web site, 51
Lawyers' Committee for Civil Rights Under Law Web site, 137
Leadership on Civil Rights Web site, 136
left-of-center ideology, 95
left-wing. *See also* liberals
  AdBusters (The Culture Jammers Network) Web site, 103
  Communications for a Sustainable Future Web site, 103
  Direct Action Network Web site, 103
  Essential Information Web site, 103
  groups/causes/issues directory, 95
  Jay's Leftist and Progressive Internet Resources Directory, 99

liberal/progressive groups information Web site, 99-101
liberalism Web site, 97-98
lobbying groups, 97
nonprofit charities, 97
online publications, 103-104
political committees, 97
ProActivist.com, 103
progressive political issues online community coffee-house, 102
social change community Web site, 96
Web sites, 244-245
Yahoo! Directory of Liberal Opinion, 101
Legal Information Institute (LII) Web site, 45
decisions, 47
legal terms, 48
legislative branch
bicameral, 262
news Web sites, 150
states, 63-64
liberals, 95. *See also* left-wing
defined, 97
group information Web site, 99-101
magazines, 245
progressives, compared, 100
Turn Left Web site, 97-98
Web sites, 244-245
Libertarian Party, 186, 255, 267
Library of Congress
Country Studies Web site, 84
THOMAS, 223
Web site, 13
LII (Legal Information Institute) Web site, 45
decisions, 47
legal terms, 48
limitations on contributions, 159, 168
Lincoln, Abraham, 171
links, 10
Lobbyforme.com Web site, 147
lobbying groups, 97, 129
local government
official Web sites, 240-241
online resources, 147
London Virtual Mayor Web site, 219

M

Macrocosm USA Web site, 95
MADD (Mothers Against Drunk Driving), 129-130, 249
Madison, James, 10
magazines
The American Prospect, 104
Bad Subjects, 104
Dissent, 104
liberal, 245
Mother Jones, 103, 208
Ms. Magazine, 104
The Nation, 104
online, 103-104
Pacific News Service, 104
The Progressive, 104
Utne Reader, 104
Massachusetts Democratic Party Web site, 161
McCain, John, 178
McIntosh, David, 179
Medicare, 31, 133
missingmoney.com Web site, 63
Montgomery County, Maryland Democratic Party Web site, 161

Mother Jones, 103, 208
Mothers Against Drunk Driving (MADD), 129-130, 249
MP3 files (Capitol Steps), 122
Ms. Magazine, 104

N

NAACP (National Association for the Advancement of Colored People), 137
Nader, Ralph, 131
  presidential campaign, 190
  Web site, 231
Nando Times Web site, 150
The Nation, 104
National Abortion Rights Action League, 138
National Archives, 9
National Association of Counties Web site, 73
National Center for State Courts Web site, 66
National Conference of State Legislatures Web site, 64
National Council of La Raza, 137
National Federation of Democratic Women Web site, 160
National Federation of Republican Women, 173
National Institute on Money in State Politics Web site, 205
National Organization for Women (NOW), 138, 250
National Political Awareness Test (NPAT), 153
National Republican Senatorial Committee (NRSC), 172
National Right to Life Committee, 138
Native American Rights Fund, 137
NATO (North Atlantic Treaty Organization), 90, 242
Natural Law Party, 187
Natural Law Party Web site, 255
NetPulse journal, 215
New Democrat Network Web site, 166
New Jersey Division of Taxation Web site, 62
New Moon Publishing Web site, 244
New York courts Web site, 66
New York State Democratic Party Web site, 161
New York Times Guide to the Supreme Court Web site, 51
New York Times Web site, 88
news
  conservatives, 114
  foreign, 87
  Free Republic, 109
  News of the Weird Web site, 123
  online resources, 151
  political, 150
  political news and information Web sites, 250-252
  The Onion, 123
  Web sites, 88
News of the Weird Web site, 123
newsgroups, 101-102
newsletters (PoliticsOnline), 215
nonfederal contributions, 159
North Atlantic Treaty Organization (NATO), 90
Northwestern University, Oyez Project, 48

notices (regulations), 38
NOW (National Organization of Women), 112, 138, 250
NPAT (National Political Awareness Test), 153
NRSC (National Republican Senatorial Committee), 172
Nuclear Files Web site, 92, 243

O

O'Bannon, Frank, 165
O'Bannon-Kernan Web site, 165
The Onion, 123, 248
online publications, 103-104
Open Secrets Web site, 203
organizations
- Americans for Tax Reform (ATR), 135
- Amnesty International, 243
- business groups, 138
- civil rights, race, and ethnicity, 136-137
- Common Cause, 207
- consumer protection, 131
- Democratic party, 157-161, 166-168
- environment, 132
- Form 990, 132
- Greenpeace, 249
- HateWatch, 137
- international, 243
- issue advocacy, 135
- liberal, 244
- lobbying, 129
- MADD, 129-130
- NAACP, 137
- non-profit, 130
- organized labor, 140
- personal issues, 137
- Public Citizen, 131
- Republican party, 171
- retirement and elder issues, 133
- Sierra Club, 132
- special interest groups, 249-250
- tax reform, 135

OSHA, 139
outreach programs (Democratic party), 158
Oyez Project Web site, 48

P

PACER Web site, 53
Pacific News Service magazine, 104
PACs (political action committees), 129, 268
- contributions, 198
- fund solicitation, 138

parties
- campaign finance law, 229
- candidate support, 195
- caucuses, 263
- Constitution Party, 190
- contributions, 198
- Democratic, 157
  - candidates, 162-166
  - county committees, 161
  - governors (in office), 160
  - organizations, 157-161
  - outreach programs, 158
  - races, 160
  - related Web sites, 252-253
  - state committees, 160-161
  - unofficial organizations, 166, 168

Green Party USA, 185
Libertarian, 186, 267
Natural Law Party, 187
other parties, 185, 190, 255
Reform Party, 188, 269
Republican, 171
candidates, 176
county level organizations, 174
George W. Bush, 177
history, 171
John McCain, 178
organizations and committees, 173
related Web sites, 254-255
Republican National Committee, 171
state candidates, 179
state level organizations, 174
Tom Campbell, 178
unofficial organizations, 180
PDF files, 22
PeaceNet, 100
People For the American Way, 138
personal issues, 137
piperinfo.com Web site, 73
Policy.com Web site, 144
political action committees. *See* PACs
political contributions, confidentiality, 159. *See also* campaigns
political parties. *See* parties, 185
Political Resources on the Net Web site, 84
Politicalwag.com Web sites, 147-149
politics
campaigns, 195
contribution information, 202-205
contribution rules, 197-200, 203
Federal Election Commission, 196
soft money contributions, 207
conservatives, 107
Enter Stage Right, 112
Free Republic, 109-111
news, 114
online resources, 114
think tanks, 113
Web directories, 109
women, 111
humor, 117, 119-120, 124
news, 150
Politics1.com Web site, 147, 149
PoliticsOnline Web site, 215
portals. *See also* Web sites
cities, 73
political, 152
Preamble to the Bill of Rights, 10
presidential debates, 189
presidents, 27
emailing, 28
executive orders, 29
related Web sites, 235
Supreme Court justices, 43
privacy issues (Internet), 147
private funding of campaigns, 164
pro-choice women, 167
ProActivist.com Web site, 103
Progressive Policy Institute Web site, 166

The Progressive magazine, 104
progressives. *See also* left-wing
  group information Web site, 99-101
  liberals, compared, 100
  political issues online community coffeehouse, 102
Project Vote Smart Web site, 153
prolife, 111
property, abandoned, 62
proposed rules (regulations), 38
Public Agenda Web site, 147
Public Citizen, 131
Public Disclosure's FECInfo Web site, 201
public funding of campaigns, 164

R

race issues, 136
RealAudio
  Capitol Steps, 122
  The Daily Feed, 120
RealPlayer, 49
Reason Foundation Web site, 187
Records of the Federal Convention of 1787, 13
Reform Party, 188, 255, 269
reforms in campaign finances, 224, 228-229
regional government, 76
registering
  Free Republic, 110
  Grassroots.com, 146
  to vote, 134
  voting online, 213
regulations
  Code of Federal Regulations (CFR), 39-40
  Federal Register, 37
  final rules, 38
  notices, 38
  proposed rules, 38
  researching, 36
  Texas, 64
Rehnquist, William, 43
reporting campaign contributions, 200
Republican Mainstream Committee, 181
Republican National Committee (RNC), 171, 229
Republican National Hispanic Assembly, 173
Republican party, 171
  candidate Web sites, 176
  county level organizations, 174
  George W. Bush, 177
  history, 171
  John McCain, 178
  National Republican Senatorial Committee, 172
  organizations and committees, 173
  related Web sites, 254-255
  Republican National Committee, 171
  state candidates, 179
  state level organizations, 174
  Tom Campbell, 178
  unofficial organizations, 180
researching, 36. *See also* searching
  Boolean logic, 40
  campaign contributions, 201
  campaign finance information, 206
  campaign finance law, 223

George W. Bush's campaign donor database, 177
regulations, 36, 39-40
source reliability, 87
Supreme Court, 45
decisions, 47
FindLaw Web site, 49
legal terms, 48
Supreme Court Historical Society Web site, 50
retirement issues, 133
right-wing Web sites, 246-247
RightBot Web site, 109
Rightgrrl Web site, 111, 246
RightPages search engine, 108
rings (Web), 99
RNC (Republican National Committee), 171
Roll Call Web site, 150
runoff elections, 269
Russia, travel concerns, 86

S

satire, 247
scandals (Watergate), 159
schools, finding online, 75
searching. *See also* researching
Avalon Project, 12
Boolean logic, 40
cities on the Internet, 72
counties on Internet, 73
international organizations online, 91
keyword searches, 13
Library of Congress Web site, 13
older legislation, 24
Oyez Project Web site, 48
RightPages search engine, 108
schools on the Internet, 74
source credibility, 11
THOMAS, 20-22
Yahoo!, 75
Senate Appropriations Committee, 23
Senate Foreign Relations Committee, 23
Senate Judiciary Committee, 23-24
Senate (U.S.), 15-16
campaigns, 165
committees, 23-24, 234
emailing senators, 17
finding senators, 16
legislation from specific senators, 23
senator list, 15
Web sites, 15, 234
Service Employees International Union (SEIU) Web site, 140
Sierra Club Web site, 132
sites. *See* Web sites
Slick Times, 124, 248
small claims courts, 74
social change community Web site, 96
Social Security, 133
tax, 31
Web site, 30, 236
South Coast Air Quality Management District, 76
special interest groups
MADD, 129-130
Web sites, 249-250
state governments, 59
agencies, 61

campaign finance disclosures, 205
candidates, 165-166
committees (Democratic party), 160-161
executive branches, 60
judicial branches, 64-65
legislative branches, 63-64
Republican organizations and committees, 173
Web sites, 60, 238-240
Supreme Court, 43, 226
FindLaw Web site, 49
Historical Society Web site, 50
legal citations, 51
Legal Information Institute (LII), 45
decisions, 47
legal terms, 48
oral arguments (downloading), 49
states, 64
terms, 45
U.S. Reports, 51
Web sites, 44, 238
William Rehnquist, 43
writs of certiorari, 45

T

Tax Court, 238
taxes
domestic help, 31
reform issues, 135
terms (Supreme Court), 45
Texas House of Representatives Web site, 63
think tanks, 113, 128
third-party presidential campaigns, 190-192
THOMAS, 20
bill information, 21
bill numbers, 22
Web site, 223
Times of London Web site, 87
Town Hall Web site, 107
transcriptions (The Constitution), 10
Transparency International, 243
traveling abroad, 86
trials, 66
Trinidad and Tobago Web site, 85
Tumwater, WA Web site, 69
Turn Left Web site, 97-98
Twin Cities Metropolitan Council of Minneapolis-St. Paul, 76

U

Uniform Resource Locators (URLs), 8-10
United Farm Workers (UFW), 140, 250
United Nations
General Assembly, 89
Web site, 88
United States Court of Federal Claims Web page, 53
United States Court of International Trade Web site, 53
United States Tax Court Web site, 53
University of Oklahoma Law Center Web site, 12
URLs (Uniform Resource Locators), 8-10
U.S. Capitol historical information, 235

U.S. Chamber of Commerce, 138
U.S. House of Representatives
  committees, 235
  Web sites, 234
U.S. Reports, 51
U.S. Senate. *See* Senate (U.S.)
U.S. State Department's Travel Warnings and Consular Information Sheets Web site, 86
USAToday Web site, 51
USConstitution.net, 11
Usenet archive Web site, 102
Usenet Information Center Web site, 102
Usenet newsgroups, 101-102
Utne Reader, 104

V

venues, 65
video (Freedom Channel), 151
visas, 86
volunteers (campaign), 163-164, 216
voting
  candidate ballot access, 188
  congress records, 145
  nonpartisan research, 153
  online, 213-215
  registering, 134, 213
VoxCap Network, 143

W

Washington Post Web site, 51, 150
Watergate scandal, 159
Web directories (conservative), 109
Web rings, 99
Web sites
  AARP, 133
  AdBusters (The Culture Jammers Network), 103
  Adversity Net, 137
  AFL-CIO, 139
  agencies, 236
  Al Gore, 162-164
  Al Gore for president, 229
  Alternative Press Center's Alternative Press Index, 104
  American embassies, 87
  American Enterprise Institute, 113
  Americans for Tax Reform (ATR), 135
  Amnesty International, 243
  Annenberg Public Center Web site, 152
  Avalon Project at Yale Law School, 12
  BBC, 88
  BeAVoter.org, 134
  Bill of Rights, 10
  bookmarks, 11
  BushInsecurity.com, 218
  Cafe Progressive, 102
  California Democratic Party, 161
  California Department of Motor Vehicles, 61
  campaign finances, 256-258
  Capitol Steps, 121
  Census Bureau, 33-34, 236
  Center for Democracy and Technology (CDT), 128
  Center for Equal Opportunity, 137
  CFIC, 206

Chile, 81
Christian Coalition of America, 138
CIA World Factbook, 83
cities, 72
civil rights, 137
Claremont Institute, 114
Club for Growth, 182
Coin-Operated Congress, 208
College Democrats, 160
Colorado courts, 64
Commission on Presidential Debates, 189
Common Cause, 128, 207
Commonwealth of Massachusetts, 59
Communications for a Sustainable Future, 103
ConEye, 247
Congressional Budget Office, 24, 235
Congressional Research Service, 25
CongressVote.com, 145
conservative, 107, 112, 246-247
The Constitution, 9
Cook County Illinois Republican Central Committee, 175
cookiecentral.com, 111
cookies, 111
Council of State Governments, 64
courts, 237
The Daily Feed, 120
Dave Barry for president, 118
Democratic Congressional Campaign Committee, 165
Democratic Governors, 166
Democratic Governors' Association, 160
Democratic Leadership Council, 166
Democratic Party of Wisconsin Online, 161
Democratic party related, 160, 252-253
Democratic Senatorial Campaign Committee, 165
Democrats 2000, 168
Department of Education, 35
Department of State, 35
Direct Action Network, 103
DNC, 157-159
DNet, 166
Doonesbury, 119
DSCC, 159
Eagle Forum, 138
election.com, 213-215
Electronic Frontier Foundation (EFF), 127
embassies (foreign), 87
EmbassyWeb.com, 87
EMILY's List, 167-168
Emory School of Law, 12
English-language versions, 80
Enter Stage Right, 112
EO, 29
Essential Information, 103
FBI, 34, 236
Federal Election Commission, 196
Federal Judiciary, 51
feminist, 244
FindLaw, 49
Food and Drug Administration

(FDA), 35
foreign government, 79
Founding.com, 234
frames, 81
Free Republic, 109, 246
Freedom Channel, 150
Freedom of Information Act (FOIA), 35
Gay and Lesbian Victory Fund, 138
General Accounting Office, 25
George W. Bush, 176-177
George W. Bush for president, 230
Global Information Access Net (GIANT), 91
GOPAC, 180
Government Printing Office, 36
govWorks.com, 152
Grassroots.com, 145-146
Green Party international, 186
Greenpeace, 249
HateWatch, 137
Heartland Institute, 113
Hillary2000, 165
HillaryNo.com, 218
historical, 233
home schooling information, 75
House Commerce Committee, 24
House Committee in Standards of Official Conduct, 23
House Judiciary Committee, 24
House of Representatives, 17
House Ways and Means Committee, 23
Human Rights Campaign, 138
Human Rights Watch, 92
humorous, 117-120, 124, 247-248
IGC Internet Progressive Gateway, 99-101
Immigration and Naturalization Service (INS), 35
independent candidate, 217
IntellectualCapital.com, 144
international government/ politics, 241
International Herald Tribune, 88
international law, 91
Internet privacy issues, 128
Interpol, 92, 243
IRS, 32-33, 236
Jay's Leftist and Progressive Internet Resources Directory, 99
labor organizations, 140
Las Vegas, NV, 70
law, 237
Lawyers' committee for Civil Rights Under Law, 137
Leadership on Civil Rights, 136
Legal Information Institute (LII), 45
- decisions, 47
- legal terms, 48

Legislative Process, 18
liberal, 244-245
Libertarian Party, 186
Library of Congress, 13
- Country Studies, 84
- THOMAS, 223

links, 10
Lobbyforme.com, 147
local/city government, 240-241
London Virtual Mayor, 219
Macrocosm USA, 95
MADD (Mothers Against Drunk Driving), 129-130, 249
Massachusetts Democratic Party, 161
McIntosh-Clark slate for governor, 179
Metropolitan Council of Minneapolis-St. Paul, 76
missingmoney.com, 63
Missouri Department of Education and Secondary Education, 75
Montgomery County, Maryland Democratic Party, 161
National Abortion Rights Action League, 138
National Association of Counties, 73
National Center for State Courts, 66
National Conference of State Legislatures, 64
National Federation of Democratic Women, 160
National Institute on Money in State Politics, 205
National Organization for Women (NOW), 138, 250
National Right to Life Committee, 138
NATO, 90, 242
New Democrat Network, 166
New Jersey Division of Taxation, 62
New York State Democratic Party, 161
New York Times, 88
news, 88
News of the Weird, 123
Nuclear Files, 92, 243
O'Bannon-Kernan, 165
The Onion, 123
Online Exhibit Hall, 7
Open Secrets, 203
OSHA, 139
other party related, 255
Oyez Project, 48
PACER, 53
People For the American Way, 138
piperinfo.com, 73
Policy.com, 144
political information and commentary, 250-252
political news, 150-151
Political Resources on the Net, 84
PoliticsOnline, 215
portals, 152
presidential campaigns, 231
presidential information, 235
privacy issues, 147
ProActivist.com, 103
Progressive Policy Institute, 166
Project Vote Smart, 153
Public Agenda, 147
Public Citizen, 131
public Disclosure's FECInfo, 201
Ralph Nader, 231

Reform Party, 189
Republican candidates, 176
Republican Mainstream Committee, 181
Republican National Committee, 171
Republican party, 178
Republican party organizations and committees, 173
Republican party related, 254-255
RightBot, 109
Rightgrrl, 111, 246
schools, 74
search engines (Yahoo!), 75
Senate Appropriations Committee, 23
Senate Foreign Relations Committee, 23
Senate Judiciary Committee, 23
Slick Times, 124
Social Security Online, 30-31
South Coast Air Quality Management District, 76
special interest groups, 249-250
states, 238, 240
    courts, 66
    governments, 60
    taxes, 62
Supreme Court, 44, 237-238
Supreme Court Historical Society, 50
Supreme Court information, 51
Texas House of Representatives, 63
THOMAS, 20
Times of London, 87
Tom Campbell for Senate, 178
Town Hall (Heritage Foundation), 107
Transparency International, 243
Trinidad and Tobago, 85
Tumwater, WA, 69
Turn Left, 97-98
U.S. Chamber of Commerce, 138
U.S. Courts of Appeals, 54
U.S. House of Representatives, 234
U.S. Senate, 15, 234
U.S. State Department's Travel Warnings and Consular Information Sheets, 86
unclaimed property, 62
United Nations, 88
United States Court of Federal Claims, 53
United States Court of International Trade, 53
United States Tax Court, 53
University of Oklahoma Law Center, 12
URLs, 8
USConstitution.net, 11
Usenet archive, 102
Usenet Information Center, 102
Virginia's Department of Taxation, 61
voter registration, 134
VoxCap Network, 143
Web rings index, 99
whatis.com, 8
White House, 27, 224

whitehouse.net, 117
Women's Leadership Forum, 160
world affairs, 243
Worldwide Governments on the WWW, 80
Yahoo! Directory of Liberal Opinion, 101
Young Democrats, 160
Young Republicans, 173
ZNet, 96
Weekly Politicker newsletter, 215
White House Web site, 27, 224
whitehouse.net Web site, 117
Women For Gore, 163
women's issues, 111
Women's Leadership Forum Web site, 160
WomensNet, 100
world government. *See* international government
Worldwide Governments on the WWW Web site, 80
writing
congress members, 19
senators, 17
state legislators, 64
writs of certiorari, 45

Y – Z

Yahoo! Directory of Liberal Opinion Web site, 101
Yahoo! search engine, 75
Young Democrats Web site, 160
Young Republicans Web site, 173

ZNet Web site, 96, 244

Tell Us What You Think!

As the reader of this book, *you* are our most important critic and commentator. We value your opinion and want to know what we're doing right, what we could do better, what areas you'd like to see us publish in, and any other words of wisdom you're willing to pass our way.

You can email or write me directly to let me know what you did or didn't like about this book—as well as what we can do to make our books stronger.

Please note that I cannot help you with technical problems related to the topic of this book, and that due to the high volume of mail I receive, I might not be able to reply to every message.

When you write, please be sure to include this book's title and author as well as your name and phone or fax number. I will carefully review your comments and share them with the authors and editors who worked on the book.

Email: `internet_sams@mcp.com`

Mail: Mark Taber
Associate Publisher
Sams Publishing
201 West 103rd Street
Indianapolis, IN 46290 USA